The Learning Annex

presents

Small Business Basics

The Learning **Annex**

presents

Small Business Basics

Your Complete Guide to a Better Bottom Line

Barbara Weltman

WILEY

John Wiley & Sons, Inc.

Published by John Wiley & Sons, Inc., Hoboken, New Jersey.
Published simultaneously in Canada.

For general information on our other products and services, or technical support, please contact our Customer Care Department within the United States at 800-762-2974, outside the United States at 317-572-3993 or fax 317-572-4002.

Wiley also publishes its books in a variety of electronic formats. Some content that appears in print may not be available in electronic books. For more information about Wiley products, visit our web site at www.wiley.com.

Library of Congress Cataloging-in-Publication Data:

ISBN-10 0-471-71403-8
ISBN-13 978-0-471-71403-3

Printed in the United States of America.

10   9   8   7   6   5   4   3   2   1

contents

Preface   vii

Introduction   xi

PART 1 ORGANIZATION

Chapter 1: Business Organization   3

Chapter 2: Tax Year and Accounting Methods   19

Chapter 3: Recordkeeping for Business Income
and Deductions   29

PART 2 BUSINESS INCOME AND LOSSES

Chapter 4: Income or Loss from Business Operations   41

Chapter 5: Capital Gains and Losses   63

Chapter 6: Gains and Losses from Sales of
Business Property   81

PART 3 BUSINESS DEDUCTIONS AND CREDITS

Chapter 7: Car and Truck Expenses   95

Chapter 8: Repairs and Maintenance   115

Chapter 9: Bad Debts   123

Chapter 10: Rents   131

Chapter 11: Taxes and Interest   138

Chapter 12: First-Year Expensing and Depreciation,
Amortization, and Depletion   151

Chapter 13: Retirement Plans   183

Chapter 14: Casualty and Theft Losses   199

Chapter 15: Home Office Deductions   211

Chapter 16: Medical Coverage and Other Deductions   222

Chapter 17: Deductions for Alternative Minimum Tax   234

Chapter 18: Roundup of Tax Credits   240

Index   247

preface

According to the Internal Revenue Service (IRS), about 80 percent of small businesses use paid professionals to handle their tax returns. So why do you need to read up on taxes? The answer is simple: You, and not your accountant or other financial advisor, run the business, so you can't rely on someone else to make decisions critical to your activities. You need to be informed about tax-saving opportunities that continually arise so you can strategically plan to take advantage of them. Being knowledgeable about tax matters also saves you money; the more you know, the better able you are to ask your accountant key tax and financial questions that can advance your business, as well as to meet your tax responsibilities.

This is a great time to be a small business. Not only is small business the major force in our economy but it also is the benefactor of new tax rules that make it easier to write off expenses and minimize the taxes you owe. This is the seventh edition of this book, and it has been revised to include all of the new rules taking effect for 2004 returns. It also provides information about future changes scheduled to take effect in order to give you an overall view of business tax planning. Most importantly, it addresses the many tax questions I have received from readers as well as visitors to my web sites, <www.bwideas.com> and <www.barbaraweltman.com>.

This book focuses primarily on federal income taxes. But businesses may be required to pay and report many other taxes, including state income taxes, employment taxes, sales and use taxes, and excise taxes. Some information about these taxes is included in this book to alert you to your possible obligations so that you can then obtain further assistance if necessary.

It is important to stay alert to future changes. Be sure to check on any final action before you complete your tax return or take any steps that could be affected by these changes. Changes can also be found at my web site.

HOW TO USE THIS BOOK

The purpose of this book is to make you acutely aware of how your actions in business can affect your bottom line from a tax perspective. The way you organize your business, the accounting method you select, and the types of payments you make all have an impact on when you report income and the extent to which you can take deductions. This book is not designed to make you a tax expert. It is strongly suggested that you consult with a tax adviser before making certain important decisions that will affect your ability to claim tax deductions. I hope that the insight you gain from this book will allow you to ask your adviser key questions to benefit your business.

In Part 1, you will find topics of interest to all businesses. First, there is an overview of the various forms of business organization and an explanation of how these forms of organization affect reporting of income and claiming tax deductions. The most common forms of business organization include independent contractors, sole proprietors, and sole practitioners—individuals who work for themselves and do not have any partners. If self-employed individuals join with others to form a business, they become partners in a partnership. Sometimes businesses incorporate. A business can be incorporated with only one owner or with many owners. A corporation can be a regular corporation (*C corporation*), or it can be a small business corporation (*S corporation*). The difference between the C and S corporations is the way in which income of the business is taxed to the owner (which is explained in detail in Part 1). There is also a relatively new form of business organization called a *limited liability company* (LLC). Limited liability companies with two or more owners generally are taxed like partnerships even though their owners enjoy protection from personal liability. The important thing to note is that each form of business organization will affect what deductions can be claimed and where to claim them. Part 1 also explains tax years and accounting methods that businesses can select as well as important recordkeeping rules.

Part 2 details how to report various types of income your business may receive. In addition to fees and sales receipts—the bread-and-butter of your business—you may receive other types of ordinary income such as interest income, dividends, and rents. You may have capital gain transactions as well as sales of business assets. But you may also have losses—from operations or the sale of assets. Special rules govern the tax treatment of these losses. Each chapter discusses the types of income to report and special rules that affect them.

Part 3 focuses on specific deductions and credits. It will provide you with guidance on the various types of deductions and credits you can use to reduce your business income. Each type of write-off is explained in detail.

One way to stay abreast of tax and other small business developments that can affect your business throughout the year is by subscribing to *Barbara Weltman's Big Ideas for Small Business*™, a monthly newsletter geared for small business owners and their professional advisers. You can receive three free issues of the newsletter by visiting <www.bwideas.com> and entering "Wiley" in the discount code box on the subscription form.

I would like to thank Sidney Kess, Esq. and CPA, for his valuable suggestions in the preparation of the original tax deduction book; Donna LeValley, Esq., for reviewing the new materials; and Elliott Eiss, Esq., for his expertise and constant assistance with this and other projects.

Barbara Weltman

November 2004

introduction

Small businesses are big news today. They employ 51 percent of the country's private sector workforce, produce 51 percent of private sector output, and now contribute more than half of the nation's gross national product. Small businesses create 75 percent of all new jobs.

Small businesses fall under the purview of the Internal Revenue Service's (IRS) Small Business and Self-Employed Division (SB/SE). This new division handles businesses with assets under $10 million and services approximately 45 million tax filers, more than 33 million of whom are full-time or partially self-employed. The SB/SE division accounts for about 40 percent of the total federal tax revenues collected. The goal of this IRS division is customer assistance to help small businesses comply with the tax laws.

There is an IRS web site devoted exclusively to small business and self-employed persons <www.irs.gov/business/small/index.htm>. Here you will find special information for your industry—agriculture, automotive, child care, construction, entertainment, gaming, gas retailers, manufacturing, real estate, restaurants, and even tax professionals are already covered, and additional industries are set to follow. You can see the hot tax issues for your industry, find special audit guides that explain what the IRS looks for in your industry when examining returns, and links to other tax information.

As a small business owner, you work, try to grow your business, and hope to make a profit. What you can keep from that profit depends in part on the income tax you pay. The income tax applies to your net income rather than to your gross income or gross receipts. You are not taxed on all the income you bring in by way of sales, fees, commissions, or other payments. Instead, you are essentially taxed on what you keep after paying off the expenses of providing the services or making the sales that are the crux of your business. Deductions for these expenses operate to fix the amount of income that will be subject to tax. So deductions, in effect, help to determine the tax you pay and the profits you keep. And tax credits, the number of which has been expanded in recent years, can offset your tax to reduce the amount you ultimately pay.

SPECIAL RULES FOR SMALL BUSINESSES

Sometimes it pays to be small. The tax laws contain a number of special rules exclusively for small businesses. But what is a small business? The Small Business Administration (SBA) usually defines small business by the number of employees—size standards range from 50 employees to 1,500 employees, depending on the industry or the SBA program (these new size standards are currently under review). For tax purposes, however, the answer varies from rule to rule, as explained throughout the book. Sometimes it depends on your revenues and sometimes on the number of employees as noted throughout the book.

Reporting Income

While taxes are figured on your bottom line—your income less certain expenses—you still must report your income on your tax return. Generally all of the income your business receives is taxable unless there is a specific tax rule that allows you to exclude the income permanently or defer it to a future time.

When you report income depends on your method of accounting. *How* and *where* you report income depends on the nature of the income and your type of business organization. Over the next several years, the declining tax rates for owners of pass-through entities—sole proprietorships, partnerships, limited liability companies (LLCs), and S corporations—requires greater sensitivity to the timing of business income as these rates decline.

What Is a Tax Deduction Worth to You?

The answer depends on your tax bracket. The tax bracket is dependent on the way you organize your business. If you are self-employed and in the top tax bracket of 35 percent in 2004, then each dollar of deduction will save you 35 cents. Had you not claimed this deduction, you would have had to pay 35 cents of tax on that dollar of income that was offset by the deduction. If you have a personal service corporation, a special type of corporation for most professionals, the corporation pays tax at a flat rate of 35 percent. This means that the corporation is in the 35-percent tax bracket. So each deduction claimed saves 35 cents of tax on the corporation's income. Deductions are even more valuable if your business is in a state that imposes income tax. The impact of state income tax and special rules for state income taxes are not discussed in this book. However, you should explore the tax rules in your state and ascertain their impact on your business income.

When Do You Claim Deductions?

Like the timing of income, the timing of deductions—when to claim them—is determined by your tax year and method of accounting. Your form of business organization affects your choice of tax year and your accounting method.

Even when expenses are deductible, there may be limits on the timing of those deductions. Most common expenses are currently deductible in full. However, some expenses must be capitalized or amortized, or you must choose between current deductibility and capitalization. Capitalization generally means that expenses can be written off ratably as amortized expenses or depreciated over a period of time. Amortized expenses include, for example, fees to incorporate a business and expenses to organize a new business. Certain capitalized costs may not be deductible at all, but are treated as an additional cost of an asset (*basis*).

Credits versus Deductions

Not all write-offs of business expenses are treated as deductions. Some can be claimed as tax credits. A tax credit is worth more than a deduction since it reduces your taxes dollar for dollar. Like deductions, tax credits are available only to the extent that Congress allows. In a couple of instances, you have a choice between treating certain expenses as a deduction or a credit. In most cases, however, tax credits can be claimed for certain expenses for which no tax deduction is provided. Business-related tax credits, as well as personal credits related to working or running a business, are included in this book.

Tax Responsibilities

As a small business owner, your obligations taxwise are broad. Not only do you have to pay income taxes and file income tax returns, but you also must manage payroll taxes if you have any employees. You may also have to collect and report on state and local sales taxes. Finally, you may have to notify the IRS of certain activities on information returns.

It is very helpful to keep an eye on the tax calendar so you will not miss out on any payment or filing deadlines, which can result in interest and penalties. You might want to view and print out or order at no cost from the IRS its Publication 1518, *Small Business Tax Calendar* (go to <www.irs.gov/businesses/small/article/0,,id=101169,00.html>).

You can obtain most federal tax forms online at <www.irs.gov>.

part I

organization

chapter 1

business organization

If you have a great idea for a product or a business and are eager to get started, do not let your enthusiasm be the reason you get off on the wrong foot. Take a while to consider how you will organize your business. The form of organization your business takes controls how income and deductions are reported to the government on a tax return. Sometimes you have a choice of the type of business organization; other times circumstances limit your choice. If you have not yet set up your business and do have a choice, this discussion will influence your decision on business organization. If you have already set up your business, you may want to consider changing to another form of organization.

For a further discussion on worker classification, see IRS Publication 15-A, *Employer's Supplemental Tax Guide*.

SOLE PROPRIETORSHIPS

If you go into business for yourself and do not have any partners, you are considered a *sole proprietor*. You may think that the term *proprietor* connotes a storekeeper. For purposes of tax treatment, proprietor means any unincorporated business owned entirely by one person. The designation also applies to independent contractors.

There are no formalities required to become a sole proprietor; you simply conduct business. You may have to register your business with your city, town, or county government by filing a simple form stating that you are doing business as the "Quality Dry Cleaners" or some other business name. This is sometimes referred to as a DBA.

From a legal standpoint, as a sole proprietor, you are personally liable for any debts your business incurs. For example, if you borrow money and default on a loan, the lender can look not only to your business equipment and other business property but also to your personal stocks, bonds, and other property. Some states may give your house homestead protection; state or federal law may protect your pensions and even Individual Retirement Accounts (IRAs). Your only protection for your personal assets is adequate insurance against accidents for your business and other liabilities and paying your debts in full.

Independent Contractors

One type of sole proprietor is the *independent contractor*, an individual who provides services to others outside an employment context. The providing of services becomes a business, an independent calling. In terms of claiming business deductions, classification as an independent contractor is generally more favorable than classification as an employee. (See "Tax Treatment of Income and Deductions in General," later in this chapter.) Therefore, many individuals whose employment status is not clear may wish to claim independent contractor status. Also, from the employer's perspective, hiring independent contractors is more favorable because the employer is not liable for employment taxes and need not provide employee benefits. Federal employment taxes include Social Security and Medicare taxes under the Federal Insurance Contribution Act (FICA) as well as unemployment taxes under the Federal Unemployment Tax Act (FUTA).

The Internal Revenue Service (IRS) aggressively tries to reclassify workers as employees in order to collect employment taxes from employers. The key to worker classification is control. In order to prove independent contractor status, you, as the worker, must show that you have the right to control the details and means by which your work is to be accomplished. Various behavioral, financial, and other factors can be brought to bear on the issue of whether you are under someone else's control. You can learn more about worker classification in IRS Publication 15-A, *Employer's Supplemental Tax Guide*.

By statute, certain employees are treated as independent contractors for employment taxes even though they continue to be treated as employees for income taxes. Other employees are treated as employees for employment taxes even though they are independent contractors for income taxes.

There are two categories of employees that are, by statute, treated as nonemployees for purposes of federal employment taxes. These two categories are real estate salespersons and direct sellers of consumer goods. These employees are considered independent contractors (the ramifications of which are discussed later in this chapter). Such workers are deemed independent contractors if at least 90 percent of the employees' compensation is determined by their output. In other words, they are independent contractors if they are paid by commission and not a fixed salary. They must also perform their services under a written contract that specifies they will not be treated as employees for federal employment tax purposes.

Statutory Employees

Some individuals who consider themselves to be in business for themselves—reporting their income and expenses as sole proprietors—may still be treated as employees for purposes of employment taxes. As such, Social Security and Medicare taxes are withheld from their compensation. These individuals include:

- Corporate officers
- Agent-drivers or commission-drivers engaged in the distribution of meat products, bakery products, produce, beverages other than milk, laundry, or dry-cleaning services
- Full-time life insurance salespersons
- Homeworkers who personally perform services according to specifications provided by the service recipient
- Traveling or city salespersons engaged on a full-time basis in the solicitation of orders from wholesalers, retailers, contractors, or operators of hotels, restaurants, or other similar businesses

Full-time life insurance salespersons, homeworkers, and traveling or city salespersons are exempt from FICA if they have made a substantial investment in the facilities used in connection with the performance of services.

One-Member Limited Liability Companies

Every state allows a single owner to form a limited liability company (LLC) under state law. From a legal standpoint, an LLC gives the owner protection from personal liability (only business assets are at risk from the claims of creditors) as explained later in this chapter. But from a tax standpoint, a one-member LLC is treated as a "disregarded entity" (the owner can elect to have the LLC taxed as a corporation, but there is probably no compelling reason to do so). If the owner is an individual (and not a corporation), all of the income and expenses of the LLC are reported on Schedule C of the owner's Form 1040, just like a sole proprietorship.

Tax Treatment of Income and Deductions in General

Sole proprietors, including independent contractors and statutory employees, report their income and deductions on Schedule C, see Profit or Loss From Business. The net amount (profit or loss after offsetting income with deductions) is then reported as part of the income section on page one of your Form 1040. Such individuals may be able to use a simplified form for reporting business income and deductions: Schedule C-EZ, Net Profit From Business. Individuals engaged in farming activities report business income and deductions on Schedule F, the net amount of which is then reported in the income section on page one of your Form 1040. Individuals who are considered employees cannot use Schedule C to report their income and claim deductions.

PARTNERSHIPS AND LIMITED LIABILITY COMPANIES

If you go into business with others, then you cannot be a sole proprietor. You are automatically in a *partnership* if you join together with one or more people to share the profits of the business and take no formal action. Owners of a partnership are called *partners*.

There are two types of partnerships: *general partnerships* and *limited partnerships*. In general partnerships, all of the partners are personally liable for the debts of the business. Creditors can go after the personal assets of any and all of the partners to satisfy partnership debts. In limited partnerships, only the general partners are personally liable for the debts of the business. Limited partners are liable only to the extent of their investments in the business plus their share of recourse debts and obligations to make future investments.

---

example

If a partnership incurs debts of $10,000 (none of which are recourse), a general partner is liable for the full $10,000. A limited partner who initially contributed $1,000 to the limited partnership is liable only to that extent. He or she can lose the $1,000 investment, but creditors cannot go after personal assets.

General partners are jointly and severally liable for the business's debts. A creditor can go after any one partner for the full amount of the debt. That partner can seek to recoup a proportional share of the debt from other partner(s).

Partnerships can be informal agreements to share profits and losses of a business venture. More typically, however, they are organized with formal partnership agreements. These agreements detail how income, deductions, gains, losses, and credits are to be split (if there are any special allocations to be made) and what happens on the retirement, disability, bankruptcy, or death of a partner. A limited partnership must have a partnership agreement that complies with state law requirements.

Another form of organization that can be used by those joining together for business is a limited liability company (LLC). This type of business organization is formed under state law in which all owners are given limited liability. Owners of LLCs are called *members*. Most states also permit limited liability partnerships (LLPs)—LLCs for accountants, attorneys, doctors, and other professionals—which are easily formed by existing partnerships filing an LLP election with the state. And Delaware now permits multiple LLCs to operate under a single LLC umbrella called a series LLC. The debts and liabilities of each LLC remain separate from those of the other LLCs, something that is ideal for those owning several pieces of real estate—each can be owned by a separate LLC under the master LLC.

As the name suggests, the creditors of LLCs can look only to the assets of the company to satisfy debts; creditors cannot go after members and hope to recover their personal assets. For federal income tax purposes, LLCs are treated like partnerships unless the members elect to have the LLCs taxed as corporations. Tax experts have yet to come up with any compelling reason for LLCs to choose corporate tax treatment, but if it is desired, the businesses just check the box on IRS Form 8832, Entity Classification Election. For purposes of our discussion throughout the book, it will be assumed that LLCs have not chosen corporate tax treatment and so are taxed the same way as partnerships.

Tax Treatment of Income and Deductions in General

Partnerships and LLCs are *pass-through* entities. They are not separate taxpaying entities; instead, they pass income, deductions, gains, losses, and tax credits through to their owners. The owners report these amounts on their individual returns. While the entity does not pay taxes, it must file an information return with IRS Form 1065, U.S. Return of Partnership Income, to report the total pass-through amounts. The entity also completes Schedule K-1 of Form 1065, a copy of which is given to each owner. The K-1 tells the owner his or her allocable share of partnership/LLC amounts. Like W-2 forms used by the IRS to match employees' reporting of their compensation, the IRS now employs computer matching of Schedules K-1 to ensure that owners are properly reporting their share of their business's income.

There are two types of items that pass through to an owner: trade or business income or loss and separately stated items. A partner's or member's share is called the *distributive share*. Trade or business income or loss takes into account most ordinary deductions of the business—compensation, rent, taxes, interest, and so forth. Guaranteed payments to an owner are also taken into account when determining ordinary income or loss. From an owner's perspective, deductions net out against income from the business, and the owner's allocable share of the net amount is then reported on the owner's Schedule E of Form 1040.

Separately stated items are stand-alone items that pass through to owners apart from the net amount of trade or business income. These are items that are subject to limitations on an individual's tax return and must be segregated from the net amount of trade or business income. They are reported along with similar items on the owner's own tax return.

Examples of separately stated items include capital gains and losses, Section 179 expense deductions, investment interest deductions, charitable contributions, and tax credits.

When a partnership or LLC has substantial expenses that exceed its operating income, a loss is passed through to the owner. A number of different rules operate to limit a loss deduction. The owner may not be able to claim the entire loss. Limitations on losses are discussed in Chapter 4

S CORPORATIONS AND THEIR SHAREHOLDER-EMPLOYEES

S corporations are like regular corporations (called *C corporations*) for business law purposes. They are separate entities in the eyes of the law and exist independently from their owners. For example, if an owner dies, the S corporation's existence continues. S corporations are formed under state law in the same way as other corporations. The only difference between S corporations and other corporations is their tax treatment for federal income tax purposes.

For the most part, S corporations are treated as pass-through entities for federal income tax purposes. This means that, as with partnerships and LLCs, the income and loss pass through to owners, and their allocable share is reported by S corporation shareholders on their individual income tax returns.

> **note**
>
> State laws vary on the tax treatment of S corporations for state income tax purposes. Be sure to check the laws of any state in which you do business.

S corporation status is not automatic. A corporation must elect S status in a timely manner. This election is made on Form 2553, Election by Small Business Corporations to Tax Corporate Income Directly to Shareholders. It must be filed with the IRS no later than the fifteenth day of the third month of the corporation's tax year.

Remember, if state law also allows S status, a separate election may have to be filed with the state. Check with all state law requirements.

Tax Treatment of Income and Deductions in General

For the most part, S corporations, like partnerships and LLCs, are pass-through entities. They are generally not separate taxpaying entities. Instead, they pass through to their shareholders' income, deductions, gains, losses, and tax credits. The shareholders report these amounts on their individual returns. The S corporation files a return with the IRS—Form 1120S, U.S. Income Tax Return for an S Corporation—to report the total pass-through amounts. The S corporation also completes Schedule K-1 of Form 1120S, a copy of which is given to each shareholder. The K-1 tells the shareholder his or her allocable share of S corporation amounts. The K-1 for S corporation shareholders is similar to the K-1 for partners and LLC members.

Unlike partnerships and LLCs, however, S corporations may become taxpayers if they have certain types of income. There are only three types of income that result in a tax on the S corporation. These three items cannot be reduced by any deductions and result only if the corporation had been a C corporation for some time before the S election: built-in gains, passive investment income, and LIFO recapture (explained in Chapter 4).

C CORPORATIONS AND THEIR SHAREHOLDER-EMPLOYEES

A *C corporation* is an entity separate and apart from its owners; it has its own legal existence. Though formed under state law, it need not be formed in the state in which the business operates. Many corporations, for example, are formed in Delaware or Nevada because the laws in these states favor the corporation, as opposed to the investors (shareholders). However, state law for the state in which the business operates may still require the corporation to make some formal notification of doing business in the state. The corporation may also be subject to tax on income generated in that state.

For federal tax purposes, a C corporation is a separate taxpaying entity. It files its own return (Form 1120, U.S. Corporation Income Tax Return) to report its income or losses (or Form 1120-A, U.S. Corporation Short-Form Income Tax Return, for corporations with gross receipts under $500,000). Shareholders do not report their share of the corporation's income.

Personal Service Corporations

Professionals who incorporate their practices are a special type of C corporation called **personal service corporations (PSCs).**

Personal service corporation (PSC)   A C corporation that performs personal services in the fields of health, law, accounting, engineering, architecture, actuarial science, performing arts, or consulting and meets certain ownership and service tests.

Personal service corporations are subject to special rules in the tax law. Some of these rules are beneficial; others are not. Personal service corporations are subject to a flat tax rate of 35 percent and certain other restrictions.

Tax Treatment of Income and Deductions in General

The C corporation reports its own income and claims its own deductions on Form 1120, U.S. Corporation Income Tax Return. Shareholders in C corporations do not have to report any income of the corporation (and cannot claim any deductions of the corporation).

Distributions from the C corporation to its shareholders are personal items for the shareholders. For example, if a shareholder works for his or her C corporation and receives a salary, the corporation deducts that salary against corporate income. The shareholder reports the salary as income on his or her individual income tax return. If the corporation distributes a dividend to the shareholder, again, the shareholder reports the dividend as income on his or her individual income tax return. In the case of dividends, however, the corporation cannot claim a deduction. This, then, creates a two-tier tax system, commonly referred to as *double taxation*. First, earnings are taxed at the corporate level. Then, when they are distributed to shareholders as dividends, they are taxed again, this time at the shareholder level.

Other Tax Issues for C Corporations

In view of the favorable corporate rate tax structure (compared with the individual tax rates), certain tax penalties prevent businesses from using this form of business organization to optimum advantage.

- **Personal holding company penalty.** Corporations that function as a shareholder investment portfolio rather than as an operating company may fall subject to the personal holding corporation (PHC) penalty tax of the highest personal income tax rate—15 percent in 2004—on certain undistributed corporate income.

- **Accumulated earnings tax.** Corporations may seek to keep money in corporate accounts rather than distribute it as dividends to shareholders with the view that an eventual sale of the business will enable shareholders to extract those funds at capital gain rates. Unfortunately, the tax law imposes a penalty on excess accumulations at the highest personal income tax rate—15 percent in 2004. Excess accumulations are those above an exemption amount ($250,000 for most businesses, but only $150,000 for PSCs) *plus* amounts for the reasonable needs of the business.

EMPLOYEES

If you do not own any interest in a business but are employed by one, you may still have to account for business expenses. Your salary or other compensation is reported as wages in the income section as seen on page one of your Form 1040. Your deductions (with a few exceptions), however, can be claimed only as miscellaneous itemized deductions on Schedule A. These deductions are subject to two limitations. First, the total is deductible only if it exceeds 2 percent of adjusted gross income. Second, high-income taxpayers have an overall reduction of itemized deductions when adjusted gross income exceeds a threshold amount.

Under the 2-percent rule, only the portion of total miscellaneous deductions in excess of 2 percent of adjusted gross income is deductible on Schedule A. *Adjusted gross income* is the tax term for your total income subject to tax (gross income) minus business expenses (other than employee business expenses), capital losses, and certain other expenses that are deductible even if you do not claim itemized deductions, such as qualifying IRA contributions or alimony. You arrive at your adjusted gross income by completing the Income and Adjusted Gross Income sections on page one of Form 1040.

---

example

You have business travel expenses that your employer does not pay for and other miscellaneous expenses (such as tax preparation fees) totaling $2,000. Your adjusted gross income is $80,000. The amount up to the 2-percent floor, or $1,600 (2 percent of $80,000), is disallowed. Only $400 of the $2,000 expenses is deductible on Schedule A.

The second deduction limitation applies to higher-income taxpayers whose adjusted gross income exceeds a threshold amount that is adjusted annually for inflation. For example, for 2004 the limitation applies to taxpayers with adjusted gross income over $142,700, or over $71,350 if married and filing separately. If the limitation applies, itemized deductions other than medical expenses, investment interest, casualty or theft losses, and gambling losses are generally reduced by 3 percent of the excess of adjusted gross income over the annual threshold.

If you fall into a special category of employees called *statutory employees*, you can deduct your business expenses on Schedule C instead of Schedule A.

FACTORS IN CHOOSING YOUR FORM OF BUSINESS ORGANIZATION

Throughout this chapter, the differences of how income and deductions are reported have been explained, but these differences are not the only reasons for choosing a form of business organization. When you are deciding on which form of business organization to choose, many factors come into play.

Personal Liability

If your business owes money to another party, are your personal assets—home, car, investment—at risk? The answer depends on your form of business organization. You have personal liability—your personal assets are at risk—if you are a sole proprietor or a general partner in a partnership. In all other cases, you do not have personal liability.

Thus, for example, if you are a shareholder in an S corporation, you do not have personal liability for the debts of your corporation.

Profitability

All businesses hope to make money. But many sustain losses, especially in the start-up years. The way in which a business is organized affects how losses are treated.

Pass-through entities allow owners to deduct their share of the company's losses on their personal returns (subject to limits discussed in Chapter 4). If a business is set up as a C corporation, only the corporation can deduct losses. Thus, when losses are anticipated, for example in the start-up phase, a pass-through entity generally is a preferable form of business organization.

Fringe Benefits

The tax law gives employees of corporations the opportunity to enjoy special fringe benefits on a tax-free basis. This same opportunity is not extended to sole proprietors, partners, LLC members, and even S corporation shareholders who own more than 2 percent of the stock in their corporations.

If the business can afford to provide these benefits, the form of business becomes important. All forms of business can offer tax-favored retirement plans.

Nature and Number of Owners

With whom you go into business affects your choice of business organization. For example, S corporations restrict the number of shareholders and who those shareholders can be.

If you have a business already formed as a C corporation and want to start another corporation, you must take into consideration the impact of special tax rules for multiple corporations.

Tax Rates

Both individuals and C corporations (other than PSCs) can enjoy graduated income tax rates. The top tax rate paid by sole proprietors and owners of other pass-through businesses is 35 percent for 2004. The top corporate tax rate imposed on C corporations is also 35 percent. Personal service corporations are subject to a flat tax rate of 35 percent. But remember, even though the C corporation has a lower top tax rate, there is a two-tier tax structure with which to contend if earnings are paid out to you—tax at the corporate level and again at the shareholder level.

While the so-called double taxation for C corporations is eased by the cut the tax rate on dividends, there is still some double tax because dividends remain nondeductible at the corporate level. The rate on dividends is 15 percent (5 percent for shareholders in the 10 percent and 15 percent tax brackets; zero for these taxpayers in 2008).

The tax rates on capital gains also differ between C corporations and other taxpayers. This is because capital gains of C corporations are not subject to special tax rates (they are taxed the same as ordinary business income), while owners of other types of businesses may pay tax on the business's capital gains at no more than 15 percent.

Social Security and Medicare Taxes

Owners of businesses organized any way other than as a corporation (C or S) are not employees of their businesses. As such, they are personally responsible for paying Social Security and Medicare taxes (called *self-employment taxes* for owners of unincorporated businesses). This tax is made up of the employer and employee shares of Social Security and Medicare taxes.

However, owners of corporations have these taxes applied only against salary actually paid to them. Owners of unincorporated businesses pay self-employment tax on net earnings from self-employment. This essentially means profits, whether they are distributed to the owners or reinvested in the business.

Restrictions on Accounting Periods and Accounting Methods

As you will see in Chapter 2, the tax law limits the use of fiscal years and the cash method of accounting for certain types of business organizations.

Multistate Operations

Each state has its own way of taxing businesses subject to its jurisdiction. The way in which a business is organized for federal income tax purposes may not necessarily control for state income tax purposes. For example, some states do not recognize S corporation elections and tax such entities as regular corporations. A company must file a return in each state in which it does business and pay income tax on the portion of its profits earned in that state. Doing business as a pass-through entity means that each owner would have to file a tax return in each state the company does business.

Audit Chances

Each year the IRS publishes statistics on the number and type of audits it conducts. The rates for 2003, the most recent year for which statistics are available, show a slight increase in audit activity for most types of business returns.

The chances of being audited vary with the type of business organization, the amount of income generated by the business, and the geographic location of the business. While the chance of an audit is not a significant reason for choosing one form of business organization over another, it is helpful to keep these statistics in mind.

Filing Deadlines and Extensions

How your business is organized dictates when its tax return must be filed, the form to use, and the additional time that can be obtained for filing the return. Table 1.1 lists the filing deadlines for calendar-year

TABLE 1.1 Filing Deadlines, Extensions, and Forms

Type of Entity	Return Due Date	Income Tax Return	Automatic Filing Extension	Form to Request Filing Extension
Sole proprietorship	April 15	Schedule C of Form 1040	August 15	Form 4868
Partnership/LLC	April 15	Form 1065	July 15	Form 8736
S corporation	March 15	Form 1120S	September 15	Form 7004
C corporation	March 15	Form 1120	September 15	Form 7004

businesses, the available automatic extensions, and the forms to use in filing the return or requesting a filing extension.

Tax Treatment on Termination

The tax treatment on the termination of a business is another factor to consider. While the choice of entity is made when the business starts out, you cannot ignore the tax consequences that this choice will have when the business terminates. The liquidation of a C corporation produces a double tax—at the entity and owner levels. The liquidation of an S corporation produces a double tax *only* if there is a built-in gains tax issue—created by having appreciated assets in the business when an S election is made. However, the built-in gains tax problem disappears 10 years after the S election so termination after that time does not result in a double tax.

If the termination of the business results in a loss, different tax rules come into play. Losses from partnerships and LLCs are treated as capital losses (explained in Chapter 5). A shareholder's losses from the termination of a C or S corporation may qualify as a Section 1244 loss—treated as an ordinary loss within limits (explained in Chapter 5).

FORMS OF BUSINESS ORGANIZATION COMPARED

Which form of business organization is right for your business? The answer is really a judgment call based on all the factors previously discussed. You can, of course, use different forms of business organization for your different business activities. For example, you may have a C corporation and personally own the building in which it operates—directly or through an LLC. Or you may be in partnership for your professional activities, while running a sideline business as an S corporation.

CHANGING YOUR FORM OF BUSINESS

Suppose you have a business that you have been running as a sole proprietorship. Now you want to make a change. Your new choice of business organization is dictated by the reason for the change. If you are taking in a partner, you would consider these alternatives: partnership, LLC, S corporation, or C corporation. If you are not taking in a partner, but want to obtain limited personal liability, you would consider an

LLC, an S corporation, or a C corporation. If you are looking to take advantage of certain fringe benefits, such as medical reimbursement plans, you would consider only a C corporation.

Whatever your reason, changing from a sole proprietorship to another type of business organization generally does not entail tax costs on making the changeover. You can set up a partnership or corporation, transfer your business assets to it, obtain an ownership interest in the new entity, and do all this on a tax-free basis. You may, however, have some tax consequences if you transfer your business liabilities to the new entity.

But what if you now have a corporation or partnership and want to change your form of business organization? This change may not be so simple. Suppose you have an S corporation or a C corporation. If you liquidate the corporation to change to another form of business organization, you may have to report gain on the liquidation. In fact, gains may have to be reported both by the business and by you as owner.

Before changing your form of business organization it is important to review your particular situation with a tax professional. In making any change in business, consider the legal and accounting costs involved.

tax year and accounting methods

Once you select your form of business organization, you must decide how you will report your income. There are two key decisions you must make: What is the time frame for calculating your income and deductions (called the tax year or accounting period), and what are the rules that you will follow to calculate your income and deductions (called the accounting method). In some cases, your form of business organization restricts you to an accounting period or accounting method. In other cases, however, you can choose which method is best for your business.

For a further discussion on tax years and accounting methods, see IRS Publication 538, *Accounting Periods and Methods*. Inventory rules are discussed in Chapter 4.

ACCOUNTING PERIODS

You account for your income and expenses on an annual basis. This period is called your *tax year*. There are two methods for fixing your tax year: *calendar* and *fiscal*. Under the calendar year, you use a 12-month period ending on December 31. Under the fiscal year, you use a 12-month period ending at the end of any month other than December.

You select your tax year when you first begin your business. You do not need IRS approval for your tax year; you simply use it to govern when you must file your first return. You use the same tax year thereafter.

A short two year may occur in the first or final year of business. For example, if you closed the doors to your business on May 1, 2004, even though you operated on a calendar year. Your final tax year is a short year because it is only seven months. You do not have to apportion or prorate deductions for this short year because the business was not in existence for the entire year. Different rules apply if a short year results from a change in accounting period.

Seasonal Businesses

Seasonal businesses should use special care when selecting their tax year. It is often advisable to select a tax year that will include both the period in which most of the expenses as well as most of the income is realized. For example, if a business expects to sell its products primarily in the spring and incurs most of its expenses for these sales in the preceding fall, it may be best to select a fiscal year ending just after the selling season, such as July or August. In this way, the expenses and the income that are related to each other will be reported on the same return.

Limits on Use of the Fiscal Year

C corporations, other than personal service corporations (PSCs), can choose a calendar year or a fiscal year, whichever is more advantageous. Other entities, however, cannot simply choose a fiscal year even though it offers tax advantages to its owners. In general, partnerships, limited liability companies (LLCs), S corporations, and PSCs must use a **required year.** Since individuals typically use a calendar year, their business must also use a calendar year.

Required year   For S corporations, this is a calendar year; for partnerships and LLCs, it is the same year as the tax year of the entity's owners. When owners have different tax years, special rules determine which owner's tax year governs.

The entity can use a fiscal year even though its owners use a calendar year if it can be established to the satisfaction of the IRS that there is a **business purpose** for the fiscal year.

Business purpose   This is shown if the fiscal year is the natural business year of the entity. For a PSC, for example, a fiscal year is treated as a natural business year if, for three consecutive years, 25 percent or more of its gross receipts for the 12-month period ending on the fiscal year end are received within the last two months of the year.

Section 444 Election for Fiscal Year

If an entity wants to use a fiscal year that is not its natural business year, it can do so by making a Section 444 election. The only acceptable tax years under this election are those ending September 30, October 31, and November 30. The election is made by filing Form 8716, Election to Have a Tax Year Other Than a Required Tax Year, by the earlier of the due date of the return for the new tax year (without regard to extensions) or the fifteenth day of the sixth month of the tax year for which the election will be effective.

If the election is made, then partnerships, LLCs, and S corporations must make certain *required payments* designed to give to the federal government the tax that has been deferred by reason of the special tax year. The payment is calculated using the highest individual income tax rate plus 1 percentage point. (the rate for 2004 is 36 percent). The required payment is made by filing Form 8752, Required Payment or Refund Under Section 7519 for Partnerships and S Corporations, by May 15 of the calendar year following the calendar year in which the election begins.

Personal service corporations that make a Section 444 election need not make a required payment. Instead, these corporations must make *required distributions* by distributing certain amounts of compensation to employee-owners by December 31 of each year for which an election is in effect. Required distributions are figured on Part I of Schedule H of Form 1120, Section 280H Limitations for a Personal Service Corporation.

Pass-Through Business on a Fiscal Year

Owners in pass-through entities who are on a calendar year report their share of the business's income, deductions, gains, losses, and credits from the entity's tax year that ends in the owners' tax year.

> **example**
>
> You are in a partnership that uses a fiscal year ending October 31. The partnership's items for its 2004 fiscal year ending October 31, 2004, are reported on your 2004 return. The portion of the partnership's income and deductions from the period November 1, 2004, through December 31, 2004, are part of its 2005 fiscal year, which will be reported on your 2005 return.

Change in Tax Year

If your business has been using a particular tax year and you want to change to a different one, you must obtain IRS approval to do so. Depending on the reason for the change, approval may be automatic or discretionary. You can request a change in your tax year by filing Form 1128, Application to Adopt, Change, or Retain a Tax Year. You must also include a user fee (an amount set by the IRS) for this request.

ACCOUNTING METHODS

There are two principal methods of accounting: *cash basis* and *accrual basis*. Use of a particular method determines when a deduction can be claimed. However, restrictions apply for both methods of accounting. Also, the form of business organization may preclude the use of the cash method of accounting even though it may be the method of choice.

Cash Method

Cash method is the simpler accounting method. Income is reported when it is actually or constructively received and a deduction can be claimed when and to the extent the expense is paid.

> **example**
>
> You are a consultant. You perform services and send a bill. You report the income when you receive payment. Similarly, you buy business cards and stationery. You can deduct this expense when you pay for the supplies.

Actual receipt is the time when income is in your hands. Constructive receipt occurs when you have control over the income and can reduce it to an actual receipt.

> **example**
>
> You earn a fee for services rendered but ask your customer not to pay you immediately. Since the customer was ready and able to pay immediately, you are in constructive receipt of the fee at that time.

Payments received by check are income when the check is received even though you may deposit it some time later. However, if the check bounces, then no income results at the time the check was received. You only report income when the check is later honored.

You may not be able to deduct all expenses when they are paid because there are some limitations that come into play. Generally, you cannot deduct advance payments (so-called prepaid expenses) that relate to periods beyond the current tax year.

Prepayments may occur for a number of expenses. You may prepay rent, insurance premiums, or interest. Generally, prepayments that do not extend beyond 12 months are currently deductible.

In the case of interest, no deduction is allowed for prepayments by businesses. For example, if you are required to pay points to obtain a mortgage on your office building, these points are considered to be prepaid interest. You must deduct the points ratably over the term of the loan.

If you pay off the mortgage before the end of the term (you sell the property or refinance the loan), you can then write off any points you still have not deducted.

Restrictions on the Use of the Cash Method

You cannot use the cash method of accounting if you maintain inventory unless you qualify for a small business exception. If you are barred from using the cash method, you must use the accrual method or another method of accounting.

Small Inventory-Based Business Exception

Even though you maintain inventory, you are permitted to use the cash method if your average annual gross receipts for the three prior years do not exceed $10 million. You can use the cash method of accounting even though you use the accrual method for financial accounting purposes (for example, on profit and loss statements). However, you do not qualify for this exception if your principal business activity is retailing, wholesaling, manufacturing (other than custom manufacturing), mining, publishing, or sound recording.

In addition to the inventory limitation, certain types of business organizations generally cannot use the cash method of accounting. These include corporations other than S corporations, partnerships that have a corporation (other than an S corporation) as a partner, and tax shelters.

Farming Exception

A farming business with gross receipts of $25 million or less can use the cash method.

PSC Exception

A qualified personal service corporation (PSC) (see Chapter 1) can use the cash method of accounting.

Small Business Exception

Corporations other than S corporations and partnerships that have a corporation (other than an S corporation) as a partner can use the cash method of accounting if they are considered to be a small business even if they do not qualify for the inventory-based exception above. A small business for this purpose is one that has average annual **gross receipts** of $5 million or less in at least one of three prior taxable years. In view of the gross receipt rule, you can see that a business may be able to use the cash method for one year but be precluded from using it in the following year.

Gross receipts   All the income is taken in by the business without offsets for expenses. For example, if a consultant receives fees of $25,000 for the year and has expenses of $10,000, gross receipts are $25,000.

Accrual Method of Accounting

Under the accrual method, you report income when it is earned rather than when it is received, and you deduct expenses when they are incurred rather than when they are paid. There are two tests to determine whether there is a fixed right to receive income so that it must be accrued and whether an expense is treated as having been incurred for tax purposes.

All Events Test

All events that fix the income and set the liability must have occurred. Also, you must be able to determine the amount of the income or expense with reasonable accuracy.

Economic Performance Test

In order to report income or deduct an expense, economic performance must occur. In most cases, this is rather obvious. If you provide goods and services, economic performance occurs when you provide the goods or services. By the same token if goods or services are provided to you, economic performance occurs when the goods or services are provided to you. Thus, for example, if you buy office supplies, economic performance occurs when the purchase is made and the bill is tendered. You can accrue the expense at that date even though you do not pay the bill until a later date.

There is an exception to the economic performance test for certain recurring items (items that are repeated on a regular basis). A deduction for these items can be accrued even though economic performance has not occurred.

There is a special rule for real estate taxes. An election can be made to ratably accrue real property taxes that are related to a definite period of time over that period of time. Any real property taxes that would normally be deductible for the tax year that apply to periods prior to your election are deductible in the year of the election.

Two-and-a-Half-Month Rule

If you pay salary, interest, or other expenses to an unrelated party, you can accrue the expense only if it is paid within two and a half months after the close of the tax year.

> **example**
>
> You declare a year-end bonus for your manager (who is not related to you under the rules discussed). You are on the calendar year. You can accrue the bonus in the year in which you declare it if you actually pay it no later than March 15.

Related Parties

If expenses are paid to related parties, such as certain family members, a special rule applies. This rule, in effect, puts an accrual taxpayer on the cash basis so that payments are not deductible until actually paid. Related parties are defined in Chapter 5.

If you fall under this related party rule, you cannot deduct the expense until payment is actually made and the related party includes the payment in his or her income.

> **example**
>
> You have an accrual business in which your child is an employee. Your business is on the calendar year. On December 31, 2004, you declare a year-end bonus of $5,000 for your child. You may not accrue the bonus until you pay the $5,000 to your child and your child includes the payment as income. Therefore, if you write a check on January 15, 2005, for the bonus and your child cashes it that day, you can accrue the expense in 2005.

Accounting Methods for Long-Term Contracts

For businesses involved in building, constructing, installing, or manufacturing property where the work cannot be completed within one year, special accounting rules exist. These rules do not affect the amount of income or expenses to be reported—they merely dictate the timing of the income or expenses.

Generally, you must use the percentage-of-completion method to report income and expenses from these long-term contracts. Under this method, you must estimate your income and expenses while the contract is in progress and report a percentage of these items relative to the portion of the contract that has been completed. However, income and expenses are not fully accounted for until the earlier of completion of the job and acceptance of the work or the buyer starts to use the item and 5 percent or less of the total contract costs remain to be completed. Small contractors may use the completed contract method under which income and expenses are accounted for when the work is done.

Other Accounting Methods

The cash and accrual methods of accounting are the most commonly used methods. There are, however, other accounting methods. For example, if you sell property and receive payments over time, you generally can account for your gain on the *installment method*. More specifically, the installment method applies if one or more payments are received after the year of the sale. *Gain* is reported when payments are received. This method can be used by taxpayers who report other income and expenses on the cash or accrual method (see Chapter 6).

Other accounting methods include, for example: Special Accounting for Multi-Year Service Warranty Contracts and Special Rules for Farmers.

Accounting for Discounts You Receive

When vendors or other sellers give you cash discounts for prompt payment, there are two ways to account for this discount, regardless of your method of accounting. They are:

- Deduct the discount as a purchase in figuring the cost of goods sold.
- Credit the discount to a special discount income account you set up in your records. Any balance in this account at the end of the year is reported as other income on your return.

Trade discounts are not reflected on your books or tax returns. These discounts are reductions from list price or catalog prices for merchandise you purchase. Once you make the choice, you must continue to use it in future years to account for all cash discounts.

UNIFORM CAPITALIZATION RULES

Regardless of your method of accounting, special tax rules limit your ability to claim a current deduction for certain expenses. These are called the *uniform capitalization rules*, sometimes referred to as the

UNICAP rules for short. The uniform capitalization rules are a form of accounting method that operates in coordination with the accrual method, but overrides it. In essence, these rules require you to add to the cost of property certain expenses—instead of currently deducting them. The cost of these expenses, in effect, are recovered through depreciation or amortization, or as part of the costs of goods sold when you use, sell, or otherwise dispose of the property. The uniform capitalization rules are complex. Important things to recognize are whether you may be subject to them and that expenses discussed throughout this book may not be currently deductible because of the application of the uniform capitalization rules.

CHANGE IN ACCOUNTING METHOD

If you want to change your method of accounting (for example, from the accrual method to the cash method), you must file Form 3115, Application for Change in Accounting Method, during the year for which the change is to be effective. (Instructions on how and where to file this form are included in instructions to the form.) Some changes are automatic—just by filing you are ensured that your change is recognized; other changes require the consent of the IRS.

Periodically the IRS modifies its list of automatic changes (for example, see Revenue Procedures 99-49 and 2002-9). These include changing to a required accounting method from an incorrect one, switching to the cash method by an eligible small inventory-based business, and deducting the cost of "smallwares" (such as dishes and glassware) in the year they are first put to use by restaurants.

recordkeeping for business income and deductions

Recordkeeping is a tiresome and time-consuming task. Still, you have little choice but to do it. You need records to determine your gain or loss when you sell property. And as a general rule, you must be able to back up your deductions with certain clear proof, such as receipts, canceled checks, and other documentation. If you do not have this proof, your deductions may be disallowed. Certain deductions require specific evidence. Other deductions are based on more general means of proof.

This chapter is concerned with recordkeeping for income tax purposes. However, it is equally important to maintain good records to help you to manage your business efficiently and to apply for business loans. For further information on recordkeeping, see IRS Publication 334, *Tax Guide for Small Business (for Individuals Who File Schedule C or C-EZ)*; IRS Publication 552, *Recordkeeping for Individuals*; and IRS Publication 583, *Starting a Business and Keeping Records*.

GENERAL RECORDKEEPING

The tax law does not require you to maintain books and records in any particular way. It does, however, require you to keep an accurate and complete set of books for each business you operate. Statistics show that this can be an awesome task averaging 10 hours each week (that amounts to about 520 hours each year) for small business owners.

Set up your books when you begin your business. Your books are based on your choice of tax year and accounting method, as explained in Chapter 2. You also need to choose a bookkeeping method—single-entry or double-entry. If you are a service business, single-entry bookkeeping may be sufficient. However, if your business involves inventory or is complicated, double-entry should be used.

Your books should be set up with various accounts in order to group your income and expenses. The broad categories of accounts include income, expenses, assets, liabilities, and equity (or net worth). Within these accounts you can keep various subaccounts. For example, in an account called Expenses you can have subaccounts for advertising, bad debts, interest expense, taxes, rents, repairs, and more. In fact, your subaccounts should reflect the various income and deduction topics discussed throughout this book.

Keeping Records by Computer

Computer-generated records save time—an important commodity for the small business owner—and generally are more accurate than handwritten entries. The IRS accepts computer-generated records if they are legible and provide all the necessary information. You are required to keep a description of the computerized portion of your accounting system. You must keep this documentation as long as you keep the records themselves, showing the controls used to prevent the unauthorized addition, alteration, or deletion of retained records.

Use recordkeeping software that facilitates recordkeeping both for tax purposes as well as for financial matters. Using programs such as Simple Start or Quickbooks from Intuit enables you to forward data to your tax professional as well as transfer information into tax return preparation programs at tax time, saving you both time and money.

Your books alone do not entitle you to deductions; you need supporting evidence. This evidence includes sales slips, invoices, canceled checks, paid bills, time sheets for part-time help, duplicate deposit slips, brokerage statements on stock purchases and sales, and other documents that help to explain a particular entry in your books. Certain deductions—travel and entertainment expenses and charitable contributions—require specific types of supporting evidence, as explained later in this chapter. The IRS considers your own memoranda or sketchy records to be inadequate when claiming deductions. Keep these records and documentation in an orderly fashion.

Keep your files in a safe place. For example, keep a copy of computer files off premises, and store paper files in a fireproof safe. If you lose files with receipts because they were not stored safely, you may lose deductions and face penalties as well. If you "lose" records before or during an audit, you may be charged with a hefty fraud penalty. If, despite your best efforts, files and records are lost or destroyed by a casualty (such as a fire, storm, earthquake, or flood), you may be permitted to reconstruct records if you can prove those records existed before the casualty. Of course, reconstruction takes considerable time, and it is probably impossible to reconstruct all of your expenses.

Electronic Imaging Systems

Storage of receipts and other records in paper form makes retrieval of wanted items difficult. This is especially so for large companies, but it can be problematic for smaller businesses as well. Recognizing the problem, the IRS now allows books and records to be maintained by **electronic imaging systems**.

Electronic imaging system   A system that prepares, records, transfers, indexes, stores, preserves, retrieves, and reproduces books and records by electronically imaging hard copy to an electronic storage media or transferring computerized books and records to an electronic storage media using a technique such as COLD (computer output to laser disk). This technique allows books and records to be viewed or reproduced without the use of the original program.

If an electronic imaging system is used, it must ensure accurate and complete transfer of the hard copy or the computerized books and records.

SPECIFIC SUBSTANTIATION REQUIREMENTS FOR CERTAIN EXPENSES

Travel and Entertainment Expenses

The tax law imposes special substantiation requirements for claiming travel, entertainment, and car expenses. These car rules are discussed in Chapter 7.

Charitable Contributions

If you make contributions up to $75, your canceled check is considered to be adequate substantiation of your contributions. A receipt from the charity is also considered adequate substantiation. If you make contributions over $75 but not more than $250, your canceled check or a receipt from the charity also remains sufficient. What is more, the charity will notify you in writing on a disclosure statement if you received any goods or services by virtue of your contribution (e.g., your contribution entitles you to attend a charity dinner). The disclosure statement will state the amount of the benefit you are entitled to receive. You then subtract this benefit from your contribution and deduct only the net amount.

If you make donations of $250 or more, your canceled check is not considered to be adequate substantiation. You must get a written receipt or acknowledgment from the charity by the due date of your return (or the extended due date if you receive a filing extension) describing your contribution (the amount of cash contributed or a description of property contributed). Each payment to the same charity is treated as a separate payment unless you designed the payment plan to avoid this substantiation requirement.

---

example

If you gave a charity $100 in February, $100 in June, and $100 in November, your canceled check is considered adequate substantiation of the donation unless you arranged these contributions to avoid having to obtain a written receipt or acknowledgment.

If a property donation is valued at over $5,000, you may also be required to obtain an appraisal and keep a record of this appraisal.

RECORDS FOR DEPRECIATION, BASIS, CARRYOVERS, AND PREPAID EXPENSES

For some tax items you must keep a running account, because deductions will be claimed not only in the current year but also in years to come.

Depreciation

Depreciation allows you to recover the cost of property over the life of that property by deducting a portion of the cost each year. In order to claim your annual deductions, you must keep certain records:

- Costs and other information necessary to calculate your depreciation
- Capital improvements to depreciable assets
- Depreciation deductions already claimed
- Adjustments to basis as a result of depreciation deductions

This information not only is necessary for depreciation purposes but will also be needed to calculate gain or loss and any depreciation recapture on the sale or other disposition of a depreciable asset. The same recordkeeping rules apply to amortization and depletion deductions.

Basis

Basis is the cost of property or some other value assigned to property. Basis is used for several purposes: It is the amount on which depreciation deductions are based, as well as the amount used to determine gain or loss on the sale or other disposition of property.

The basis of property can vary from its basis upon acquisition. Some items increase basis; others decrease it. Keep track of changes in basis from:

- Depreciation deductions or first-year expensing
- Casualty deductions relating to the property
- Certain tax credits
- Capitalized costs

Carryovers

A number of deductions may be limited in a current year, but you may be able to carry over any unused portion to other years. In order to take advantage of carryover opportunities, you must keep records of deductions you have already taken and the years in which they were taken. What is more, you must maintain relevant records for the carryover periods:

- *At-risk losses.* Losses disallowed because of the application of the at-risk rules (see Chapter 4) can be carried over indefinitely.

- *Capital losses.* There is no limit on the carryover period for individuals. There is a five-year limit on carryover losses for corporations.

- *Charitable contributions.* Individuals who cannot fully use current charitable contributions because of adjusted gross income limits can carry over the unused deductions for a period of five years. C corporations that cannot fully use current charitable contributions because of the 10-percent-of-taxable-income limit can carry over the unused deductions for a period of five years.

- *Home office deductions.* Individuals who maintain an office in their home and whose home office deductions are limited in the current year by gross income earned in the home office can carry forward unused deductions indefinitely

- *Investment interest.* Individuals (including partners, LLC members, and S corporation shareholders) may be limited in their current deduction for investment interest by the amount of their net investment income. Excess investment interest can be carried forward indefinitely. There is no limitation on corporations, so there is no carryover.

- *Net operating losses.* When operating losses cannot be used in full in the current year, they may be applied against income in certain other years. The carryover period depends on the year in which the net operating loss arise; it can be as long as 10 years back and 20 years forward.

- *Passive activity losses.* Losses disallowed because of the application of the passive activity loss rules (*suspended losses*) can be carried forward indefinitely. The same rules apply to credits from passive activities.

■ *Cash basis and prepayment.* Depreciation and carryovers are not the only tax items that may run beyond the current tax year. If you are on the cash basis and prepay certain expenses, you may not be allowed a current deduction for your outlays. You may be required to deduct the expenses ratably over the period of time to which they relate. Some examples of commonly prepaid expenses that may have to be deducted ratably including insurance premiums, prepaid interest, rents, and subscriptions.

You need to keep a running record of Section 1231 losses—losses on the sale of certain business assets. This is because of a special recapture rule that applies to net ordinary losses from Section 1231 property. Section 1231 losses are explained in more detail in Chapter 6.

Finally, you need to keep track of tax credits that are not completely used in the current year. Tax credits that are part of the general business credit (such as the research credit, empowerment zone credit, employer Social Security credit, and the disabled access credit) are subject to a carryback and carryforward period depending on the year in which the excess credits result (up to 20 years).

HOW LONG YOU SHOULD MAINTAIN RECORDS

Your books and records must be available at all times for inspection by the IRS. You should keep these books and records at least until the time when the IRS's ability to question your deductions runs out. This time is called the *statute of limitations.* In general, the statute of limitations is either three years after the due date of your return or two years after the date the tax was paid—whichever is later. Some records must be kept even longer. You need to keep records to support the basis in property owned by the business. You also need to keep records for depreciation and carryovers, as discussed earlier.

Tax Returns

Keep copies of tax returns to help you prepare future returns, as well as to help you if your return is questioned by the IRS. It is a good idea to keep old tax returns indefinitely, along with proof that you filed it (for example, a certified receipt).

Keep a record of the basis of property used in your business for as long as you own the property, plus the statute of limitations on filing the return for the year in which property is sold or otherwise disposed of. For example, if in 2004 you buy equipment that you will sell in 2006, keep records on the basis of the property until 2010 (three years from the due date of the return for the year in which the property was sold).

Employer Records

If you have employees, you are required to keep records on employment taxes for at least four years after the due date of the return or after the tax is paid, whichever is later. Keep copies of all returns you have filed and the dates and amount of tax deposits you have made. Your records should also show your *employer identification number (EIN)*, a nine-digit number assigned to each business and used to report the payment of employment taxes and to file certain returns.

If you are just starting your business and do not have an EIN, you can obtain one instantaneously online at <www.irs.gov/businesses /small/article/0,,id=102767,00.html> or by filing Form SS-4, Application for Employer Identification Number, with the IRS service center in the area in which your business is located. Application by mail takes several weeks. An SS-4 can be obtained from the IRS web site at <www.irs.gov> or by calling a special business phone number (1-800-829-4933) or the special Tele-TIN phone number. The number for your service center is listed in the instructions to Form SS-4. If you call for a number, it is assigned immediately, after which you must send or fax a signed SS-4 within 24 hours.

Income Tax Withholding

You must keep records of each employee's name, address, and Social Security number, the amount of each wage payment, the amount of each payment subject to income tax withholding, and the amount of income tax withheld. You must also keep copies of all employees' withholding allowance certificates (Form W-4). Similarly, you must keep any earned income credit advance payment certificates (Form W-5) filed with you by low-income wage earners who want to receive an advance on their earned income credit.

Other Employment Taxes

Similar records must be kept for each employee for Social Security and Medicare taxes, as well as for federal unemployment taxes (FUTA).

part 2

business income and losses

chapter 4

income or loss from business operations

The fees you earn for your services or the receipts you collect from the sale of goods are the bread-and-butter income of your business. Hopefully your pricing policies are realistic and you have a strong customer or client base so that you can make a profit.

Even if sales are healthy, expenses can outrun receipts, resulting in a loss for the business. You will not know whether you have net income or loss until all of the expenses discussed throughout the book have been taken into account. If there is a net loss, then limitations may come into play on when and the extent to which business losses can be deducted.

For further information about business income and losses, see IRS Publication 225, *Farmer's Tax Guide*, IRS Publication 334, *Tax Guide for Small Business*, Publication 541, *Partnerships*, IRS Publication 542, *Corporations*, and IRS Publication 911, *Direct Sellers*. A further discussion of the hobby loss rules may be found in IRS Publication 535, *Business Expenses*. For information on the at-risk rules and passive activity loss limitations, see IRS Publication 925, *Passive Activity and At-Risk Rules*.

BUSINESS INCOME

Whether you work full-time or part-time, income received for your business activity is part of your business income. How you report it depends on your accounting method (explained in Chapter 2).

Where you report it depends on how your business is organized. For example, self-employed individuals report income on Schedule C or Schedule C-EZ or on Schedule F if the business is farming. Partnerships and LLCs report income on Form 1065, S corporations use Form 1120S, and C corporations report income on Form 1120.

Payment Methods

Most business transactions are in cash. For tax purposes the term *cash* includes checks and credit card charges. However, in some cases, payments may take a different form.

Payments in Kind

If you exchange your goods or services for property, you must include the fair market value of the property you received in income. Bartering does not avoid the requirement to report income. This is true whether you barter directly—one-on-one—or receive property through a barter exchange that gives you credit for the goods or services you provide. Bartering is reported to the IRS on Form 1099-B, Proceeds from Broker and Barter Exchange Transactions.

Payments in Services

If you exchange your goods or services for someone else's services, you are also taxed on the value of the services you receive. If services are exchanged for services, you both can agree to the value of the services you report as income.

Consignments

If items owned by others are consigned to you for sale, do not include these items in your inventory. Instead, report income from any commissions or profits you are entitled to upon sale.

If you consign your goods to others, do not report this arrangement as a sale. You report income from the sale of consigned goods when they are sold by the consignee. Do not remove the items from your inventory until a sale by the consignee.

Kickbacks

Amounts you receive as kickbacks are included in income. However, do not include them as a separate income item if you properly treat these amounts as a reduction to the cost of goods sold, a capital expenditure, or an expense item.

Loans

If you obtain business loans, do not include the proceeds in income. They are merely loans that must be repaid according to the terms of the loan agreement.

INCOME FOR SERVICE BUSINESSES

If your main business activity is providing services to customers and clients, you are in a service business. As such, reporting business income is generally a simple matter. You report as income all of your revenues from performing services according to your method of accounting. Since most service businesses are on the cash basis, income usually is reported when fees are collected.

1099 Income

If you are an independent contractor, your clients or customers are required to report income paid to you on Form 1099-MISC, Miscellaneous Income. This informs the IRS of income you have received. Income is required to be reported on Form 1099 if annual payments are at least $600, but you are required to report on your tax return *all* income you receive (even if no 1099 has been issued).

Advances and Prepayments

If you receive income for services to be performed in the future, you report the income if you have free and unrestricted use of the money.

Accrual basis businesses receiving advance payments may defer the reporting of income to the following year *if* services are to be performed by the end of that year (the income is accrued at the time the services are performed). However, no deferral is permitted beyond the year after the year of receiving the advance.

Similarly, accrual basis businesses receiving advance payments for service agreements (including agreements that include incidental parts or materials) can defer the income if the services will be performed by the end of the next year.

INCOME FROM THE SALE OF GOODS

Reporting income from the sale of goods involves a two-step process. First you must figure your *gross receipts*—amounts received from sales (determined by your method of accounting). Then you must subtract from gross receipts your **cost of goods sold.**

Cost of goods sold The cost of buying raw materials and producing finished goods. Essentially it is the cost of buying inventory or manufacturing inventory.

Cost of Goods Sold

Cost of goods sold is determined each year by adjusting beginning inventory for changes made during the year. Inventory at the beginning of the year (generally your closing inventory reported on last year's return) is increased by adding any inventory purchases or manufactured items purchased that year. Include purchases, the cost of labor, and other costs required to be included under the uniform capitalization (UNICAP) rules. Decrease this figure by sales from inventory.

To know what your opening inventory and closing inventory is, you need to take a physical inventory. A physical inventory must be taken at reasonable intervals and the actual count must be used to adjust the inventory figures you have been maintaining all along. Generally, a physical inventory is taken at year-end. You are permitted to estimate year-end inventory by factoring in a reasonable allowance for shrinkage (for example, loss due to theft that you failed to detect). If you make such an estimate, then you must take a physical count on a consistent basis and adjust—upward or downward—the actual inventory count.

There are four methods for reporting inventory. They are:

1. Cost

2. Lower of cost or market method

3. Write-down of subnormal goods

4. Other inventory methods

Resellers—those who buy items for sale to others—use certain rules and methods to assign the cost of these items to those sold during the year:

- *First-in, First-out (FIFO).* An item sold is deemed to be the first item booked into inventory. For example, if you bought 10 widgets on three occasions at a cost of 10¢ each, 15¢ each, and 20¢ each and you sell 15, under FIFO you have sold 10 at 10¢ each and 5 at 15¢ each.

- *Last-in, First-out (LIFO).* An item sold is deemed to be the last item booked into inventory. In the widge example, you have sold 10 at 20¢ each and 5 at 15¢ each.

- *Specific identification method.* The actual cost of the items is used. This method generally is used when a business owns large or unique items (for example, an antique store would use this method for its objects since items are not identical and cannot be commingled).

Small businesses are allowed to use a simplified value LIFO method that makes it easier to determine the value of inventory. If you elect FIFO, you must use the lower of cost or market method to report inventory. If you elect LIFO, you must use cost to report inventory.

Gross Profits

Gross profits from the sale of goods is the difference between the gross receipts (sales revenues) and the cost of goods sold (as well as other allowances). If you remove items from inventory for your personal use, be sure to adjust your figures accordingly.

You generally cannot use the installment method of accounting to report the sale of inventory items—even if you receive payment on an installment plan. You report the sale according to your usual method of accounting so that on the accrual basis you pick up the income in full in the year of sale even though the full payment will not be received at that time.

Other Income for Direct Sellers

In addition to income from sales of products to customers, direct sellers may receive income from commissions, bonuses, or percentages you receive for sales and the sales of others who work under you, as well as prizes, awards, and gifts resulting from your sales activities.

INCOME FROM FARMING

When a business earns its income from sales of livestock and produce, payments from agricultural programs and farm rents and other similar sources, it is considered a farming business. Since most small farms use the cash method of accounting to report income and expenses, the following discussion is limited to this method of accounting. However, if items regularly produced in the farming business or used in the farming business are sold on an installment basis, the sale can be reported on the installment method, deferring income until payment is received.

While many income items of farms are similar to nonfarm businesses, there are some items unique to farming that enjoy special treatment:

- *Sales of livestock (including poultry) and produce.* The sale of livestock classified as Section 1231 property may result in Section 1231 gain or loss (explained in Chapter 6). If crops are sold on a deferred payment contract, you report the income when payment is received.

- *Sales of livestock caused by drought, flood or other weather conditions.* While such sales are generally reported in the current year, you can opt to report them in the following year if you can show that you would not have sold the livestock this year but for the weather conditions *and* you are eligible for federal assistance because of the weather conditions. You must file a separate election with your tax return for the year of the weather conditions for each class of animals (e.g., cattle, sheep). Alternatively, deferral is indefinite if proceeds are reinvested in similar livestock within four years.

- *Rents, including crop shares.* Generally, rents are not treated as farm income but rental income and these rents are not part of your net income or loss from farming. However, rents are treated as farm income if you materially participate in the management or operations of the farm (material participation is explained later in this chapter).

- *Agricultural payments* (cash, materials, services or commodity certificates) from government programs generally are included in income. If you later refund or repay a portion of the payments, you can deduct these amounts at that time. For details on how to treat specific government payments, see IRS Publication 225, *Farmer's Tax Guide*.

- *Patronage dividends* from farm cooperatives through which you purchase farm supplies and sell your farm products are included in income.

- *National Tobacco Settlement payments* to landowners, producers, and tobacco quota owners in Alabama, Florida, Georgia, Indiana, Kentucky, Maryland, Missouri, North Carolina, Ohio, Pennsylvania, South Carolina, Tennessee, Virginia, and West Virginia.

Farmers who pledge part or all of their production to secure a Commodity Credit Corporation (CCC) loan can make a special election to treat the loan proceeds as income in the year received and obtain a basis in the commodity for the amount reported as income. Farmers who do not make this election must report market gain as income.

Farmers may exclude payments received under the Agricultural Management Assistance Program and the Soil and Water Conservation Assistance Program.

Farm Income Averaging

You can choose to figure the tax on your farming income (*elected farm income*) by averaging it over the past three years. If you make this election, it will lower the tax on this year's income if income was substantially lower in the three prior years. However, it does not always save taxes to average your farming income—it is a good idea to figure your tax in both ways (the usual way and averaging) to determine which method is more favorable to you.

The same averaging option applies to commercial fishermen.

INVESTMENT-TYPE INCOME

Operating income from a business includes certain investment-type income, such as interest on business bank accounts and rents from leasing property. Except for C corporations, these items are not listed separately on the return but instead reported together as other income. How to report this income can be found later in this chapter. Capital gains are discussed in Chapter 5 and other gains from the sale of business property are discussed in Chapter 6.

Interest Income

Interest received on business bank accounts and on accounts or notes receivable in the ordinary course of business is a common type of ordinary business income. If the business lends money, interest received on business loans is business income.

Businesses that make below-market or interest-free loans may be deemed to receive interest, called *imputed interest* (see Chapter 11).

Dividends

Dividends payable by corporations in which the business owns shares is reported as ordinary business income. C corporations that receive dividends from domestic (U.S.) corporations can effectively exclude some or all of these dividends by claiming a special dividends-received deduction. The amount of the dividends-received deduction depends on the percentage of ownership in the corporation paying the dividend.

Rents

Rents can be generated from leasing personal property items such as equipment, formal wear, or videos. Rents can also be generated from leasing out real property.

Real Estate Rents

A business that provides services in conjunction with rentals reports rents as business income. For example, if you own a motel, you report your rentals as business income because you provide maid service and other services to your business guests.

If your tenant pays expenses on your behalf in lieu of making rental payments to you, these payments to third parties are part of your business income. For example, if your tenant pays your property taxes, you report the payment of taxes as rental income.

Prepaid Rent

Advances, including security deposits, must be reported as income if you have unrestricted right to them. If you are required by law or contract to segregate these payments, you do not have to report them as income until you are entitled to enjoy them (the restrictions no longer apply).

Lease Bonus or Cancellation Payments

Amounts your tenant pays to secure a lease (lease bonus payments) or to get out of a lease early (cancellation payments) are income to you.

Cancellation of Debt

If you owe money and some or all of your debt is forgiven by the lender, you generally must include this debt forgiveness in income. However, you do not have to include debt forgiveness in income if you are insolvent at the time of the cancellation or file for bankruptcy. Special rules apply to qualified farm debt and qualified real property business debt.

Instead of reporting the cancellation of debt as income, you may elect to reduce certain **tax attributes**. Making this election has the effect of limiting your future write-offs with respect to these tax attributes. Generally the amount excluded from income reduces the tax attributes (in a certain order) on a dollar-for-dollar or $33\frac{1}{3}$ cents basis. The election is made on Form 982, Reduction of Tax Attributes Due to Discharge of Indebtedness.

Tax attributes   These are tax aspects that provide a tax benefit in the current year or future years. They include the basis of depreciable real property, the basis of other depreciable property, net operating losses and loss carryovers, general business credit carryovers, minimum tax credit, capital losses and loss carryovers, passive activity loss and credit carryovers, and foreign tax credit carryovers.

Damages and Other Recoveries

If you receive damages for patent, copyright or trademark infringement, breach of contract, or other business-related injuries, you report the damages as business income.

MISCELLANEOUS BUSINESS INCOME

Almost any type of income earned by a business is considered to be business income. In addition to the types of income already discussed, the following are other examples of business income you must report:

- Recovery of bad debts previously deducted under the specific charge-off method
- Taxable income from insurance proceeds (such as key person insurance)
- Income adjustments resulting from a change in accounting method
- Scrap sales
- Finance reserve income
- Prizes and awards for the business
- Credit for alcohol used as fuel (for details see the instructions to Form 6478, Credit for Alcohol Used as Fuel)
- State gasoline or fuel tax refunds received in the current year
- Credit for federal tax paid on gasoline or other fuels claimed on the prior year return
- Recapture of the deduction for clean-fuel vehicles used in the business and clean-fuel refueling property (for details see IRS Publication 535, *Business Expenses*)
- Recapture of first-year expensing deduction (first-year expensing is explained in Chapter 12)
- Recapture of Sec. 280F if listed property's business use drops below 50 percent (figure recapture amount on Form 4797 in Chapter 6)
- World Trade Center grants made to businesses

Special Income Items for S Corporations

If a corporation operated as a C corporation and then converted to S status, certain unique income items may result. These items are taxed to the S corporation; they are not pass-through items taxed to the shareholders. These items include:

- *Last-in, first-out inventory recapture on the conversion from C status to S status.* Recapture results in an income adjustment payable in four equal installments, one reported on the final return of the C corporation (or the year of the transfer), and one fourth each in the first, second, and third years of the S corporation's life (or the year of the transfer and the two successive years).

- *Excess net passive income.* If there were accumulated earnings and profits (E&P) from the time when the corporation was a C corporation *and* it has passive income for the year in excess of 25 percent of gross receipts, then tax is due at the rate of 35 percent.

- *Built-in capital gains.* If the corporation has appreciated property when it converts, the appreciation to the date of conversion is reported as built-in gains if the property is sold or otherwise disposed of within 10 years of the conversion. The tax on net recognized built-in capital gains is 35 percent.

Special Income Items for C Corporations

If a C corporation converts to S status and reports inventory using LIFO, it must recapture one fourth of the resulting income adjustment, reporting it as income on its final return (the year of conversion).

If the corporation receives a tax refund of taxes deducted in a prior year, the refund must be reported as income to the extent it produced a tax benefit for the corporation.

STATE INCOME TAXES ON BUSINESS INCOME

Federal income taxes on your business income may not be your only concern. You may also be subject to state income taxes. This liability depends on whether you do business within the state. Generally, this means having a nexus (connection) to the state. This is based on having a physical presence there, which may be evidenced by maintaining an office or sending a sales force into the state; merely shipping goods into the state without some additional connection is not enough to prove a business presence within the state. You may have a nexus to more than one state, no matter how small your business is.

If there is a business connection, the business income is apportioned among the states in which you do business. Apportionment is based on a sales factor, a payroll factor, and a property factor (the states have different apportionment rules). The rules are highly complex, but there is considerable wiggle room to shift income into the state with the lowest taxes.

For more information about state income taxes, contact the tax or revenue departments of each state in which you do business.

NET OPERATING LOSSES

If deductions and losses from your business exceed your business income, you may be able to use the losses to offset income in other years. Net losses from the conduct of your business are *net operating losses* (*NOLs*).

Net operating losses are not an additional loss deduction. Rather, they are the result of your deductions exceeding the income from your business. The excess deductions are not lost; they are simply used in certain other years.

You have an NOL if you have deductions from a trade or business, deductions from your work as an employee, or deductions from casualty and theft losses.

Only individuals and C corporations can claim NOLs. Partnerships, limited liability companies (LLCs), and S corporations cannot have NOLs, since their income and losses pass through to owners. However, partners, LLC members, and S corporation shareholders can have NOLs on their individual returns. These NOLs are created by their share of the business's operating losses.

Calculating NOLs

After you have completed your tax return for the year, you may find that you have an NOL. If you are an individual, you may have an NOL if your adjusted gross income, reduced by itemized deductions or the standard deduction (but before personal exemptions), is a negative figure. C corporations may have an NOL if taxable income is a negative figure. This negative figure merely indicates a possibility of an NOL; then you must determine whether, in fact, there actually is one. This is due to the fact that certain adjustments must be made to that negative figure in arriving at an NOL. Individuals and corporations calculate NOLs in a slightly different manner.

Individuals

An NOL does not include personal exemptions, net capital losses, nonbusiness losses, or nonbusiness deductions. The NOL can be computed on Schedule A of Form 1045. This form adds back to taxable income any of these items claimed on the return and makes other adjustments required to compute the NOL. Do not add back business-related deductions, such as moving expenses and state income tax on business profits.

Corporations

The NOL for corporations generally is calculated by reducing gross income by deductions. Special rules then apply to adjust the NOL. They are:

- A full dividends-received deduction is taken into account in calculating the NOL. For example, the 70-percent or 80-percent limit is ignored.
- NOLs from other years are not taken into account in calculating a current NOL.
- Losses that fall under the passive activity rules cannot be used to calculate an NOL.

If a corporation's ownership changes hands, limits apply on the use of NOL carryforwards. The tax law does not want one corporation to acquire another for the purpose of using NOLs of the target corporation to offset the income of the acquiring corporation. These rules are highly complex.

Carrybacks and Carryovers

Net operating losses may be carried back and, if not used up, carried forward for a certain number of years. The carryback and carryforward periods depend on the year in which the NOL arose.

> For NOLs arising in tax years beginning before August 6, 1997, the carryback period was three years and the carryforward period continues to be 15 years.

> For NOLs arising in tax years beginning after August 5, 1997, generally there is a two-year carryback and a 20-year carryforward period. However, for small businesses (those with average annual gross receipts of $5 million or less during a three-year period), a three-year carryback applies to NOLs arising from government-declared disasters (e.g., for farmers and ranchers, there is a five-year carryback for all NOLs). For NOLs arising in 2001 and 2002, there is a five-year carryback. There is a 10-year carryback for NOLs arising from product liability.

If you have an NOL in 2004, you first carry the loss back to a year that is two years before the year in which the NOL arose (the NOL year), which is 2002. If it is not used up in that year, carry it to the year before the NOL year, which is 2003. If the NOL is still not used up, you can begin to carry it forward (with modifications explained below).

Keep track of each category of NOL. For example, do not lump pre-August 6, 1997, carryforwards together with post-August 5, 1997, carryforwards.

If you have carryovers from more than one year, you use the carryovers in the order in which they were incurred.

Election to Forgo Carryback

Instead of carrying a 2004 NOL back two years and then forward, you can elect to forgo the carryback and just carry forward the loss for 20 years. You make this election in the NOL year by attaching a statement to your return if you are an individual, or by checking the appropriate box on the corporate return for C corporations. Once the election is made, it cannot be changed. If you incur another NOL in a subsequent year, you must make a separate election if you also want to forgo the carryback.

The election to forgo the NOL carryback applies not only to regular income tax purposes but also to alternative minimum tax purposes.

Quick Refunds from Carrybacks

If your business is struggling, you can use an NOL carryback to generate quick cash flow. The carryback will offset income in the carryback years, and you will receive a refund of taxes paid in those years.

Individuals can file Form 1045, Application for Tentative Refund, to obtain a relatively quick refund. Corporations can expedite a refund from an NOL carryback by using a special form, Form 1139, Corporation Application for Tentative Refund, to obtain a quick refund.

A corporation that expects an NOL for the current year may extend the time for payment of tax for the immediately preceding tax year by filing Form 1139, Extension of Time for the Payment of Taxes by a Corporation Expecting a Net Operating Loss Carryback. This form is filed *after* the start of the year in which the NOL is expected but *before* the tax for the preceding year is required to be paid. Such corporations can also further extend the time for payment by filing Form 1139, explained earlier. Doing so extends the time for payment of tax for the immediately preceding tax year until the IRS has informed the corporation that it has allowed or disallowed its application in whole or in part.

You can also claim an NOL on an amended return, Form 1040X or Form 1120X. Individuals who carry back NOLs cannot recalculate self-employment tax and get a refund of this tax. The NOL applies for income tax purposes only.

LIMITATIONS ON BUSINESS LOSSES

Once you figure whether your business has sustained operating losses, you must then determine the extent to which you can deduct these losses. A number of limits apply that restrict full and immediate write-offs of business losses. Not all of the rules that follow apply to all types of businesses, so only review those rules applicable to your company.

Basis

If you own a pass-through entity, business losses claimed on your personal return cannot exceed your tax basis in the company. Losses in excess of basis can be carried forward and used in future years to the extent of basis at that time. There is no time limit on these carryforwards.

Partnerships and LLCs

Basis is determined, in part, by the way in which a partner or member acquires his interest in the entity.

- If the interest is acquired by contributing directly to the entity (typically in the start-up of the business), then basis is the cash and owner's basis of the property contributed to the entity.
- If the interest is purchased from an owner (for example, a retiring partner), then basis is the cash and value of the property paid.
- If the interest is acquired by performing services for the business, then basis is the amount of compensation reported. However, the receipt of an interest in the profits of the business (and not a capital interest) is not taxable under certain conditions and so does not give rise to any basis.
- If the interest is inherited from a deceased owner, then basis is the value of the interest for estate tax purposes (typically the value of the interest on the date of the owner's death).

If property transferred to the entity is subject to liabilities, owners increase their basis by their share of the liabilities.

After the initial determination of basis, it may be increased or decreased annually. Basis is increased by the following items (determined on a per-share, per-day basis):

- The owner's distributive share of entity income
- The owner's share of tax-exempt income (such as life insurance proceeds)
- Excess of depletion deductions over the basis of depletable property

- Additional capital contributions
- Share of new partnership liabilities (Limited partners in limited partnerships do not increase their basis by a share of liabilities assumed by the general partners.)

Basis is decreased (on a per-share, per-day basis), but not below zero, by:

- The owner's distributive share of entity losses (including capital losses)
- The owner's share of expenses that are not deductible in figuring entity income
- Distributions to the owner by the entity

S Corporations

Basis for the purpose of deducting pass-through losses means your basis in your S corporation stock—what you contributed to the corporation to acquire your shares—plus the amount of any money you loaned to the corporation. If S corporation stock is acquired by inheritance, the basis, which is generally the value of the stock on the date of the owner's death, is reduced by the portion of the value attributable to income in respect of a decedent. This is income earned by the owner prior to death that is received by and reported by the person who inherits the stock.

Guaranteeing corporate debt, which is a common practice for bank loans to S corporations, does not give rise to basis. However, if you are called on to make good on your guarantee, then you can increase your basis by the amount you pay to the bank on the corporation's behalf. A shareholder's basis is not affected by the corporation's liabilities.

After the initial determination of basis, it may be increased or decreased annually. Basis is increased by:

- The shareholder's share of the corporation's ordinary income
- The shareholder's share of separately stated items reported on the Schedule K-1 (including tax-exempt income)
- Excess of depletion deductions over the basis of depletable property
- Additional capital contributions

Basis is decreased (but not below zero) by:

- The shareholder's share of the corporation's losses
- The shareholder's share of expenses and losses that are not deductible in figuring ordinary income
- Noncapital and nondeductible corporate expenses reported on the Schedule K-1 (e.g., 50 percent of meal and entertainment costs and nondeductible penalties)
- Distributions not includible in the shareholder's income (e.g., dividends in excess of basis)

Hobby Losses

If your unincorporated business sustains losses year after year, you may not be able to deduct the losses in excess of your business income unless you can show that you have undertaken the business in order to make a profit. This limitation on losses is called the *hobby loss rule*, because it is designed to prevent individuals who collect coins and stamps, breed dogs or cats, or carry on other hobby activities from deducting what the tax law views as personal expenses. Any activity you do mainly for recreation, sport, or personal enjoyment is particularly suspect.

The hobby loss rule applies to individuals (including partners and LLC members) and S corporations. It does not apply to C corporations. For partnerships, LLCs, and S corporations whose business losses pass through to owners, the determination of whether there is a profit motive is made at the business level rather than at the owner level. In other words, the business itself must have a reasonable expectation of making a profit.

Impact of Hobby Classification

If your business is classified as a hobby, then any year in which you make a profit you must pay taxes on your entire profit. Any year you have losses (expenses exceeding income), you cannot deduct them. What is more, you cannot carry over the unused losses to claim them in another year. You lose the deduction for your losses forever.

Proving a Profit Motive

There is no hard and fast way for proving that you have a *profit motive*. Rather, a profit motive is something that is inferred on the basis of various factors. The burden of proof is on you, the taxpayer. No single factor is determinative. Some or all of the factors used to determine profit motive include whether you carry on the activity in a *businesslike manner*, whether the time and effort you put into the activity shows that you intend to make a profit, and whether you depend on the income from the activity for your livelihood.

Presumption of a Profit Motive

Your business may not be profitable, particularly in the early or start-up years. The tax law gives you a special presumption on which you can rely to show a profit motive (and delay an IRS inquiry into your activity). An activity is presumed to be engaged in for profit if you have a profit in at least three out of five years. If the activity is breeding, training, showing, or racing horses, the presumption period is two out of seven years. If you meet this presumption, then the hobby loss rules do not apply and your losses in the off years can be claimed in excess of your income from the activity.

You can rely on this presumption and avoid having the IRS question your losses by filing Form 5213, Election to Postpone Determination as to Whether the Presumption Applies that an Activity Is Engaged in for Profit. In effect, the form asks the IRS to delay a determination of your profit motive until the end of the five-year (or seven-year) period.

Is it a good idea to file Form 5213 and raise the presumption? Doing so is almost a guarantee that the IRS will look closely at your return. Should you not show a profit in the required number of years during the presumption period, you will be forced to argue that you have a profit motive despite recurrent losses. Thus, you are no better off than if you had not filed the form.

At-Risk Rules

In the past it was not uncommon for someone to invest in a business by contributing a small sum of cash and a large note on which there was no personal liability. The note increased the investor's basis against which tax write-offs could be claimed. If the business prospered, all was well and good. If the business failed, the individual lost only the small amount of cash invested. Congress felt this arrangement was unreasonably beneficial to investors and created *at-risk rules*. At-risk rules operate to limit your losses to the extent of your at-risk amounts in the activity. Your at-risk amounts are, in effect, your economic investment in the activity. This is the cash you put into a business. It also includes the adjusted basis of other property you contribute and any debts secured by your property or for which you are personally liable for repayment.

If you are subject to the at-risk rules, you do not lose your deductions to the extent they exceed your at-risk amounts; you simply cannot claim them currently. The losses can be carried forward and used in subsequent years if your at-risk amount increases. There is no limit on the carryover period. If the activity is sold, your gain from the disposition of property is treated as income from the activity and you can then offset the gain by the amount of your carried-over losses.

At-risk rules do not apply to investments in closely held C corporations that meet active business tests and that do not engage in equipment leasing or any business involving master sound recording, films, videotapes, or other artistic, literary, or musical property.

If you are subject to the at-risk rules, you must file Form 6198, At-Risk Limitations, to determine the amount of loss you can claim in the current year. You file a separate form for each activity you have an interest in.

You can treat nonrecourse financing from commercial lenders or government agencies as being at risk if the financing is secured by the real estate.

Passive Activity Loss Rules

If you work for your business full-time, you need not be concerned with the *passive activity loss (PAL) rules*. These rules apply only to a business in which you have an ownership interest but do not work in the day-to-day operations or management (i.e., **materially participate**) as well as rental real estate activities.

Passive activity   Any activity involving the conduct of a business in which you do not materially participate and all rental activities. These rules operate to limit a current deduction for losses from these activities unless certain exceptions, discussed later in this chapter, apply.

Material participation   Participation in a passive activity that satisfies one of seven tests set forth in the tax law. The basic test requires a minimum of 500 hours of participation during the year. Material participation may be allowed for as little as 100 hours of participation during the year if no other owner in the activity participates more.

There are seven tests for proving material participation. The one most relied on is whether you participate in the activity for more than 500 hours during the year.

Rental Real Estate Exceptions

There are two special rules for rental real estate activities that may allow you to claim losses in excess of rental income.

Rule 1 allows a limited amount of loss in excess of income to be deducted if participation is considered to be active (**active participation**). This limited loss deduction is called the $25,000 allowance and can be claimed by individuals whose adjusted gross income does not exceed $100,000. The allowance is phased out for those with adjusted gross income over $100,000 and is entirely eliminated when adjusted gross income is $150,000 or more. Married couples must file jointly to claim this allowance unless they lived apart for the entire year. In this case, up to $12,500 in losses can be deducted on a separate return (with a phase-out of the allowance for adjusted gross income over $50,000).

Active participation   Participation in a rental real estate activity that is less than the material participation standard. Participation in decision making may be sufficient. For example, if you set the rents, screen tenants, and review expenses, you may satisfy the active participation test. Having a managing agent to collect rents and see to property repairs does not prevent active participation by an owner.

Rule 2 allows real estate professionals to escape the PAL limitations altogether for purposes of deducting losses from their rental real estate activities. Individuals can be considered real estate professionals if they meet certain tests regarding their participation in real estate activities in general, including real estate construction, conversion, management, or brokerage activities, as well as rental real estate. If a qualifying real estate professional then meets material participation tests with respect to the rental real estate, losses from the rental real estate activity escape PAL restrictions. (Details of these rules are in the instructions to Form 8582.)

How the Passive Activity Loss Rules
Limit Deductions for Expenses

If the rules apply, your losses from passive activities that exceed income from all other passive activities cannot be deducted in the current year. You can carry over your unused deductions to future years. These are called *suspended losses*, for which there is no limit on the carryover period.

You can claim all carryover deductions from an activity in the year in which you dispose of your entire interest in the activity. A disposition includes a sale to an unrelated party, abandonment of the business, or the business becoming completely worthless. Simply giving away your interest does not amount to a disposition that allows you to deduct your suspended losses.

The PAL limitation for noncorporate taxpayers is computed on Form 8582, Passive Activity Loss Limitations. Closely held C corporations subject to the PAL rules must file Form 8810, Corporate Passive Activity Loss and Credit Limitations. Similar rules apply to tax credits from passive activities. The limitation on tax credits from passive activities for noncorporate taxpayers is computed on Form 8582-CR, Passive Activity Credit Limitations.

chapter 5

capital gains and losses

Companies may sell assets other than inventory items. These sales may result in gains or losses that are classified as capital gains or losses. Similarly, companies may exchange assets, also producing capital gains or losses unless tax-free exchange rules apply. Further, owners may sell their interests in the business for gain or loss.

Capital gains generally are treated more favorably than other types of income. However, C corporations do not realize any significant tax benefit from capital gains. What's more, capital losses may be subject to special limitations.

The treatment of gains and losses from Section 1231 property and income resulting from depreciation recapture are discussed in Chapter 6.

For further information about capital gains and losses, see IRS Publication 537, *Installment Sales*, IRS Publication 544, *Sales and Other Dispositions of Assets*, and IRS Publication 550, *Investment Interest and Expenses*.

WHAT ARE CAPITAL GAINS AND LOSSES

The tax law generally looks more favorably on income classified as capital gains than on other types of income—at least for pass-through entities. On the flip side, the tax law provides special treatment for capital losses. To understand how capital gains and losses affect your business income you need to know what items are subject to capital gain or loss treatment and how to determine gains and losses.

Capital Assets

If you own property used in or owned by your business (other than Section 1231 property discussed in Chapter 6, or Section 1244 stock discussed later in this chapter), gain or loss on the disposition of the property generally is treated as capital gain or loss. *Capital gains and losses* are gains and losses taken on **capital assets**.

Capital assets   Property held for investment and other property not otherwise excluded from capital asset treatment. For example, your interest in a partnership or stocks and securities is treated as a capital asset.

Most property is treated as capital assets. Excluded from the definition of capital assets are inventory, accounts receivable, depreciable business property, copyrighted materials, and government publications.

Determining the Amount of Your Gain or Loss

The difference between the **amount received** for your property on a sale, exchange, or other disposition, and your **adjusted basis** in the property is your gain or loss.

Amount received   The cash, fair market value of property, and relief of liability you get when you dispose of your property. For example, if you own a computer system for your business and you upgrade with a new system and sell your old system to another business, any cash you receive is considered an amount received. Upon the sale, you receive $5,000 cash, plus the buyer agrees to pay the remaining balance of $2,000 on a bank loan you took to buy the system; your amount received is $7,000 ($5,000 cash, plus $2,000 liability relieved).

Adjusted basis   This is your basis in the property, adjusted for certain items. Start with the original cost if you bought the property (the cash and other property you paid to acquire it). Even if the cash did not come out of your pocket—for example, if you took a loan—the cash you turn over to the seller is part of your basis. Adjust the basis by reducing it for any depreciation claimed (or that could have been claimed) and any casualty loss you claimed with respect to the property. For example, if your original computer system cost you $10,000, and you claimed $2,000 depreciation, your adjusted basis is $8,000.

You adjust basis—upward or downward—for certain items occurring in the acquisition of the asset or during the time you hold it. Amounts that *increase* basis include improvements or additions to property; legal fees to acquire property or defend title to it; selling expenses (e.g., a real estate broker's fee or advertising costs); and unharvested crops sold with the land.

Amounts that *decrease* basis include such items as depreciation and casualty losses that have been deducted. You do not adjust basis for selling expenses and related costs. These amounts are factored into the amount received (they reduce the amount received on the transaction).

Determining Basis on Assets Transferred Between You and Your Entity

The entity takes over your basis in any assets you contribute in a non-taxable transaction. Thus, if you contribute property to your partnership, the partnership assumes your basis in the property. Similarly, if you contribute property to your corporation as part of a tax-free incorporation, the corporation takes over your basis in the property. The rules for determining the basis in interests in pass-through entities are explained in Chapter 4.

Figuring Gain or Loss

When the amount received exceeds the adjusted basis of the property, you have a gain. When the adjusted basis exceeds the amount received, you have a loss.

Sale or Exchange Requirement

In order to obtain capital gain or loss treatment on the disposition of a capital asset, you generally must sell or exchange property. Typically, you sell your property, but other transactions may qualify for sale or exchange treatment. For example, if your corporation redeems some or all of your stock, you may be able to treat the redemption as a sale or exchange. Capital losses are subject to limitation on current deductibility as explained later in this chapter.

If you dispose of property in some way other than a sale or exchange, gain or loss generally is treated as ordinary gain or loss. For example, if you abandon business property, your loss is treated as ordinary loss, even though the property is a capital asset. However, if the property is foreclosed on or repossessed, your loss may be a capital loss. Ordinary losses are deductible without regard to the results from other transactions and can be used to offset various types of income (such as interest income).

Holding Period

Whether gains and losses are short-term or long-term depends on how long the asset disposed of has been held. If the holding period is more than one year, then gain or loss is long-term. If the holding period is one year or less, then the gain or loss is short-term.

If the business buys an asset, the holding period commences at that time (technically on the day after the acquisition date). If you transfer property to your business, the company's holding period includes your holding period if the transfer is viewed as a nonrecognition transaction (for example, a tax-free incorporation).

---

example

You form a corporation and transfer ownership of your truck and other items to the corporation in exchange for all of its stock. You acquired your truck on June 1, 2003, and transfer it to the corporation on July 1, 2004. On November 1, 2004, the corporation sells the truck. Its gain or loss on the sale of the truck is long-term because the holding period for the truck is more than one year—measured from the time you acquired it.

If a partnership makes an in kind (property) distribution to you, include the partnership's holding period in your holding period. However, if the distribution is from the partnership's inventory, then you cannot add the partnership's holding period to yours if you sell the property within five years.

Transfers to a Partnership or Limited Liability Company

If you transfer an asset to your company, the company takes on your holding period since this is a nontaxable transaction. If you sell an asset to your company, the company starts its own holding period since the sale generally is a taxable transaction (the company obtains a stepped up basis for the property).

Tax-Free Exchanges

Gain need not be immediately reported as income if the transaction qualifies as a tax-free exchange. The term *tax-free* is not an entirely apt description because the tax rules for these transactions merely *postpone* the reporting of gain rather than make gain permanently tax free. You reduce the basis of the property you acquire in the exchange by the gain you realized on the trade but did not have to report. Then, when you later sell the replacement property in a taxable transaction, you will report the gain on both initial exchange and the later disposition (if any).

To qualify for the tax-free exchange treatment, both the old property (the property you are giving up) and the new property (the property you are acquiring, called *replacement property*) must be business or investment property (certain property cannot be exchanged tax free). And both of the properties must be *like kind*. This means they must be of the same class of property. Depreciable tangible personal property can be either like kind or *like class* (the same General Asset Class or Product Class based on the four-digit codes in the Industrial Classification Manual of the U.S. Department of Commerce), such as a vacant lot for a factory building or a pickup truck for a panel truck used in the business.

---

example

You exchange one office building for another of equal value. Your building is worth $175,000, but has a basis of $100,000. The value of the new building is $175,000. You have a gain of $75,000, which may be postponed because of the tax-free exchange rules. The basis in the new building is $100,000 ($175,000 minus $75,000 gain not recognized). If you sell the new building in the future for $225,000, you will recognize gain of $125,000 ($75,000 deferred from the initial exchange, plus $50,000 from the appreciation of the replacement building).

If non–like-kind property is also received in the exchange, you must recognize gain to the extent of this other property, called *boot*.

---

example

Use the example of the building, except that the replacement building is only valued at $150,000 and you receive $25,000 cash to make the exchange of equal value. You must recognize gain of $25,000, the extent of the boot received. The basis of the replacement building in this case is reduced by only $50,000, and the gain not recognized.

Timing

Like-kind exchanges must be completed within set time limits. The new property must be identified within 45 days after you transfer the old property. This identification applies to up to three properties (or any number where the value of the properties is not more than double the value of the property given up). Then, the exchange must be completed (you must receive the new property) within 180 days after you transfer the old property or the due date of your return (including extensions) for the year you gave up the old property if this is earlier than 180 days after the transfer.

Since it is not always easy to locate appropriate exchange property, you may work with a qualified intermediary to locate the property, acquire it, and then exchange it with you. A *qualified intermediary* is someone (other than your attorney, accountant, broker, employee, or a related person) who makes a written agreement to acquire the property you are giving up and to transfer replacement property to you. The agreement must limit your rights to receive, pledge, borrow, or otherwise obtain the benefits of money or other property held by the qualified intermediary.

Installment Sales

Gain need not be reported all at once if the sale is structured as an installment sale. This generally allows you to report gain as payments are received. An *installment sale* occurs when at least one payment is received after the year of sale.

Under the installment method, a portion of each payment received represents a return of your investment (part of your adjusted basis) and another part represents your profit (gain). You figure the amount of gain reported each year by a ratio:

$$\text{Gross profit percentage (reportable gain)} = \frac{\text{Gross profit}}{\text{Selling price (contract price)}}$$

Election Out of Installment Reporting

You can elect to report the entire gain in the year of sale (even though payments will be received at a later time). The election does not require any special forms. You simply report your entire gain in the year of sale. But once you do so, you generally cannot change your mind later on, even if your choice proved to be the wrong one tax-wise.

---

example

You sell property worth $100,000 for five annual installments of $20,000, plus 8 percent interest. Your adjusted basis in the property is $60,000 so your gross profit is $40,000 ($100,000 – $60,000). Your gross profit percentage is 40 percent ($40,000 ÷ $100,000). This means that 40 percent of each installment represents your gain while 60 percent is a return of your investment. Thus, in the first year, $8,000 of the $20,000 payment is gain while $12,000 is a return of your investment.

Why would you want to report all of your gain in one year when you can spread it out over a number of years? Reporting the entire gain in the year of sale may be wise, for example, if you have a net operating loss carryforward that can be used to offset the gain.

Interest on Deferred Payments

Payments must bear a reasonable rate of interest. If you fail to fix a reasonable rate of interest, then a portion of each payment is deemed to represent interest rather than capital gain. *Reasonable rate of interest* usually is the applicable federal rate (AFR) of interest for the term of the installment sale (a rate adjusted monthly by the IRS).

If the seller finances the purchase, the required minimum interest rate is the lower of 9 percent ("safe harbor rate") compounded semiannually or the AFR, provided the financed amount does not exceed $4,381,300 in 2004. With interest rates running below the 9 percent safe harbor rate, charging the AFR will produce a lower allowable interest rate. If the deferred amount exceeds $4,381,300, then the required minimum interest rate is 100 percent of the AFR.

Depreciable Property

If you sell depreciable property on the installment basis, any depreciation recapture must be reported in full in the year of sale regardless of when payments are actually received. In other words, gain resulting from depreciation recapture may exceed the cash payments received in the year of the installment sale but must be reported as income anyway.

TAX TREATMENT OF CAPITAL GAINS AND LOSSES FOR PASS-THROUGH ENTITIES

Capital gains and losses are separately stated items that pass through separately to owners. They are not taken into account in figuring the entity's total income (or loss). The reason for this distinction is to allow individual owners to apply the capital gain and loss rules on individual tax returns.

The impact of pass-through treatment of capital gains and losses is that owners may have favorable capital gains rates applied to their share of the business's capital gains. Similarly they may offset pass-through gains and losses from their business against their personal gains and losses.

---

example

In 2004, a shareholder in an S corporation has pass-through capital loss from his corporation of $10,000. He also has a $10,000 capital gain distribution from a mutual fund he owns in his personal investment account. He can offset the business gain by his personal loss on his individual income tax return.

Tax Rates on Capital Gains

Owners who are individuals pay tax on their share of capital gains as they would on their gains from personal investments. Thus, long-term capital gains generally are subject to a basic capital gains rate of 15 percent. However, owners in the 10-percent and 15-percent tax brackets pay only 5 percent on their share of capital gains. These rates apply to sales and exchanges in 2004 as well as to payments received on installment sales made in prior years.

Short-Term Gain

This type of gain is subject to the same tax rates as ordinary income. Owners in a pass-through entity may pay different tax rates on the same share of short-term capital gain.

---

example

An LLC with two equal owners sells at a profit a capital asset held for six months. In 2004, one owner may be in the 35-percent tax bracket while another is in the 25-percent tax bracket. Even though each owner receives an equal share of the gain, one owner pays a greater amount of tax on that gain than the other according to each owner's own tax bracket.

Unrecaptured Gain

Gain from the sale of real property on which straight line depreciation was taken results in unrecaptured gain (the amount of straight line depreciation). This portion of capital gain is taxed at the rate of 25 percent if the owner is in a tax bracket higher than the 15-percent tax bracket.

If property with unrecaptured gain is sold on the installment basis (discussed later in this chapter), then the first payment is deemed to reflect unrecaptured gain. When this amount has been fully reported, all additional amounts are capital gains subject to the lower rates detailed above.

Capital Losses

Special rules determine how capital losses of individuals may be used. These rules are discussed later in this chapter.

TAX TREATMENT OF CAPITAL GAINS AND LOSSES FOR C CORPORATIONS

C corporations must follow the rules discussed throughout this chapter on reporting capital gains and losses separately from their other income. These gains and losses are detailed on the corporation's Schedule D. However, C corporations at present realize no benefit from capital gains. *Net gains*, capital gains in excess of capital losses, are simply added to other business income. In effect, capital gains are taxed at the same rate of the corporation's other income. In the past, C corporations enjoyed a favorable tax rate on their capital gains and it may be possible that this treatment will be restored in the future.

LOSS LIMITATIONS

In some cases, even if you sell or exchange property at a loss, you may not be permitted to deduct your loss. If you sell, exchange, or even abandon a Section 197 intangible (see Chapter 14 for a complete discussion of the amortization of Section 197 intangibles), you cannot deduct your loss if you still hold other Section 197 intangibles that you acquired in the same transaction. Instead, you increase the basis of the Section 197 intangibles that you still own. This means that instead of deducting your loss in the year you dispose of one Section 197 intangible, you will deduct a portion of the loss over the remaining recovery period for the Section 197 intangibles you still hold.

Similarly, you cannot deduct losses on sales or exchanges of property between related parties (defined later). This related party rule prevents you from deducting a loss if you sell a piece of equipment to your spouse. However, the party acquiring the property from you (the original transferee, or in this case, your spouse) can add to the basis the amount of loss you were not allowed to deduct in determining gain or loss on a subsequent disposition of the property.

---

example

You sell your partnership interest to your daughter for $7,500. Your basis in the interest is $10,000. You cannot deduct your $2,500 loss. However, if your daughter then sells the partnership interest for $12,000, her gain is minimized to the extent of your nondeductible loss. Her tentative gain is $4,500 ($12,000 amount received less basis of $7,500). The amount of gain she must report is $2,000 ($4,500 tentative gain less $2,500 nondeductible loss).

Related Parties

The tax law defines who is considered a *related party*. This includes not only certain close relatives (spouses, siblings, parents, children, grandparents, and grandchildren), but also certain businesses you control. A *controlled entity* is a corporation in which you (and your family) own, directly or indirectly, more than 50 percent of the value of all outstanding stock, or a partnership in which you own, directly or indirectly, more than 50 percent of the capital interest or profits interest.

Businesses may be treated as related parties. These relationships include:

- A corporation and partnership if the same persons own more than 50 percent in the value of the outstanding stock of the corporation and more than 50 percent of the capital interest or profits interest in the partnership.
- Two corporations that are members of the same controlled group (one corporation owns a certain percentage of the other, or owners own a certain percentage of each corporation).
- Two S corporations if the same persons own more than 50 percent in value of the outstanding stock in each corporation.
- Two corporations, one of which is an S corporation, if the same person owns more than 50 percent in value of the outstanding stock of each corporation.

Special rules also apply to transactions between partners and their partnerships. It is important to note that what you may view as a related party may not be treated as such for tax purposes. Thus, for example, your in-laws and cousins are not treated as related parties. If you sell property to an in-law or cousin at a loss, you are not prevented from deducting the loss.

Loss Limits on Individuals

You can deduct capital losses against capital gains without limit. Short-term losses from sales of assets held one year or less are first used to offset short-term gains otherwise taxed up to 35 percent in 2004. Similarly, long-term losses from sales of assets held more than one year offset long-term gains otherwise taxed as low as 15 percent (5 percent for those in the 10-percent and 15-percent tax brackets), depending on when the transaction occurred. Losses in excess of their category are then used to offset gains starting with those taxed at the highest rates. For example, short-term losses in excess of short-term capital gains can be used to offset long-term capital gains from the sale of qualified small business stock, 50 percent of such gain of which is otherwise taxed at up to 28 percent (for an effective tax rate of 14 percent). However, if your capital losses exceed your capital gains, you can deduct only $3,000 of losses against your other income (such as salaries, dividends, and interest income).

If married persons file separate returns, the capital loss offset to other income is limited to $1,500. If you do not use up all of your capital losses, you can carry over any unused amount and claim it in future years. There is no limit on the carryover period for individuals.

Loss Limits on Corporations

If your corporation realizes capital losses, they are deductible only against capital gains. Any capital losses in excess of capital gains can be carried back for three years and then, if not used up, carried forward for up to five years. If they are not used within the five-year carryover period, they are lost forever.

The carryback may entitle your corporation to a refund of taxes from the carryback years. The corporation can apply for this refund by filing Form 1120X, Amended U.S. Corporation Income Tax Return. A corporation cannot choose to forgo the carryback in order to simply carry forward the unused capital losses.

Special rules not discussed here apply in calculating the corporation's carryback and carryforward.

SALES OF BUSINESS INTERESTS

The type of interest you own governs the tax treatment accorded to the sale of your interest.

Sole Proprietorship

If you sell your incorporated sole proprietorship, you are viewed as selling the assets of the business. The sale of all the assets of a business are discussed in Chapter 6.

Partnerships and LLCs

Partnerships

Gain or loss on the sale of your partnership interest is treated as capital gain *except* to the extent any gain relates to **unrealized receivables** and inventory items. Gain in this case is ordinary income.

Unrealized receivables   These are amounts not previously included in income that represent a right to payments for noncapital assets, which include inventory, services rendered, and services to be rendered.

If you receive items that were inventory to the partnership, they may be treated as capital assets to you. However, if you dispose of the items within five years, then any gain with respect to these items is ordinary income, not capital gain.

LLCs

Generally, the rules governing the sale of a partnership interest apply with equal force to the sale of an interest in an LLC. However, there are two special situations to consider:

1. *Sale of multiple-owner LLC to a single buyer.* The entity is treated as making a liquidating distribution of all of its assets to its owners. This means that gain in excess of basis is capital gain *except* to the extent of unrealized receivables and substantially appreciated inventory. Losses on a liquidating distribution can be recognized if only cash is received and it is less than your basis in your interest or cash, unrealized receivables or substantially appreciated inventory are distributed and they are less than your basis in your interest.

2. *Sale of a single-member LLC to multiple buyers.* This entity is treated as selling its assets and then contributing them to the new entity comprised of multiple buyers (treated as a partnership). You recognize gain or loss on the deemed sale of your interest to the buyers. There is no gain or loss recognition upon the contribution of the assets to the new entity.

S and C Corporations

When you sell your stock in a corporation, you recognize capital gain or loss. The amount of your gain or loss is the difference between your adjusted basis in the stock and the amount received in exchange.

If another corporation acquires 80 percent or more of the stock in your corporation within a 12-month period, it can elect to treat the stock purchase as if they had purchased the underlying asset. If so, your corporation must recognize gain or loss as if it had sold its assets for fair market value. From the buyer's perspective, this enables the corporation to step-up the basis of its assets as if it were a new corporation. The purchase price is allocated to the assets as explained in Chapter 6.

SPECIAL SITUATIONS

Sale of Qualified Business Stock

Tax laws encourage investments in small businesses by offering unique tax incentives. If you own stock in a corporation treated as a **small business**, you may be able to defer your gain or exclude it entirely.

Small business   For purposes of deferring or excluding gain on the sale of stock, a small business is a C corporation with gross assets of no more than $50 million when the stock is issued. The small business must be an active business and not a mere holding company. The stock must have been issued after August 10, 1993.

Deferring Gain

If you own stock in a small business for more than six months and sell it, you can defer any tax on the gain—called Section 1202 gain after the section in the Internal Revenue Code—by acquiring other small business stock within 60 days of the sale. If you reinvest only part of your proceeds, you can defer gain to the extent of your reinvestment.

Excluding Gain

If you own stock in a small business for more than five years, and sell it you can exclude one-half of your gain. The other half of the gain that is taxable is subject to tax at up to a 28 percent capital gain tax rate (unless you are in the 10-percent or 15-percent tax bracket). Thus, the effective tax rate on the sale of small business stock is 14 percent (50 percent of 28 percent).

The amount of the exclusion related to stock from a particular company is limited to the greater of 10 times your basis in the stock or $10 million ($5 million if married filing separately) minus any gain on stock from the same company excluded in a prior year.

Deferring Gain from Publicly Traded Securities by Investing in a Specialized Small Business Investment Company

If you own publicly traded securities, gain from their sale can be deferred by rolling over the proceeds into qualified small business stock. In this case qualified small business stock is stock or a partnership interest in a specialized small business investment company (SSBIC). The rollover must be completed within 60 days. The amount of the gain deferred under this option reduces the basis in the stock or partnership interest you acquire.

This deferral option is limited annually to $50,000 ($25,000 if married filing separately). This deferral option has a lifetime limit of $500,000 ($250,000 if married filing separately).

Zero Percent Gain from Community Renewal Property

If you own a community renewal business that invests in business assets within a specialty designated renewal community and hold the assets for more than five years, you do not have to pay *any* tax on your gain (40 authorized community renewal areas have been designated by the Secretaries of Housing and Urban Development and Agriculture). However, any portion of the gain attributable to periods before January 1, 2002, is ineligible for this special treatment and is taxed in the usual way.

Section 1244 Losses

If you own stock in a company considered to be a small business and you realize a loss on this stock, you may be able to treat the loss as an ordinary loss (within set limits). This loss is referred to as a *Section 1244 loss* because it is the section in the Internal Revenue Code.

Ordinary loss treatment applies to both common stock issued at any time and preferred stock issued after July 18, 1984. You can claim an ordinary loss if you sell or exchange the stock or if it becomes worthless. This special tax rule for small business stock presents another win-win situation for owners. If the company does well and a disposition of the stock produces a gain, it is treated as capital gain. If the company does not do well and the disposition of the stock results in a loss, the loss is treated as ordinary loss, which is fully deductible against your other income (such as salary, dividends, and interest income).

Qualifying for Ordinary Loss Treatment

The corporation issuing the stock must be a small business. This means that it can have equity of no more than $1 million at the time the stock is issued. This equity is the amount of cash or other property invested in the company in exchange for the stock. The stock must be issued for cash and property other than stock and securities. This definition of small business stock applies only to the loss deduction under Section 1244. Other definitions of small business stock apply for other purposes under the tax law.

You must acquire the stock by purchase. The ordinary loss deduction is allowed only to the original purchaser of the stock. If you inherit stock in a small business, receive it as a gift, or buy it from someone who was the original purchaser of the stock, you do not qualify for ordinary loss treatment.

Most important, the corporation must have derived over half its gross receipts during the five years preceding the year of your loss from business operations, and not from passive income. If the corporation is in business for less than five years, then only the years in which it is in business are considered. If the corporation's deductions (other than for dividends received and NOL) exceed gross income, the five-year requirement is waived.

Limit on Ordinary Loss Deduction

You can treat only the first $50,000 of your loss on small business stock as an ordinary loss. The limit is raised to $100,000 on a joint return, even if only one spouse owned the stock. However, losses in excess of these dollar limits can be treated as capital losses, as discussed earlier in this chapter.

The ordinary loss deduction can be claimed only by individuals. If a partnership owns Section 1244 stock and sustains a loss, an ordinary loss deduction can be claimed by individuals who were partners when the stock was issued. If the partnership distributes stock to partners and the partners then realize a loss on the stock, they cannot treat the loss as an ordinary loss. If an S corporation owns Section 1244 stock and sustains a loss, it cannot pass the loss through to its shareholders in the same way that partnerships can pass the loss through to their partners.

Worthless Securities

If you buy stock or bonds (collectively called *securities*) in a corporation and they become worthless, special tax rules apply. In general, loss on a security that becomes worthless is treated as a capital loss. If the stock is Section 1244 stock, you can claim an ordinary loss deduction, as explained earlier.

To claim a deduction, you must be able to show that the securities are completely worthless. If they still have some value, you cannot claim the loss. You must show that there is no reasonable possibility of receiving repayment on a bond or any value for your stock. Insolvency of the corporation issuing the security is certainly indicative of worthlessness. However, even if a corporation is insolvent, there may still be some value to your securities. The corporation may be in a bankruptcy restructuring arrangement designed to make the corporation solvent again someday. In this instance, the securities are not considered to be worthless.

You can claim a deduction for worthless securities only in the year in which worthlessness occurs. Since it is difficult to pinpoint when worthlessness occurs, you have some flexibility. The tax law allows you seven years to go back and amend a prior return to claim a deduction for worthless securities.

---

example

In 2005 you learn that stock you owned in a business became worthless in 2001. In general, you have seven years from the due date of your 2001 return, or April 15, 2009, to amend your 2001 return to claim the loss deduction.

If you own stock in an S corporation that becomes worthless, you must first adjust the basis in the stock for your share of corporate items of income, loss, and deductions. If there is any excess basis remaining, you can then claim the excess as a loss on worthless securities.

chapter 6

gains and losses from sales of business property

Businesses hold a unique category of assets called *Section 1231 property*. This category is named after the section in the Internal Revenue Code that created them. Upon the disposition of these assets, you can realize the best of both possible worlds—capital gain treatment for profitable sales and ordinary loss treatment for sales that result in a loss. Gain may be recognized all at once or deferred through an installment sale.

You may also realize gains or losses from other transactions involving business property, including involuntary conversions, abandonment or repossession of property, or the sale of all of the assets of the business.

Complex rules govern the overall treatment of these transactions. (The treatment of capital gains and losses from other property is also discussed in Chapter 5.) The purpose of this chapter is to alert you to the basic rules governing certain sales of business property. If any transaction applies to your business, you may wish to delve deeper with the assistance of a tax professional.

For further information about capital gains and losses, see IRS Publication 537, *Installment Sales*, and IRS Publication 544, *Sales and Other Dispositions of Assets*.

SECTION 1231 GAINS AND LOSSES

Certain assets used in business are granted special tax treatment. This treatment seeks to provide a win-win situation for a business. If a sale or other disposition of these assets (called **Section 1231 property**) results in a net gain, the gain can be treated as capital gain. If a net loss results, the loss is an ordinary loss.

Section 1231 property   Property held for more than one year and used in a business or held for the production of rents or royalties, such as real property, equipment, and inventory.

Determining Section 1231 Gains or Losses

You must use a *netting process* to determine your Section 1231 gains or losses. This means combining all gains and losses from the sale or other disposition of Section 1231 property. If your Section 1231 gains exceed your Section 1231 losses, then all of your gains and losses are treated as capital gains and losses. On the other hand, if your Section 1231 losses equal or exceed your Section 1231 gains, all of your gains and losses are treated as ordinary gains and losses.

If you sell appreciated Section 1231 property to a *related person*, gain that would otherwise be capital gain is recharacterized as ordinary income if the property is depreciable property in the hands of the buyer. Related persons for this purpose means a person and all entities that are controlled entities. A *controlled entity* is explained in Chapter 5.

Losses

The fact that your Section 1231 losses for the year equal or exceed Section 1231 gains does not automatically ensure ordinary loss treatment. You must check to see whether a special recapture rule applies. Under the recapture rule, net Section 1231 gain is treated as ordinary income to the extent it does not exceed **nonrecaptured** net Section 1231 **losses** taken in prior years.

Nonrecaptured losses   Total of net Section 1231 losses for the five most recent preceding tax years that have not been applied (recaptured) against any net Section 1231 gains in those years.

The recapture rules for Section 1231 gains and losses are extremely complex. They are designed to prevent you from being able to time gains and losses from year to year so that you take your gains as capital gains and your losses as ordinary losses. (Do not confuse these recapture rules with those that apply to depreciation which are discussed later in this chapter.) The recapture rules, in effect, treat your gains and losses as occurring in the same year so that what would ordinarily have been treated as capital gains is partially or fully treated as ordinary income.

INSTALLMENT SALES

If you sell property and receive at least one payment after the year of sale, you have automatically transacted an installment sale. You report your gain over the period in which you receive payment *unless* you elect to report all of the gain in the year of sale. Installment reporting does not apply to losses. This is called the installment method. You can use it regardless of your other accounting method for reporting income. Installment reporting does not affect the amount of gain you report, nor the characterization of that gain. It merely affects the timing of reporting the gain.

Recapture

If part of the gain on an installment sale relates to depreciation recapture, this gain must be reported up front, regardless of the payments received.

RECAPTURE

Certain write-offs you may take can come back to haunt you. The benefit you enjoy now may have to be repaid at a later time. For instance, if you claim certain *depreciation* on business assets (explained in Chapter 12)—a write-off of the cost of the assets over a set time—you must *recapture* the benefit when you dispose of the assets. Recapture in some instances is merely a matter of recharacterizing gain—instead of capital gain the recapture amount is treated as ordinary income. However, in other instances, recapture means reporting income that would not otherwise be due.

Recaptured Depreciation

If you claim accelerated depreciation on realty (generally this applies to realty placed in service before 1987), then you must recapture (report as ordinary income) the portion of gain relating to the excess of accelerated depreciation.

- For equipment and other personal property, recapture all of depreciation claimed (to the extent of gain).
- For nonresidential realty depreciated under The Accelerated Cost Recovery System (ACRS) (placed in service after 1981 and before 1987), recapture the excess of ACRS depreciation in excess of straight-line depreciation. Different rules apply to pre-ACRS property.

Unrecaptured Depreciation

If you claim a home office deduction for business use of a portion of your home (these rules are explained in Chapter 15), you do *not* have to apportion your gain; in effect, you can apply the home sale exclusion to your entire gain. However, all depreciation claimed on a home office after May 6, 1997 is unrecaptured depreciation—it must all be reported as gain upon the sale of the home. This gain is taxed at a maximum of 25 percent.

Recapture on Installment Reporting

When to report recapture on an installment sale depends on the type of recapture involved:

- *For recaptured depreciation*—All of the depreciation must be reported in full in the year of sale. This recapture is reported without regard to the proceeds received in the year of sale.
- *For unrecaptured depreciation*—The gain, with respect to each installment payment received, is reported first at the 25 percent

rate. Once unrecaptured depreciation has been fully reported, the balance of any gain is reported at the basic capital gains rate (generally 15 percent).

---

example

You purchased realty for $100,000 that you depreciated by $20,000 (for a basis of $80,000). In July 2004, you then sell the property for $130,000, payable in five equal annual installments. Of these installments, $10,000 of gain must be reported each year. (*Gain* is the difference between $130,000 received for the property and $80,000 basis.) Thus, gain on the first two installments is taxed at 25 percent. Gain on the three remaining installments will be taxed at 15 percent.

INVOLUNTARY CONVERSIONS

If business property is destroyed or stolen, condemned or disposed of through threat of condemnation and you receive insurance proceeds or other funds to compensate you for your loss, you have suffered an *involuntary conversion. Condemnations* are the taking of your property for public purposes, such as building roads or putting up utility poles—in effect a forced sale. Threat of condemnation occurs when you learn from a government official or other authorized person that the government intends to take your property. If you do not sell it to the government, it will be condemned.

If the funds you receive for the involuntary conversion of your property exceed your **adjusted basis** in the involuntarily converted property, you have a gain that is currently taxable unless you qualify to postpone your gain (explained later). If the funds you receive are less than your adjusted basis in the involuntarily converted property, you have a loss that is currently deductible (subject to usual loss limitation rules discussed in this chapter and in Chapter 5).

Adjusted basis   This is your basis in the property, adjusted for certain items. Start with your original cost if you bought the property (the cash and other property you paid to acquire it). Even if the cash did not come out of your pocket, for example, if you took a loan, the cash you turn over to the seller is part of your basis. Then, adjust the basis by reducing it for any depreciation claimed (or that could have been claimed) and any casualty loss you claimed with respect to the property. For example, if your original computer system cost you $10,000 and you claimed $2,000 depreciation, your adjusted basis is $8,000. (Other basis adjustments are explained in Chapter 5.)

In reporting condemnation awards, you can reduce your receipts by any legal fees or other expenses you incurred to obtain the payment as well as any special assessments levied against the part of the property if only a portion of the property was condemned. If amounts are withheld from the award to pay off your mortgage or outstanding taxes, you treat these amounts as payment you receive. Also add to the amount any severance payments you receive for the decrease in the value of the property you retain if only a portion of the property was condemned. The portion of gain relating to severance damages can be postponed in the same way as direct payments for the condemned property.

In figuring your gain or loss from an involuntary conversion, certain payments related to the event are not taken into account (they are treated separately). Relocation payments from the federal government or an assistance program are tax-free payments and interest on a condemnation award is reported separately as interest income (see Chapter 4).

Election to Postpone Gain

You make the election to postpone gain by acquiring replacement property within set time limits. In deciding whether or not to postpone gain, keep in mind that you do not have to use the insurance proceeds or other funds to acquire the replacement property—you need only invest a similar amount. You can, for example, spend the proceeds and take a loan to buy the replacement property. First, consider the advantage and disadvantage to help you decide whether or not you want to postpone gain.

- *Advantage*—Postponing gain allows you to use the proceeds undiminished by taxes on your gain.
- *Disadvantage*—You must reduce the basis of the replacement property by the amount of gain not immediately recognized. This results in a lower basis for purposes of figuring depreciation on the replacement property as well as for determining gain or loss on the disposition of the property.

Replacement Property

Replacement property is property that is similar or related in service or use to the involuntarily converted property. *Similar or related* means that the functions of the old and replacement properties are related. For example, if one piece of machinery is destroyed in a storm and you buy a new machine to perform the same work in your business, the new machine is clearly replacement property.

You need not buy the property directly. You are treated as acquiring replacement property if you buy at least an 80 percent interest in a corporation that owns property similar or related in service or use to the involuntarily converted property. However, you cannot buy replacement property from a *related party*—a business you control or a close relative—if the gain is more than $100,000. You can buy replacement property from a related party if the gain is $100,000 or less.

If your business property is destroyed in a disaster within an area qualifying for federal disaster relief, acquiring *any* tangible property for your business is treated as similar or related even if the functions of the old and new property are entirely different.

Replacement Time Limits

You must decide whether or not to postpone gain by acting with set time limits to place replacement property in service for your business. Generally you have until the end of the two years following the close of the year in which gain from the involuntary conversion was realized to acquire replacement property.

If business property has been condemned (or sold under threat of condemnation), the replacement period is three years from the close of the year in which the gain from condemnation (or threat of condemnation) was realized. However, if you buy replacement property by acquiring a controlling interest in a corporation, then the two-year replacement period applies.

---

example

In February 2004, a machine is destroyed by a storm and insurance proceeds you receive produce a gain. You can postpone the reporting of this gain by obtaining replacement property no later than December 2006.

If you decide you want to postpone gain but time is running out on buying replacement property, you can request an extension. For example, if you have already found property but have yet to close on the sale, ask for more time to do so. Address your request to the local district director of the IRS. Do not let the replacement period expire without submitting your extension request—it may be almost impossible to obtain an extension at this late date.

ABANDONMENT, FORECLOSURE, AND REPOSSESSION OF PROPERTY

Disposing of business property by abandonment, foreclosure, or repossession generally produces taxable results.

Abandonment

If you abandon business property, you *automatically* have a loss that is treated as an ordinary loss. The amount of your loss is the adjusted basis of the abandoned property. However, if you effectively abandon inventory that has become unsalable because it is obsolete or defective, you do not report it as a loss. Instead, you adjust your inventory valuation to reflect the actual value of the items, which may be merely their scrap value.

If the property you are abandoning is subject to a debt for which you are personally liable and the debt is canceled, you have ordinary income to the extent of this debt cancellation. Report this income separately from the abandonment loss—do not net one against the other.

Foreclosure or Repossession

If you cannot pay a loan or the mortgage on your business property, the lender will recoup this amount by *foreclosing* on the property or *repossessing* it. Foreclosure and repossession are treated as a sale or exchange for tax purposes, producing gain or loss on the transaction. This is the case even if you voluntarily transfer the property back. The amount realized usually is the debt you no longer have to pay. The difference between this amount and the adjusted basis in the property is the amount of your gain or loss.

- *If the debt is recourse debt* (you are personally liable for it)—do not include the debt cancellation in the amount realized (you report the debt cancellation separately as income). *Exception:* If the value of the property is less than the canceled debt, then the amount realized includes the debt cancellation to the extent of the value of the property.

- *If the debt is nonrecourse debt* (you are not personally liable for it)—include the full debt cancellation in the amount realized, regardless of the property's value.

---

example

The business bought a car for $30,000, financing $25,000 of the purchase price. The business stops paying the loan when there is still $20,000 outstanding and the adjusted basis of the car is $22,040. The lender repossesses the car and walks away from the remaining debt. If the debt is nonrecourse, report $2,040 as a loss (the difference between the amount realized of $20,000 and the adjusted basis of the car, $22,040).

---

example

Continuing with the car example, except that the debt is recourse. The value of the car at the time of the repossession is $19,000. In this instance, report a loss of $3,040 (the difference between the amount realized of $19,000 less $22,040). But you must also report income of $1,000 (the amount of the canceled debt in excess of the value of the car).

Lender's Perspective

If you are the lender and foreclose or repossess property because of nonpayment, you recognize gain or loss on the transaction. This is so whether or not the debtor cooperates and voluntarily transfers the property back to you.

Real Property

Generally, your gain is the difference between the total payments you have already received for the property and the gain you already reported as income. However, your reportable gain on a foreclosure or repossession is limited to the gross profit on your original gain minus any gain already reported. Reduce your profit by any costs related to the foreclosure or repossession, such as legal fees, court costs, and costs of recording or clearing title to the property.

Your basis in the reacquired property is your original basis in the property, increased by any gain recognized on the receipt of principal and foreclosure/repossession, and decreased by any principal payments received.

---

example

You foreclose on an office building for nonpayment of the mortgage you hold on the property you sold. You figure your basis in the building as follows:

Original basis	$200,000
Plus: Gain reported on principal received	+18,000
Plus: Gain on foreclosure	+27,000
Less: Principal received	(–90,000)
New basis	$155,000

Equipment and Other Personal Property

If you sold property on the installment method and repossess it for nonpayment, report gain or loss on the transaction, which is the difference between your basis in the installment obligations and the value of the property you repossess. Reduce the basis in the installment obligations by any costs for the repossession. Increase the value of the property by anything you receive from the debtor upon the repossession, such as a partial payment.

What is your basis in the installment obligations? This depends on how you originally opted to report the sale. If you used the installment method, your basis in the installment obligations is the unpaid balance of the installment obligations divided by your gross profit percentage.

SALE OF ALL THE ASSETS OF THE BUSINESS

If you sell your business by selling all of its assets, the rules for reporting gain or loss are really no different from a single asset sale. You allocate the purchase price of the sale to each of the assets, including goodwill or going concern value, in order to determine your gain or loss.

You usually arrive at this allocation through negotiations between you and the buyer.

Asset classes include the following:

- *Class I assets*—cash, demand deposits, and similar bank accounts.

- *Class II assets*—certificates of deposit, government securities, readily marketable stock or securities, and foreign currency.

- *Class III assets*—tangible assets (such as equipment, furniture, and fixtures) and intangible assets not in Classes IV or V (such as accounts receivable).

- *Class IV assets*—Section 197 assets (other than goodwill and going concern value) such as patents, copyrights, licenses, permits, franchises, trademarks, and covenants not to compete. (Section 197 assets are discussed in Chapter 12.)

- *Class V assets*—goodwill and going concern value.

The sale price is allocated in descending order—first to Class I assets, then Class II assets, and so on. There is no debate on allocating part of the purchase price to assets in the first two classes since the value of the assets is not in dispute. But as a seller, you generally want to allocate as much of the remaining purchase price to assets that will produce the most favorable tax results to you. For example, if you can allocate an amount to goodwill, you will achieve capital gain treatment.

In contrast, if such amount is allocated to inventory, you have ordinary income. However, the buyer has competing interests and wants to allocate as much as possible to depreciable assets. That would give him or her the opportunity to maximize depreciation deductions and not to allocate to goodwill, the amount of which is only recoverable upon a future sale of the business. Ultimately, the price you receive for the assets will reflect negotiations that include the allocation process.

part 3

business deductions and credits

chapter 7

car and
truck expenses

Americans are highly mobile, and the car is the method of choice for transportation. If you use your car for business, you may write off various costs. There are two methods for deducting costs: the actual expense method and the standard mileage allowance.

For further information about deductions with respect to business use of your car, see IRS Publication 463, *Travel, Entertainment, Gift, and Car Expenses*.

DEDUCTING CAR EXPENSES IN GENERAL

The discussion in this chapter applies to **cars** used partly or entirely for business.

Car Any four-wheel vehicle made primarily for use on public streets, roads, and highways that has an unloaded gross vehicle weight of 6,000 pounds or less (the manufacturer can provide this information). A truck or van is treated as a car if its unloaded gross weight is 6,000 pounds or less. Excluded from the definition is an ambulance, hearse, or combination thereof used in business and any vehicle used in business for transporting people or for compensation or hire.

The law allows you to choose between two methods for deducting business-related expenses of a car: the actual expense method or the standard mileage allowance, both of which are detailed in this chapter.

Choosing Between the Actual Expense Method and the Standard Mileage Allowance

Read over the rules on the *actual expense method* and the *standard mileage allowance*. For the most part, the choice of method is yours. In some cases, however, you may not be able to use the standard mileage rate. Where you are not barred from using the standard mileage rate and can choose between the methods, which is better? Obviously, it is the one that produces the greater deduction. However, there is no easy way to determine which method will produce the greater deduction. Many factors will affect your decision, including the number of miles you drive each year and the extent of your actual expenses. See the example's comparison.

---

example

You buy or lease a car for $15,000 and use it 100 percent for business. In 2004, the first year the car is in service, you drive 1,500 miles per month. If you use the standard mileage allowance, your car deduction for 2004 is $6,750 (18,000 miles × 37.5¢). If your actual costs exceed this amount, it may be advisable to use the actual expense method. If they are less than $6,750, the standard mileage allowance may be better.

In making your decision, bear in mind that the standard mileage allowance simplifies recordkeeping for business use of the car.

You should make the decision in the first year you own the car. This is because a choice of the actual expense method for the first year will forever bar the use of the standard mileage allowance in subsequent years. If you use the standard mileage rate, you can still use the actual expense method in later years. However, if the car has not yet been fully depreciated (using the deemed depreciation rates discussed later), then, for depreciation purposes, you must use the straight-line method over what you estimate to be the car's remaining useful life.

ACTUAL EXPENSE METHOD

The *actual expense method* allows you to deduct all of your out-of-pocket costs for operating your car for business, plus an allowance for depreciation if you own the car. Actual expenses include:

Depreciation	Lease fees	Repairs
Garage rent	Licenses	Tires
Gas	Oil	Tolls
Insurance	Parking fees	Towing

For individuals, whether interest on a car loan is deductible depends on employment status. If you are an employee who uses a car for business, you cannot deduct interest on a car loan; the interest is treated as nondeductible personal interest. However, if you are self-employed, the interest may be treated as business interest. For corporations, interest on a car loan is fully deductible.

If you pay personal property tax on a car used for business, the tax is deductible by an employee only as an itemized deduction. Personal property tax is not grouped with other car expenses. Instead, it is listed on an individual's Schedule A as a personal property tax.

If your car is damaged, destroyed, or stolen, the part of the loss not covered by insurance may be deductible. If the car was used entirely for business, the loss is treated as a fully deductible casualty or theft loss. If it was used partly for personal purposes, the loss may be treated as a casualty or theft loss, but the portion of the loss allocated to personal purposes is subject to certain limitations. See Chapter 14 for a discussion of casualty and theft losses.

Fines for traffic violations, including parking violations, are not deductible even when they were incurred in the course of business-related travel.

Depreciation

If you own your car and use it for business, you may recoup part of the cost of the car through a deduction called *depreciation*. The amount of depreciation depends on a great many factors. First, it depends on whether you use the depreciation allowance or claim a Section 179 deduction (discussed later in the chapter). It also varies according to the year in which you begin to use your car for business, the cost of the car, and the amount of business mileage for the year as compared with the total mileage for the year. Depreciation is covered in Chapter 12 as well.

Business Use versus Personal or Investment Use

Whether you claim a depreciation allowance or a Section 179 deduction, you can do so only with respect to the portion of the car used for business. For example, if you use your car 75 percent for business and 25 percent for personal purposes, you must allocate the cost of the car for purposes of calculating depreciation. The allocation is based on the number of miles driven for business compared to the total number of miles driven for the year.

---

example

In 2004 you buy a car for $16,000 and drive it 20,000 miles. Of this mileage, 15,000 miles were for business; 5,000 miles were personal. For purposes of depreciation, you must allocate $12,000 for business use. It is this amount on which you figure depreciation.

If you use a car for investment purposes, you can add the miles driven for investment purposes when making an allocation for depreciation.

Depreciation Allowance

A depreciation allowance is simply a deduction calculated by applying a percentage to the **basis** of the car. Cars are treated as five-year property under the Modified Accelerated Cost Recovery System (MACRS), the depreciation system currently in effect, as discussed in Chapter 12. As such, you would think that the cost of the car could be recovered through depreciation deductions over a period of five years. However, this is generally not the case because of a number of different rules that exist. These rules all operate to limit the amount of depreciation that can be claimed in any one year and to extend the number of years for claiming depreciation.

Basis Generally, this is the original cost of the car. If a car is bought in part with the trade-in of an old car, the basis of the new car is the adjusted basis of the old car plus any cash payment you make. Basis is reduced by any first-year expense deduction, any clean fuel vehicle deduction, and any qualified electric vehicle tax credit. It is adjusted downward for any depreciation deductions.

Depreciation can take several forms. There is *accelerated depreciation* under MACRS, which results in greater deductions in the early years of ownership and smaller deductions in the later years. There is *straight-line depreciation*, which spreads depreciation deductions evenly over the years the car is expected to last (the fixed number of years may, in fact, have no relation to the actual number of years the car is in operation). Depreciation is discussed in Chapter 12. There is *bonus depreciation*, an additional first-year deduction figured before the regular depreciation allowance (discussed later in this chapter and in Chapter 12). The bonus depreciation rate is 50 percent (although a 30 percent rate can be elected). And there is the *first-year expense deduction*, discussed later in this chapter, which is in lieu of depreciation. It takes the place of depreciation for the first year. Any part of the car not recovered through the first-year expense deduction can then be recovered through depreciation deductions in subsequent years.

Business Use

In order for you to claim an accelerated depreciation deduction or a first-year expense, the car must be used more than 50 percent for business. Compare the miles driven during the year for business with the total miles driven. If more than 50 percent of the mileage represents business use, accelerated depreciation (or the first-year expense deduction below) can be claimed.

If you satisfy the 50-percent test, you may also add to business mileage any miles driven for investment purposes when calculating the depreciation deduction. You may not add investment mileage in order to determine whether you meet the 50-percent test. If you fail the 50-percent test (you use the car 50 percent or less for business), you can deduct depreciation using only the straight-line method (see "Listed Property" in Chapter 12).

What if the percentage of business use changes from year to year? Where business use in the year the car is placed in service is more than 50 percent but drops below 50 percent in a subsequent year, you must also change depreciation rates. Once business use drops to 50 percent or below, you can use only the straight-line method thereafter. The depreciation rate is taken from the table for the straight-line method found in IRS Publication 946, *How to Depreciate Property*, as if the car had not qualified for accelerated depreciation in a prior year.

Where business use drops to 50 percent or less, you may have to include in income an amount called *excess depreciation*. This is the amount of depreciation (including the first-year expense deduction) claimed when the car was used more than 50 percent for business over the amount of depreciation that would have been allowable had the car not been used more than 50 percent in the year it was placed in service. In addition to including excess depreciation in income, you must increase the basis of your car by the same amount.

Dollar Limit on Depreciation Deduction

The law sets a *dollar limit* on the amount of depreciation that can be claimed on a car used for business (see Table 7.1). The dollar limit is intended to limit depreciation that could be claimed on a nonluxury car.

TABLE 7.1 Dollar Limit on Depreciation on Passenger Cars

Year Placed in Service	2000	2001	2002	2003	2004
2000	$5,000				
2001	2,950	$3,060*			
2002	1,775	5,000	$7,660		
2003	1,775	2,950	4,900	$7,660**	
2004	1,775	1,775	2,950	4,900	$10,610***
2005	1,775	1,775	1,775	2,950	4,800
2006	1,775	1,775	1,775	1,775	2,850
2007	1,775	1,775	1,775	1,775	1,675

*For cars placed in service after September 11, 2001, the limit is $7,660.
**For cars placed in service after May 5, 2003, the dollar limit is $10,710.
***If the car has been pre-owned (so that it does not qualify for bonus depreciation), the dollar limit is $2,960 for the first year.

In essence, the government does not want to underwrite the cost of buy-ing high-priced cars. However, in reality the dollar limits do not really correlate with luxury cars, since the average cost of a new American car purchased topped $28,000 in April 2003. Still, the dollar limits are a factor you must reckon with in calculating your deduction limit.

The dollar limits in Table 7.1 do not apply to light trucks and vans (those weighing less than 6,000 pounds). Special (higher) limits apply as explained later in this chapter.

The dollar limit applies only to cars with a gross vehicle weight (the manufacturer's maximum weight rating when loaded to capacity) of 6,000 pounds or less. Most cars fall into this category. However, some sport utility vehicles (SUVs) are heavier. If you use an SUV as your business car, check the manufacturer's specifications to see if the weight exceeds 6,000 pounds. If so, it can be fully expensed up to $102,000 ($25,000 if placed in service after October 22, 2004).

---

example

In March 2004 you place in service a new car costing $20,000 that is used 100 percent for business. The dollar limit on depreciation for 2004 is $10,610. For 2005 it will be $4,800; for 2006 it will be $2,850, and for each year thereafter it will be $1,675 as long as you use the car for business, until the car is fully depreciated.

---

example

In 2001 you placed in service a car costing $20,000. For 2004 and all later years, your dollar limit is $1,775.

If the dollar limit applies to your business car, the amount depends on the year in which the car was placed in service and how long you have owned it. Over the years the dollar limits have been modified by law changes. For a number of years they have been adjusted for changes in the cost-of-living index. For 2004, the first-year dollar limit is $10,610 for new cars and $2,960 for pre-owned cars.

These dollar amounts apply to cars used 100 percent for business. If you use your car for personal purposes as well as for business, you must allocate the dollar limit. The method for allocating this limit is the same method used for allocating the cost of the car for purposes of depreciation, as described earlier.

---

example

In July 2004 you place in service a new car costing $30,000 that is used 75 percent for business and 25 percent for personal purposes. The full dollar limit of $10,610 is allocated 75 percent for business. Thus the 2004 dollar limit for this car is $7,958 (75 percent of $10,610).

For cars propelled primarily by electricity, the dollar limits are approximately tripled (rounding off of inflation adjustments can lead to slightly higher-than-triple figures). You may be entitled to a special tax credit for the purchase of an electric car, as explained later in this chapter. If such credit is claimed, then the basis of the car for purposes of depreciation is reduced by the amount of the credit.

Increase Your Dollar Limit

The dollar limit applies on a per-car basis. If you own two cars and use each for business, you may be able to increase your total dollar limit. Be sure to apply the percentage of business use for each car to the applicable dollar limit.

---

example

In June 2004 you buy a new car costing $25,000. Assume you drive 24,000 miles during the year, 90 percent of which (21,600 miles) is for business. Your dollar limit on depreciation is $9,549 (90 percent of $10,610).

Now, instead assume you own two cars, each costing $25,000, which you use for business. You drive car A 22,200 miles, of which 20,000 miles is for business, or 90 percent. You drive car B 4,400 miles, of which 2,200 is for business, or 50 percent. Your dollar limit for car A is $9,549 ($10,610 × .90). Your dollar limit for car B is $5,305 ($10,610 × .50). Your total depreciation deduction is $14,854 ($9,549 + 5,305). By using two cars instead of one, your depreciation limit is $4,244 greater than it would be if you used one car exclusively for business and the other for only personal driving.

Dispositions of a Car

When you sell your car, trade it in for a new one, or lose it as the result of a casualty or theft, you have to calculate your tax consequences.

Sale

If you sell your car, your gain or loss is the difference between what you receive for the car and your adjusted basis. Your adjusted basis is your original basis reduced by any first-year expensing or depreciation (up to the dollar limit each year). If the car has been fully depreciated, anything you receive for the car is all gain.

If you used the standard mileage allowance, you are considered to have claimed depreciation even though you did not have to figure a separate depreciation deduction. The standard mileage allowance automatically takes into account a deduction for depreciation. You figure your *deemed depreciation* according to the number of miles you drove the car for business each year and the years in which it was used (see Table 7.2).

---

example

You bought a car and placed it in service at the beginning of 2002. You drove the car 20,000 miles each year for business. You sell it at the end of 2004. You must adjust the basis of the car for purposes of determining gain or loss on the sale by deemed depreciation of $14,400 (20,000 miles × 12 cents/mile + 20,000 miles × 14 cents/mile + 40,000 miles × 15 cents/mile + 20,000 miles × 16 cents/mile). You reduce your original basis by the total of deemed depreciation but do not reduce the basis below zero.

If you use the actual expense method and sell the car before the end of its recovery period, you can claim a reduced depreciation deduction in the year of disposition. Calculate what the depreciation deduction would have been had you held the car for the full year. Then, if you originally placed your car in service in the first three-quarters of the year (January 1 through September 30), you can deduct 50 percent of

TABLE 7.2 Deemed Depreciation

Year*	Rate per Mile
2003–2004	16 cents
2001–2002	15
2000	14
1994–1999	12

*Different rates per mile apply to cars that used the standard mileage rate prior to 1999.

the amount that would have been allowed. If you originally placed your car in service in the last quarter of the year (October 1 through December 31), you can deduct an amount calculated by applying the percentage in Table 7.3 to what would have been allowed.

Trade-In

Generally, no gain or loss is recognized if you trade in your car to buy another car for business. Such a trade is treated as a like-kind exchange. This nonrecognition rule applies even if you pay cash in addition to your trade-in or if you finance the purchase. However, if the dealer gives you money back (because the new car costs less than the trade-in), you may have gain to recognize. The gain recognized will not exceed the amount of cash you receive.

If you buy a car by trading in another car, your basis for purposes of determining first-year expensing is only the amount of consideration paid; it does not include the basis of the trade-in. But for purposes of

TABLE 7.3 Depreciation in Year of Sale*

Month Car Sold**	Percentage
January, February, March	12.5
April, May, June	37.5
July, August, September	62.5
October, November, December	87.5

*Table is not for fiscal-year taxpayers.
**Car placed in service October 1–December 31.

depreciation, including bonus depreciation, the basis of the trade-in is included in the basis of the new car.

---

example

You buy a new car that costs $15,000 by paying $9,000 cash and receiving $6,000 for the trade-in of your old car. The adjusted basis of the old car is $5,000. Your basis for purposes of calculating depreciation is $14,000 ($5,000 adjusted basis of the old car, plus $9,000).

Sale or Trade-In?

If your car is fully depreciated, a trade-in avoids what would otherwise be a taxable gain. But the price for this legal tax avoidance is the loss of future depreciation deductions on the new car you receive on the trade-in. This factor may not be significant if you use the standard mileage rate (discussed in the next section) to deduct car expenses.

Casualty or Theft

If your car is damaged or stolen and insurance or other reimbursements exceed the adjusted basis of the car, you have a tax gain. However, if you use the reimbursements to buy another car for business or to repair the old car within two years of the end of the year of the casualty or theft, then no gain is recognized. The basis of the new car for purposes of depreciation is its cost less any gain that is not recognized.

STANDARD MILEAGE ALLOWANCE

Instead of keeping a record of all your expenses and having to calculate depreciation, you can use a *standard mileage allowance* to determine your deduction for business use of your car. You can use the standard mileage allowance in 2004 whether you own or lease the car (in prior years you could not use the standard mileage allowance if you leased your car). The cents-per-mile allowance takes the place of a deduction for gasoline, oil, insurance, maintenance and repairs, vehicle registration fees, and depreciation (if you own the car) or lease payments (if you lease the car). Towing charges for the car are separately deductible in addition to the standard mileage allowance. Parking fees and tolls are also allowed in addition to the standard mileage allowance. Deductible parking fees include those incurred by visiting clients and customers or while traveling away from home on business. Fees to park your car at home or at your place of work are nondeductible personal expenses.

In 2004 the standard mileage allowance for business use of a car is 37.5 cents per mile. (Rural letter carriers who use their cars to deliver mail can deduct the amount paid to them by the U.S. Postal Service as an equipment maintenance allowance.) This rate is adjusted annually for inflation.

Standard Mileage Rate Barred

You cannot use the standard mileage rate when:

- You use the car for hire (such as a taxi).
- You operate more than four cars at the same time (such as in a fleet operation). This limit does not apply to the use of more than four cars on an alternate basis. For example, if you own cars and vans and alternate the use of these vehicles for business use, then you are not barred from using the standard mileage rate to account for the expenses of the business use for the vehicles.
- You have already claimed MACRS or a first-year expense deduction on the car.

Standard Mileage Rate or Actual Expense Method?

As discussed earlier in this chapter, which method is preferable for you depends on a number of variables. The most important is the number of business miles you drive each year. As a rule of thumb, those who drive a great number of miles each year frequently find the standard mileage rate offers the greater deduction. It is also important to note that the standard mileage rate is not dependent on the price of the car. Less expensive cars can claim the same deduction as more expensive cars, assuming each is driven the same number of business miles.

LEASING A CAR FOR BUSINESS

It is becoming increasingly popular to lease a car rather than to buy it. If you use the car entirely for business, the cost of leasing is fully deductible. If you make advance payments, you must spread these payments over the entire lease period and deduct them accordingly. You cannot depreciate a car you lease, because depreciation applies only to property that is owned. However, you can choose to deduct the standard mileage rate in lieu of actual expenses (including lease payments).

Lease with an Option to Buy

When you have this arrangement, are you leasing or buying the car? The answer depends on several factors, including the intent of the parties to the transaction. When the factors support a lease arrangement, the payments are deductible. If, however, the factors support a purchase agreement, the payments are not deductible.

Inclusion Amount

If the car price of a leased car exceeds a certain amount and you deduct your actual costs (you do not use the standard mileage rate), you may have to include in income an *inclusion amount*. The inclusion amount, which is simply an amount that you add to your other income, applies if a car is leased for more than 30 days and its value exceeds a certain amount, based on the value of the car as of the first day of the lease term. At the start of the lease, you can see what your inclusion amount will be for that year and for all subsequent years. The inclusion amount is based on a percentage of the **fair market value** of the car at the time the lease begins. Different inclusion amounts apply to gas-driven cars and to electric cars.

Fair market value   The price that would be paid for the property when there is a willing buyer and seller (neither being required to buy or sell) and both have reasonable knowledge of all the necessary facts. Evidence of fair market value includes the price paid for similar property on or about the same date.

The inclusion amount applies only if the fair market value of the car when the lease began was more than $15,800 in 1997 to 1998, $15,500 in 1999 to 2002, $18,000 in 2003, and $17,500 in 2004.

Inclusion amounts are taken from IRS tables, which can be found in the appendix to IRS Publication 463, *Travel, Entertainment, Gift, and*

Car Expenses. Use the table that applies to the year in which the car is first leased. The full amount in the table applies if the car is leased for the full year and used entirely for business. If the car is leased for less than the full year, or if it is used partly for personal purposes, the inclusion amount must be allocated to business use for the period of the year during which it was used.

---

example

The inclusion amount for your car is $500. You used your car only six months of the year (a leap year). You must include $250 in income (183/366 of $500).

There are separate inclusion amount tables for trucks and vans and for electric cars first leased in 2004. This information can be found in IRS Rev. Proc. 2004-20.

Should You Lease or Buy?

The decision to lease or buy a car used for business is not an easy one. There are many financial advantages to leasing. Most important is that you need not put forth more than a small amount of up-front cash to lease, whereas a purchase generally requires a significant down payment. However, as a practical matter, if a car is driven extensively (more than 15,000 miles per year), leasing may not make sense because of the annual mileage limit and the charge for excess mileage. In such cases, owning may be preferable. Take into consideration that at the end of the lease term you own nothing, whereas at the end of the same period of time with a purchased car you own an asset that can be sold or traded in for a newer model.

Whether there are any tax advantages is difficult to say. With leasing, you deduct the entire lease charge; with a purchase, you may be subject to limits on depreciation.

The only way to know whether leasing or buying is more advantageous tax-wise is to run the numbers. Project your deductible costs of leasing versus your costs of purchasing the car.

ARRANGING CAR OWNERSHIP

If you have a corporation, should you or your corporation own the car you will use for business? From a tax standpoint, it is generally wise to have the corporation own the car because the corporation can fully deduct the expenses of the car (subject, of course, to the dollar limit on depreciation). If you own the car, your deductions can be claimed only as itemized deductions subject to a floor of 2 percent of your adjusted gross income.

For insurance purposes, it may also be more advantageous to have the corporation own the car. If the corporation owns more than one vehicle, it can command better insurance rates than an individual who owns only one or two cars. Also, if the car is involved in an accident, the corporation's insurance rates are not affected. If you own the car and it is in an accident, your personal insurance rates will be increased.

Finally, if there is a lawsuit involving the car, it is generally preferable to have the corporation sued rather than you personally, since a recovery against the corporation is limited by corporate assets.

EMPLOYEE USE OF AN EMPLOYER-PROVIDED CAR

If your employer gives you a car to use for business, you may be able to deduct certain expenses. Your deduction is limited to the actual expenses of operating the car that were not reimbursed by your employer. The amount of the deduction depends on the amount your employer includes in your income and the number of business and personal miles driven. Your personal use is reported annually on your Form W-2. If your employer owns the car you use, you cannot use the standard mileage allowance for car expenses.

TRUCKS AND VANS

Trucks (including SUVs) and vans that are configured in such a way as to be used for personal purposes only minimally are not subject to the dollar limits on depreciation that apply to passenger cars weighing no more than 6,000 pounds. These trucks and vans are referred to as qualified nonpersonal use vehicles.

Modifications likely to render a truck or van a qualified nonpersonal use vehicle include having a front jump seat, permanent shelving that fills the cargo area, and advertising or a company name printed on the side.

Trucks and vans that are not qualified nonpersonal use vehicles are subject to the following rules:

- For vehicles with a gross vehicle weight rating in excess of 6,000 pounds, the dollar limits on depreciation do not apply (see the treatment of heavy SUVs earlier in this chapter). Their cost can be expensed up to $102,000 if purchased before October 23, 2004 ($25,000 if purchased after October 22, 2004) or depreciated as five-year property without any dollar limit on the annual deduction.

- For lighter vehicles, special dollar limits apply. These dollar limits are slightly higher than for passenger cars.

WRITE-OFFS FOR HYBRID AND ELECTRIC CARS

The tax law encourages the use of environmentally sensitive cars, including those powered by gas and electricity (hybrid cars) and those powered primarily by electricity.

Hybrid Cars

You may deduct up to $2,000 for the purchase of a clean-fuel car (different limits apply to trucks and vans weighing more than 10,000 pounds). The deduction applies not only to cars used for business, but also to personal cars.

The deduction is claimed in the year of purchase. If the car is not used entirely for business, then the allocable part of the deduction for personal use is claimed as an above-the-line deduction on Form 1040. No deduction is allowed for the portion of the car taken into account for purposes of first-year expensing. The deduction applies only if you are the original owner of the car; it cannot be claimed for the purchase of a used car.

The deduction relates to the incremental cost of clean fuel (electricity). Manufacturers must tell the IRS this amount and receive certification, a copy of which should be available to purchasers of these cars. To date, the IRS has given certification to the Toyota Prius, model years 2001 through 2005; the Honda Civic Hybrid, model years 2003 through 2005; the

Honda Insight, model years 2000 through 2005; the Honda Accord Hybrid, model year 2005; and the Ford Escape Hybrid, model year 2005.

Electric Cars

There are distinct rules for electric cars. The dollar limit for depreciation on electric cars is higher than for cars powered by other means. The inclusion amounts for leased electric cars are also higher than for nonelectric cars. And there is a special tax credit for the purchase of an electric car. There is a credit for **qualified electric vehicles**, which is 10 percent of the cost of the car, up to a maximum credit of $4,000 in 2004.

Qualified electric vehicle   Any motor vehicle that is powered primarily by an electric motor drawing current from rechargeable batteries, fuel cells, or other portable sources of electrical current.

You cannot claim a credit for any portion of the car for which a first-year expense deduction is claimed. You must reduce the basis of the car for purposes of depreciation and otherwise by the amount of the credit. The credit cannot exceed the amount of your tax liability, reduced by certain refundable credits.

To claim the credit, you must be the original owner of the car and must not have bought it for resale (you are not a car dealer). The credit is not limited to the portion of the car for business use. You may claim the credit for the portion of the car used for personal purposes. The credit is computed on Form 8834, Qualified Electric Vehicle Credit.

REIMBURSEMENT ARRANGEMENTS

If your employer reimburses you for the business use of your car, you may or may not need to claim deductions. The answer depends on the reimbursement arrangement with your employer.

RECORDKEEPING FOR CAR EXPENSES

Regardless of whether you use the actual expense method or the standard mileage allowance for your car (or a car that your employer provides you with), certain recordkeeping requirements apply. You must keep track of the number of miles you drive each year for business, as well as the total miles driven each year. You must also record the date of the business mileage, the designation of the business travel, and the business reason for the car expense. It is advisable to maintain a daily travel log or diary in which you record the date, the destination, the business purpose of the trip, and the number of miles driven (use the odometer readings at the start and end of the trip, and then total the miles for each trip). Be sure to note the odometer reading on January 1 each year.

If you use the actual expense method, you must also keep a record of the costs of operating the car. These include the cost of gasoline and oil, car insurance, interest on a car loan (if you are self-employed), licenses and taxes, and repairs and maintenance. Record these amounts in your expense log or diary.

If you lease a car, you must keep track of the amount of the lease payments, in addition to the number of miles driven (and the number of business miles), the dates of travel, the destinations, and the purpose for the travel.

Use a diary or log to keep track of your business mileage and other related costs. You can buy a car expense log in stationery and business supply stores. Table 7.4 is a model of an IRS sample daily business mileage and expense log.

Proving Expenses with a Mileage Allowance

Generally, required recordkeeping includes tracking the odometer at the start and end of each business trip (as well as the date, destination, and purpose of the trip). However, the IRS permits "sampling" in some situations. You are treated as having adequate substantiation if you keep records for a representative portion of the year and can demonstrate that the period for which records are kept is representative of use for the entire year.

---

example

An interior designer who runs her business from home visits clients using her personal car for this business driving. She records her mileage for the first three months of the year, which shows that the car is used 75 percent for business and 25 percent for personal driving. Invoices from her business show that business activity was nearly constant throughout the year, indicating that her driving pattern remained the same. Under these facts, she can extrapolate that 75 percent of her car expenses for the year are business-related.

TABLE 7.4 Sample Log

| Date | Destination | Business Purpose | Odometer Readings | | Miles this Trip | Expenses | |
			Start	Stop		Type	Amount
5/4/04	Local—St. Louis	Sales calls	8,097	8,188	91	Gas	$18.00
5/5/04	Indianapolis	Sales calls	8,211	8,486	275	Parking	$5.00
5/6/04	Louisville	Bob Smith (potential client)	8,486	8,599	113	Gas	$17.80
						Repair flat tire	$10.00
5/7/04	Return to St. Louis		8,599	8,875	276	Gas	$18.25
5/8/04	Local—St. Louis	Sales calls	8,914	9,005	91		
Weekly total			8,097	9,005	846		$69.05
Year-to-date total					5,883		$1,014.75

---

example

The same interior designer instead records her mileage for the first week of every month, showing 75 percent business use. Invoices show that business continued at the same rate throughout the month so that the first week's record was representative of the full month. Under these facts, she can extrapolate that 75 percent of her car expenses for the balance of the month (and throughout the year) are business-related.

Sampling may not be used if you cannot show a consistent pattern of car use. Also, not all substantiation shortcuts are acceptable. For instance, one taxpayer used mileage figured by a computer atlas to substantiate his car expenses. Unfortunately, the Tax Court rejected this method, observing that he failed to keep track of his odometer readings at the time the expenses were incurred.

If your employer pays for car expenses with a mileage allowance, it generally is considered to be proof of the amount of expenses. The amount of expenses that can be proven by use of this allowance is limited to the standard mileage allowance or the amount of a fixed and variable rate (FAVR) allowance that is not included on your W-2. The FAVR allowance includes a combination of fixed and variable costs, such as a cents-per-mile rate to cover variable operating costs (e.g., gas, oil, routine maintenance, and repairs) and a flat amount to cover fixed costs (e.g., depreciation, insurance, registration and license fees, and personal property taxes). The FAVR allowance applies only if the car is used for certain employees. Thus, use of this allowance is the employer's choice, not the employee's.

chapter 8

repairs and maintenance

Property and equipment generally need constant repairs to keep them in working order. Preventative maintenance—regular servicing of equipment—can cut down on replacement costs by allowing you to keep your current equipment longer. When your computer goes down, a service person is required to make repairs. When the air-conditioning system in your office building stops working, again, servicing is necessary. If you have property or equipment to which you make repairs, you can deduct these expenses. The only hitch is making sure that the expenses are not *capital expenditures*. Capital expenditures cannot be currently deducted but instead are added to the basis of property and recovered through depreciation or upon the disposition of the property.

For further information about deducting repairs, see IRS Publication 535, *Business Expenses*.

ORDINARY REPAIRS
Deducting Incidental Repairs in General

The cost of repairing property and equipment used in your business is a deductible business expense. In contrast, expenditures that materially add to the value of the property or prolong its life must be capitalized (added to the basis of the property and recovered through depreciation). In most cases, the distinction is clear. If you pay a repair person to service your copying machine because paper keeps getting jammed, the cost of the service call is a repair expense and is currently deductible. If you put a new roof on your office building, you usually must capitalize the expenditure and recover the cost through depreciation. Sometimes, however, the classification of an expense as a repair or a capital expenditure is not clear. For example, in one case the cost of a new roof was currently deductible where it was installed merely to repair a leak and did not change the structure of the building or add to its value.

Guidelines on Distinguishing Between a Repair and a Capital Item

Repairs are expenses designed to keep property in good working condition. This includes the replacement of short-lived parts. Typically, the cost of repairs is small compared with the cost of the property itself.

Capital items, on the other hand, are akin to original construction. They replace long-lived parts or enlarge or improve on the original property. Costs are usually substantial.

Table 8.1 includes some common examples of repairs and capital improvements.

The fact that certain repairs are necessitated by governmental directives does not change the character of the expense. If it is a required repair, it is currently deductible; if it substantially improves the property,

TABLE 8.1 Examples of Repairs versus Capital Items

Repairs	Capital Items
Painting the outside of office building	Vinyl siding the outside of office building
Replacing missing shingles on roof	Replacing entire roof unless strictly for repair purposes
Replacing compressor for air conditioner	Adding air-conditioning system
Cleaning canopy over restaurant entrance	Adding canopy over restaurant entrance
Resurfacing office floor	Replacing office floor

it is a capital expenditure. For example, in one case, rewiring ordered by local fire prevention inspectors was a capital expenditure. The same is true for capital expenditures ordered by the U.S. Public Health Service and state sanitary or health laws.

Repairs made to property damaged by a casualty are deductible if they merely restore the property to its pre-casualty condition. This is so even if a deduction is also claimed for a casualty loss to the property.

---

example

Severe flooding destroyed a business owner's property. He was not compensated by insurance. The IRS, in a memorandum to a district counsel, allowed him to deduct the cost of repairs to the property where such repairs merely restored it to its precasualty condition. In addition, he claimed a casualty loss for the same property.

Environmental Protection Agency Compliance

If you are forced to take certain actions to comply with Environmental Protection Agency (EPA) requirements, such as encapsulating or removing asbestos, be sure to understand which expenses are currently deductible and which expenses must be capitalized. Environmental remediation costs can be currently deducted. These are costs of cleanups to comply with environmental laws that effectively restore property to its original (precontamination) condition. The cost of capital improvements to comply with environmental laws, however, must be capitalized.

---

example

The cost of encapsulating asbestos in a warehouse is currently deductible. The cost of removing asbestos from a boiler room must be capitalized. (The removal makes the property substantially more attractive to potential buyers.)

REHABILITATION PLANS

If you make repairs as part of a general plan to recondition or improve property—typically, office buildings, stores, and factories—then the expenses must be capitalized. This is so even though the expenses would have been deductible if made outside a general plan of repair. This rule is called the *rehabilitation doctrine*. For example, painting generally is treated as a currently deductible repair expense. However, if you add an extension to your office building, the cost of painting the extension upon completion is a capital item under the rehabilitation doctrine.

Protecting the Deduction for Repairs

With proper planning, you can make sure that repair costs are currently deductible even though you also undertake capital expenditures. Schedule repairs separately from capital improvements so they will not be treated as one rehabilitation plan, and get separate bills for the repairs.

Tax Credits for Rehabilitation

While rehabilitation costs generally must be capitalized, in special instances you can claim a tax credit for your expenditures. If you rehabilitate a nonresidential building that was built before 1936, you can claim a credit for 10 percent of your expenditures. If you rehabilitate a certified historic structure (a building that is listed in the National Register or located in a registered historic district), the credit is 20 percent of costs. The credit is claimed in the year the property is placed in service, not the year in which the expenditures are made.

---

example

If you undertake a two-year project beginning in 2003 and do not place the building in service until 2004, the credit is taken in 2004.

Rehabilitation requires that you make substantial improvements to the building but leave a substantial portion of it intact. A *substantial portion* means that within any two-year period you select, the rehabilitation expenditures exceed the adjusted basis of the building or $5,000, whichever is greater. In the case of a pre-1936 building, at least 75 percent of the external walls must be left intact and at least 50 percent of external walls must remain as external walls. The Secretary of the Interior must certify that the rehabilitation of certified historic structures will be in keeping with the building's historic status.

The credit is claimed on Form 3468, Investment Credit. For individuals and C corporations, it is part of the general business credit computed on Form 3800, General Business Credit. The credit may be limited by the passive loss rules explained in Chapter 4. The general business credit limitations are explained in Chapter 18.

Demolition Expenses

As a general rule, the costs of demolishing a building are not deductible. Instead, they are added to the basis of the new building (that is, the building put up in the place of the demolished building). However, the costs of demolishing only a part of a building may be currently deductible. According to the IRS, if 75 percent or more of the existing external walls and 75 percent or more of the existing internal framework are both retained, the costs of demolition need not be capitalized (added to basis) but instead can be currently deducted.

SPECIAL RULES FOR IMPROVEMENTS FOR THE ELDERLY AND HANDICAPPED

The Americans with Disabilities Act (ADA) may require you to make certain modifications to your office, store, or factory if you have not done so already. You may have to install ramps, widen doorways and lavatories to accommodate wheelchairs, add elevators, or make other similar changes to your facilities to render them more accessible to the elderly and handicapped.

These modifications may be more in the nature of capital improvements than repairs. Still, the law provides two special tax incentives to which you may be entitled. One is a tax credit; the other is a special deduction. These incentives allow for a current benefit rather than requiring capitalization of expenditures that will be recovered over long periods of time.

Disabled Access Credit

Small business owners can claim a tax credit for expenditures to remove barriers on business property that impede the access of handicapped individuals and to supply special materials or assistance to visually or hearing-impaired persons.

Small business   Businesses with gross receipts of no more than $1 million (after returns and allowances) and no more than 30 full-time employees. Full-time employees are those who work more than 30 hours per week for 20 or more calendar weeks in the year.

The credit cannot exceed 50 percent of expenditures over $250 but not over $10,250. The maximum credit is $5,000.

---

example

You, as a small business owner, spend $4,000 to install ramps in your mall. You may take a tax credit of $1,875 ($4,000 – $250 = $3,750 × .50).

The dollar limit applies at both the partner and partnership levels. The same rule applies to shareholders and S corporations, as well as to members and LLCs.

Qualifying Expenditures

Qualifying expenditures are designed to meet the requirements of the ADA (see IRS Publication 535, *Business Expenses*, for a list of qualifying expenditures). For example, the cost of putting in handicapped parking spaces as required by federal law is a qualified expenditure. Many of these requirements are set forth in connection with the expense deduction for the removal of architectural and transportation barriers. However, eligible expenditures do not include those in connection with new construction. If you claim the credit, you cannot also claim a deduction for the same expenditures.

Businesses already in compliance with the ADA cannot claim the credit for equipment that may add some benefit for handicapped customers. Also, the IRS has ruled that Web-based businesses using software to enable handicapped customers to shop cannot claim the credit; it is limited to bricks-and-mortar businesses. However, a company with a physical place of business that uses a software service to communicate on-site with hearing-impaired customers qualifies for the credit.

Deduction for Removal of Architectural or Transportation Barriers

You can elect to deduct the expenses of removing architectural or transportation barriers to the handicapped and elderly. The election is made simply by claiming the deduction on a timely filed tax return.

The maximum deduction in any one year is $15,000. If your expenditures for a removal project exceed this limit, you can deduct the first $15,000 of costs and capitalize (and then depreciate) the balance.

The dollar limit applies at both the partner and partnership levels. A partner must combine his or her distributive share of these expenditures from one partnership with any distributive share of such expenditures from any other partnerships. The partner may allocate the $15,000 limit among his or her own expenditures and the partner's distributive share of partnership expenditures in any manner. If the allocation results in all or a portion of the partner's distributive share of partnership's expenditures not being an allocable deduction, then the partnership can capitalize the unallowable portion.

While the regulations on applying the dollar limits at both the partner and partnership levels do not specify other pass-through entities, presumably the same rules that apply to partners and partnerships apply as well to shareholders and S corporations.

If the election is made to expense these expenditures, then no disabled access credit can be claimed for the same expenses.

---

example

A partner's distributive share of partnership expenditures (after application of the $15,000 limit at the partnership level) is $7,500. The partner also has a sole proprietorship that made $10,000 of expenditures. The partner can choose to allocate the $15,000 limitation as follows: $5,000 to his or her distributive share of the partnership's expenditures and $10,000 to individual expenditures. If the partner provides written proof of this allocation to the partnership, the partnership can then capitalize $2,500, the unused portion of the partner's distributive share of expenditures ($7,500 distributive share less $5,000 allocated as a deduction).

Qualifying Expenditures

These are expenses that conform a facility or public transportation vehicle to certain standards that make them accessible to persons over the age of 65 or those with physical or mental disability or impairment. It does not include any expense for the construction or comprehensive renovation of a facility or public transportation vehicle or the normal replacement of depreciable property.

Recordkeeping

If you elect to deduct these expenditures, you must maintain records and documentation, including architectural plans and blueprints, contracts, and building permits to support your claims. How long these records should be kept is discussed in Chapter 3.

chapter 9

bad debts

No one thinks that the loans they make to others will go unpaid; otherwise, such loans would not be made in the first place. If, in the course of your business, you lend money or extend goods and services but fail to receive payment, you can take some comfort in the tax treatment for these transactions gone sour. You may be able to deduct your loss as a bad debt.

For further information about deducting bad debts, see IRS Publication 535, *Business Expenses*.

BAD DEBTS IN GENERAL

If you cannot collect money that is owed to you in your business, your loss may be deductible. You must prove three factors to establish a bad debt:

1. The debtor-creditor relationship
2. Worthlessness
3. Loss

The Debtor-Creditor Relationship

You must prove that there is a *debtor-creditor relationship*. This means that there is a legal obligation on the part of the debtor to pay to the creditor (you) a fixed or determinable sum of money.

If you lend money to a friend or relative, the relationship between you and the borrower is not always clear. You may, for example, lend the money with the expectation of receiving repayment but later forgive some or all of the payments. This forgiveness with a friend or relative transforms what might have been a bad debt into a gift. The law does not bar loans between relatives or friends, but be aware that the IRS gives special scrutiny to loans involving related parties.

The simplest way to prove a debtor-creditor relationship is to have a written note evidencing the loan. The note should state such terms as the amount of the loan, a stated rate of interest, a fixed maturity date, and a repayment schedule.

If you have a corporation to which you lend money, establishing the debtor-creditor relationship is crucial. Unless you can show that an advance to the corporation is intended to be a loan, it will be treated as a contribution to the capital of the corporation (which is not deductible). Make sure that the corporation carries the advance as a loan on its books.

If your corporation lends money to others, it is advisable to include this arrangement in the corporate minutes (e.g., a corporate resolution authorizing the loan and spelling out the loan terms) as well as to carry the loan on the corporation's books.

Worthlessness

You must also show that the debt has become *worthless* and will remain that way. You must be able to show that you took reasonable steps to collect the debt. It is not necessary that you actually go to court to collect the debt if you can show that a judgment would remain uncollectible. If the borrower is in bankruptcy, this is a very good indication that the debt is worthless, at least in part. Generally, the debt is considered to be worthless as of the settlement date of the bankruptcy action, but facts can show that it was worthless before this time. If you use a collection agency to attempt collection of outstanding accounts receivable or other amounts owed to you and you agree to pay the agency a percentage of what is collected, you can immediately deduct that percentage of the outstanding amount as a bad debt; your agreement establishes that that percentage will never be collected by you.

---

example

You have an open accounts receivable of $1,000. After 120 days you turn it over to a collection agency that charges 30 percent of what it collects. At the point of your agreement with the agency you are certain you will never recoup at least $300 of the outstanding amount (the fee that would be paid to the agency if it collects 100 percent of the debt) and can now deduct that amount.

   You may, in fact, deduct more if the agency collects less than the full amount of the debt. For example, if it collects $500 of the $1,000 outstanding, it is entitled to a $150 fee, so you recoup only $350 of the $1,000. Result: You deduct a total of $650 ($300 of which you deducted when the agreement with the agency was made).

Whether a loan is fully or only partially worthless affects whether you can claim a deduction for the loss. Business bad debts are deductible whether they are fully or partially worthless. If the loss is a nonbusiness bad debt, it is deductible only if the debt is fully worthless. No partial deduction is allowed for nonbusiness bad debts. The distinction between business and nonbusiness bad debts is explained later in this chapter.

Loss

You must show that you sustained a *loss* because of the debt. A loss results when an amount has been included in income but the income is never received. This might happen, for example, where an accrual method taxpayer accrues income but later fails to collect it. If you sell goods on credit and fail to receive payment, you sustain an economic loss whether you are on the accrual method or the cash method of accounting.

If you are on the cash basis and extend services but fail to collect, you cannot claim a bad debt deduction. You are not considered to have an economic loss even though you might argue that you put in your time and effort and were not justly compensated.

---

example

A cash basis accountant prepares an individual's tax return. The bill comes to $400. The accountant never receives payment. She cannot deduct the $400. The accountant never reported the $400 as income, so she is not considered to have suffered an economic loss, even though she extended services and invested her time and energy.

If you make payments to a supplier for future shipments and the supplier fails to deliver because of insolvency, you have a business bad debt, regardless of your method of accounting. Again, you have an economic loss (the money you advanced to the supplier) that gives rise to the bad debt deduction.

COLLECTION OF BAD DEBTS

Suppose you fully investigated a debt, made every effort to collect it, and finally concluded it was worthless. You claim a deduction; then, lo and behold, the debtor repays you a year or two later. You need not go back and amend your return to remove the bad debt deduction. Instead, include the recovery of the bad debt in income in the year you receive payment.

BUSINESS VERSUS NONBUSINESS BAD DEBTS

Business bad debts, as the term implies, arise in connection with a business. *Nonbusiness bad debts* are all other debts; they can arise in either a personal or investment context.

Business bad debts are deductible as ordinary losses. A C corporation's debts are always business bad debts. Nonbusiness bad debts are deductible by an individual only as short-term capital losses. As such, they are deductible only to offset your capital gains, and then up to $3,000 of ordinary income.

Business bad debts are deductible if partially or wholly worthless. Nonbusiness bad debts must be wholly worthless to be deductible.

Business Bad Debts

Business bad debts are treated as ordinary losses that offset ordinary business income. To be treated as a business bad debt, the debt must be closely related to the activity of the business. There must have been a business reason for entering into the debtor-creditor relationship.

Business bad debts typically arise from credit sales to customers. They can also be the result of loans to suppliers, customers, employees, or distributors. Credit sales are generally reported on the books of the business as accounts receivable. Loans to suppliers, customers, employees, or distributors generally are reported on the books of the business as notes receivable. When accounts receivable or notes receivable become uncollectible, this results in a business bad debt.

Valuing a Bad Debt

Accounts receivable and notes receivable generally are carried on the books at fair market value (FMV). Thus, when they go bad, they are deductible at FMV. This is so even where that value is less than the face value of the obligations.

Impact of Loans with Your Business or Associates

If you lend money to your corporation and the corporation later defaults, you cannot claim a bad debt deduction unless it was a true loan. If, as explained earlier, the advance to the corporation was in fact a contribution to its capital, then you cannot claim a bad debt deduction.

If you have a partnership that breaks up and there is money owing from the partnership, you may be forced to make payments if your partner or partners do not. This payment may be more than your share of the partnership's debts. In this case, you can claim a bad debt deduction if your partner or partners were insolvent and you were required to pay their share.

If you go out of business but still try to collect outstanding amounts owed to you, potential bad debt deductions are not lost. You can still claim them as business bad debts if the debts become worthless after you go out of business.

---

example

An attorney lent money to a friend and is later unable to collect despite a number of attempts. Since the loan had nothing to do with the attorney's business, the failure to collect results in a nonbusiness bad debt if it is wholly worthless.

Nonbusiness Bad Debts

Loans made to protect investments or for personal reasons give rise to nonbusiness bad debts when they go bad.

LOANS BY SHAREHOLDER-EMPLOYEES

When a shareholder who is also an employee of a corporation lends the corporation money but fails to receive repayment, or guarantees corporate debt and is called upon to make good on the guarantee, it is not always clear whether the resulting debt is a business bad debt or a nonbusiness bad debt.

A business bad debt must arise in the context of a business. A shareholder who lends money to the corporation is doing so to protect his or her investment. An employee who lends money to his or her corporation is doing so to protect his or her business of being an employee. In this instance, employment is treated as a business. When an individual is both a shareholder and an employee, which status governs?

According to the U.S. Supreme Court, the dominant motive for making the loan to the corporation is what makes a debt a business or nonbusiness bad debt. Where the dominant motive is to protect one's investment, then the bad debt is treated as a nonbusiness bad debt. Where the dominant motive is to protect one's employment status to ensure continued receipt of salary, then the bad debt is treated as a business bad debt.

GUARANTEES THAT RESULT IN BAD DEBTS

If you guarantee, endorse, or indemnify someone else's loan made to your business and are then called on to make good on your guarantee, endorsement, or indemnity, how do you treat this payment? If the dominant motive for making the guarantee was proximately related to your business (e.g., you guaranteed a loan to the corporation for which you work), then you claim a business bad debt. If the dominant motive for making the guarantee was to protect an investment, you claim a nonbusiness bad debt.

If the guarantee was made for a friend or relative without the receipt of consideration, no bad debt deduction can be claimed. The reason: You did not enter into the arrangement for profit or to protect an investment.

If there is more than one guarantor but only one co-guarantor pays the debt, the co-guarantor who pays the debt can claim only his or her proportional share of the obligation unless it can be proved that the other guarantors were unable to pay.

> **example**
>
> Three equal shareholders of Corporation X guarantee a bank loan made to the corporation. X defaults and one of the shareholders pays off the entire loan. That shareholder can deduct only one-third of the debt unless he can prove that the other two shareholders were unable to make any payment.

If you, as guarantor, give your own note to substitute or replace the note of the party for whom you became the guarantor, you cannot claim a bad debt deduction at that time. The deduction arises only when and to the extent you make payments on the notes.

When to Claim the Deduction

In general, a bad debt deduction in the case of a guarantee is claimed for the year in which payment is made by the guarantor. Suppose you guarantee a debt but have the right of subrogation or other right against the debtor to recoup your outlays. In this case, you claim your bad debt deduction only when the right against the debtor becomes worthless.

SPECIAL RULES FOR ACCRUAL TAXPAYERS

All taxpayers (other than certain financial institutions) use the *specific charge-off method* to account for bad debts. Under this method, business bad debts are deducted when and to the extent that they arise.

Nonaccrual-Experience Method

Taxpayers on the accrual basis have an alternative way to account for bad debts. Income that is not expected to be collected need not be accrued. If, based on prior experience, it is determined that certain receivables will not be collected, then they need not be included in gross income for the year. Since income is not taken into account, there is no need to then claim a bad debt deduction.

The *nonaccrual-experience method* applies only to accounts receivable for performing services in the fields of health, law, engineering, architecture, accounting, actuarial science, performing arts, or consulting. In addition, the business's average annual gross receipts for the three prior years cannot be more than $5 million. It cannot be used for amounts owed from activities such as lending money, selling goods, or acquiring receivables or the right to receive payments. Nor can this method be used if interest or penalties are charged on late payments. However, merely offering a discount for early payment is not treated as charging interest or a late penalty if the full amount is accrued as gross income at the time the services are provided and the discount for early payment is treated as an adjustment to gross income in the year of payment.

This method can be used under either a separate receivable system or a periodic system. The separate receivable system applies the nonaccrual-experience method separately to each account receivable; the periodic system applies it to the total of the qualified accounts receivable at the end of the year. This is a highly technical accounting rule that should be discussed with an experienced accountant. The nonaccrual-experience method is explained more fully in IRS Publication 535, *Business Expenses*.

REPORTING BAD DEBTS ON THE TAX RETURN

If you want to claim a bad debt deduction on your return, you must do more than simply enter your loss. You also must attach a statement to your return explaining each element of the bad debt. (There is no special IRS form required for making this statement.) These elements include:

- A description of the debt
- The name of the debtor
- Your family or business relationship to the debtor
- The due date of the loan
- Your efforts to collect the debt
- How you decided the debt became worthless

This reporting requirement applies only to individuals who claim bad debts on Schedule A, C, E, or F. Partnerships, LLCs, S corporations, and C corporations need not attach a statement to their returns explaining their bad debt deductions.

chapter 10

rents

From a financial standpoint, it might make more sense to rent than to buy property and equipment. Renting may require a smaller cash outlay than buying. Also, the business may not as yet have established sufficient credit to make large purchases but can still gain the use of the property or equipment through renting. If you pay rent to use office space, a store, or other property for your business, or you pay to lease business equipment, you generally can deduct your outlays.

DEDUCTING RENT PAYMENTS IN GENERAL

If you pay to use property for business that you do not own, the payments are *rent*. They may also be called *lease payments*. Rents paid for property used in a business are deductible business expenses. These include obligations you pay on behalf of your landlord. For example, if you are required by the terms of your lease to pay real estate taxes on the property, you can deduct these taxes as part of your rent payments.

The rents must be reasonable in amount. The issue of reasonableness generally does not arise where you and the landlord are at arm's length. However, the issue does come up when you and the landlord are related parties, such as family members or related companies. Rent paid to a related party is treated as reasonable if it is the same rent that would be paid to an unrelated party. A percentage rental is also considered reasonable if the rental paid is reasonable.

If the rent payments entitle you to receive equity in or title to the property at the end of some term, the payments are not rent. They may, however, be deductible in part as depreciation (see Chapter 12).

Rent to Your Corporation

If you rent property to your corporation, the corporation can claim a rental expense deduction, assuming the rents are reasonable. However, you cannot treat the rents as passive income that you could use to offset your losses from other passive activities. The law specifically prohibits you from arranging this type of rental for tax benefit.

If you rent a portion of your home to your employer, see the discussion on Rental of a Portion of Your Home for Business later in this chapter.

Rent with an Option to Buy

Sometimes it is not clear whether payments are to lease or purchase property. There are a number of factors used to make such a determination.

Nature of the Document

If you have a lease, payments made pursuant to the lease generally are treated as rents. If you have a conditional sales contract, payments made pursuant to the lease are nondeductible purchase payments. A document is treated as a conditional sales contract if it provides that you will acquire title to or equity in the property upon completing a certain number or amount of payments.

Intent of the Parties

How the parties view the transaction affects whether it is a lease or a conditional sales contract. Intent can be inferred from certain objective factors. A conditional sales contract exists if any of the following are found:

- The agreement applies part of each payment toward an equity interest.
- The agreement provides for the transfer of title after payment of a stated amount.

- The amount of the payment to use the property for a short time is a large part of the amount paid to get title to the property.

- The payments exceed the current fair rental value of the property (based on comparisons with other similar properties).

- There is an option to buy the property at a nominal price as compared with the property's value at the time the option can be exercised.

- There is an option to buy the property at a nominal price as compared with the total amount required to be paid under the agreement.

- The agreement designates a part of the payments as interest or in some way makes part of the payments easily recognizable as interest.

---

example

You lease an office building for a period of two years. The lease agreement provides that at the end of that term you have the option of buying the property and all of the payments made to date will be applied toward the purchase price. In this case, your payments probably would be viewed as payments to purchase rather than payments to lease the property.

Advance Rents

Generally, rents are deductible in the year in which they are paid or accrued. What happens if you pay rent in advance? According to the IRS, you can deduct only the portion of the rent that applies to use of the rented property for the following 12 months.

Gift-Leasebacks

If you own property you have already depreciated, you may want to create a tax deduction for your business by entering into a *gift-leaseback* transaction. Typically, the property is gifted to your spouse or children, to whom you then pay rent. In the past this type of arrangement was more popular, but the passive loss rules put a damper on deducting losses created by these arrangements. If you still want to shift income to your children (who presumably are in a lower tax bracket than you) while getting a tax deduction for your business, you may do so as long as you do not retain control over the property after the gift is given, the leaseback is in writing and the rent charged is reasonable, and there is a business purpose for the leaseback.

There are other factors to consider before entering into a gift-leaseback. Consider the impact of the kiddie tax if your children are under the age of 14. It is strongly suggested that you consult with a tax adviser before giving business property to your children and then leasing it back for use in your business.

Miscellaneous Rentals

Some payments for the use of property that you may not otherwise think of as rentals but that may be required by your business include safety deposit box rental fees and post office box rental fees.

THE COST OF ACQUIRING, MODIFYING, OR CANCELING A LEASE

The Cost of Acquiring a Lease

When you pay a premium to obtain immediate possession under a lease that does not extend beyond the tax year, the premium is deductible in full for the current year. Where the premium relates to a long-term lease, the cost of the premium is deductible over the term of the lease. The same amortization rule applies to commissions, bonuses, and other fees paid to obtain a lease on property you use in your business.

What is the term of the lease for purposes of deducting lease acquisition premiums when the lease contains renewal options? The tax law provides a complicated method for making this determination. The term of the lease for amortization purposes includes all renewal option periods if less than 75 percent of the cost is attributable to the term of the lease remaining on the purchase date. Do not include any period for which the lease may be renewed, extended, or continued under an option exercisable by you, the lessee, in determining the term of the lease remaining on the purchase date.

example

You pay $10,000 to acquire a lease with 20 years remaining on it. The lease has two options to renew, for five years each. Of the $10,000, $7,000 is paid for the original lease and $3,000 for the renewal options. Since $7,000 is less than 75 percent of the total cost, you must amortize $10,000 over 30 years (the lease term plus the two renewal option periods).

example

The circumstances are the previous example, except that $8,000 is allocable to the original lease. Since this is not less than 75 percent of the total cost, the entire $10,000 can be amortized over the original lease term of 20 years.

The Cost of Modifying a Lease

If you pay an additional rent to change a lease provision, you amortize this additional payment over the remaining term of the lease.

The Cost of Canceling a Lease

If you pay to get out of your lease before the end of its term, the cost generally is deductible in full in the year of payment. However, where a new lease is obtained, the cost of canceling the lease must be capitalized if the cancellation and new lease are viewed as part of the same transaction.

example

A company leased a computer system for five years. To upgrade its system, the company canceled the original lease and entered into a new one with the same lessor. Because the termination of the old lease was conditioned on obtaining a new lease, the cost of termination had to be capitalized (i.e., added to the cost of the new lease and deducted ratably over the term of the new lease).

IMPROVEMENTS YOU MAKE TO LEASED PROPERTY

If you add a building or make other permanent improvements to leased property, you can depreciate the cost of the improvements using Modified Accelerated Cost Recovery System (MACRS) depreciation. (For a further discussion of depreciation, see Chapter 14.) The improvements are depreciated over their recovery period, a time fixed by law. They are not depreciated over the remaining term of the lease. However, leasehold improvements after October 22, 2004, can be amortized over 15 years rather than depreciated.

If you acquire a lease through an assignment and the lessee has made improvements to the property, the amount you pay for the assignment is a capital investment. Where the rental value of the leased land has increased since the beginning of the lease, part of the capital investment is for the increase in that value; the balance is for your investment in the permanent improvements. You amortize the part of the increased rental value of the leased land; you depreciate the part of the investment related to the improvements.

If you enter into a lease after August 5, 1997, for retail space for 15 years or less and you receive a construction allowance from the landlord to make additions or improvements to the space, you are not taxed on these payments provided they are fully used for the purpose intended.

RENTAL OF A PORTION OF YOUR HOME FOR BUSINESS

If you rent your home and use part of it for business, you may be able to deduct part of your rent as a business expense. This part of the rent is treated as a home office deduction if you meet certain requirements. See Chapter 15 for details on the home office deduction.

LEASING A CAR

If you lease a car for business use, the treatment of the rental costs depends upon the term of the lease. If the term is less than 30 days, the entire cost of the rental is deductible. Thus, if you go out of town on business and rent a car for a week, your rental costs are deductible.

If the lease term exceeds 30 days, the lease payments are still deductible if you use the car entirely for business. If you use it for both business and personal purposes, you must allocate the lease payments and deduct only the business portion of the costs. However, depending on the value of the car at the time it is leased, you may be required to include an amount in gross income called an inclusion amount (see Chapter 7).

If you make advance payments, you must spread these payments over the entire lease period and deduct them accordingly. You cannot depreciate a car you lease, because depreciation applies only to property that is owned.

Lease with an Option to Buy

When you have this arrangement, are you leasing or buying the car? The answer depends on a number of factors, including the intent of the parties to the transaction, whether any equity results from the arrangement, whether any interest is paid, and whether the fair market value (FMV) of the car is less than the lease payment or option payment when the option to buy is exercised.

If the factors support a finding that the arrangement is a lease, the payments are deductible. If, however, the factors support a finding that the arrangement is a purchase agreement, the payments are not deductible.

chapter 11

taxes and interest

Taxes and interest are two types of expenses that are hard to avoid. In the course of your business activities, you may pay various taxes and interest charges.

For further information about deducting taxes and interest, see IRS Publication 535, *Business Expenses*.

DEDUCTIBLE TAXES
General Rules

In order to deduct taxes, they must be imposed on you. The tax must be owed by the party who pays it. If your corporation owns an office building, it is the party that owes the real property taxes. If, as part of your lease, you are obligated to pay your landlord's taxes, you can deduct your payment as an additional part of your rent; you do not claim a deduction for taxes, since you are not the owner of the property.

Taxes must be paid during the year if you are on a cash basis. If you pay taxes at year end by means of a check or even a credit card charge, the tax is deductible in the year the check is sent or delivered or the credit charge is made. This is so even though the check is not cashed until the following year or you do not pay the credit card bill until the following year. If you pay any tax by phone or through your computer, the tax is deductible on the date of payment reported on the statement issued by the financial institution through which the payment is made. If you contest a liability and do not pay it until the issue is settled, you cannot deduct the tax until it is actually paid. It may be advisable to settle a disputed liability in order to fix the amount and claim a deduction. If you pay tax after the end of the year for a liability that relates to the prior year, you deduct the tax in the year of payment.

---

example

An S corporation on a calendar year, using the cash basis method, pays its state franchise fee for 2004 in March 2005. The payment is deductible on the S corporation's 2005 income tax return, not on its 2004 return.

Real Estate Taxes

In general, real property taxes are deductible. Assessments made to real property for the repair or maintenance of some local benefit (such as streets, sidewalks, or sewers) are treated as deductible taxes.

If you acquire real property for resale to customers, you may be required under uniform capitalization rules to capitalize these taxes. The uniform capitalization rules are discussed in Chapter 2.

Special rules apply when real estate is sold during the year. Real property taxes must be allocated between the buyer and seller according to the number of days in the real property tax year. The seller can deduct the taxes up to, but not including, the date of sale. The buyer can deduct the taxes from the date of sale onward.

Accrual basis taxpayers can deduct only taxes accruing on the date of sale. An accrual basis taxpayer can elect to accrue ratably real property taxes related to a definite period of time over that period of time.

---

example

X Corporation, a calendar-year taxpayer on the accrual basis, owns an office building on which annual taxes are $1,200 for the fiscal year beginning July 1, 2004 through June 30, 2005. If X elects to ratably accrue taxes, $600 of the taxes is deductible in 2004, the balance in 2005.

The election to accrue taxes ratably applies for each separate business. If one business owns two properties, an election covers both properties. The election is binding and can be revoked only with the consent of the IRS. You make the election by attaching a statement to your return for the first year that real property taxes are due on property that includes the businesses for which the election is being made, the period of time to which the taxes relate, and a computation of the real property tax deduction for the first year of the election. The election must be filed with your income tax return (including extensions) on time.

If you have already owned property for some time but want to switch to the ratable accrual method, you must obtain the consent of the IRS. To do so, file Form 3115, Change in Accounting Method, within the year for which the change is to be effective.

State and Local Income Taxes

A corporation that pays state and local income taxes can deduct the taxes on its return. Taxes may include state corporate income taxes and any franchise tax (which is a tax for operating as a corporation and has nothing to do with being a franchise business).

A self-employed individual who pays state and local taxes with respect to business income reported on Schedule C can deduct them only as an itemized deduction on Schedule A. Similarly, an employee who pays state and local taxes with respect to compensation from employment can deduct these taxes only on Schedule A.

Self-Employment Tax

Businesses do not pay self-employment tax; individuals do. Sole proprietors, general partners (whether active or inactive), and certain LLC members pay self-employment tax on their net earnings from self-employment (amounts reported on Schedule C or as self-employment income on Schedule K). Limited partners do not pay self-employment tax on their share of income from the business. However, limited partners are subject to self-employment tax if they perform any services for the business or receive any guaranteed payments. LLC members who are like general partners pay self-employment tax; those like limited partners do not. The IRS was precluded from issuing regulations defining a limited partner before July 1, 1998. To date, the IRS has still not issued any regulations nor given any indication when it would.

The tax rate for the Social Security portion of self-employment tax is 12.4 percent and, in 2004, applies to net earnings from self-employment up to $87,900. The Medicare tax rate is 2.9 percent; it applies to *all* net earnings from self-employment (there is no limit for the Medicare portion of self-employment tax).

Those who pay self-employment tax are entitled to deduct one-half of the tax as an adjustment to gross income on their personal income tax returns. The deduction on page one of Form 1040 reduces your gross income and serves to lower the threshold for certain itemized deductions.

Owners of S corporations who are also employees of their businesses do not pay self-employment tax on their compensation—they are employees of the corporation for purposes of employment tax (see "Employment Taxes" subsection). Individuals who both are self-employed and have an interest in an S corporation cannot use losses from the S corporation to reduce net earnings from self-employment.

Personal Property Tax

Personal property tax on any property used in a business is deductible. Personal property tax is an *ad valorem tax*—a tax on the value of personal property. For example, a *floor tax* is a property tax levied on inventory that is sitting on the floor (or shelves) of your business. Registration fees for the right to use property within the state in your trade or business are deductible. If the fees are based on the value of the property they are considered a personal property tax.

Sales and Use Taxes

Sales tax to acquire a depreciable asset used in a trade or business is added to the basis of the asset and is recovered through depreciation. If sales tax is paid to acquire a nondepreciable asset, it is still treated as part of the cost of the asset and is deducted as part of the asset's expense. For example, sales tax on business stationery is part of the cost of the stationery and is deducted as part of that cost (not as a separate sales tax deduction). Sales tax paid on property acquired for resale is also treated as part of the cost of that property.

Sales tax you collect as a merchant or other business owner and turn over to the state is deductible only if you include it in your gross receipts. If the sales tax is not included, it is not deductible.

When sales tax is imposed on the seller or retailer and the seller or retailer can separately state the tax or pass it on to the consumer, then the consumer, rather than the seller or retailer, gets to deduct the tax. When the consumer is in business the tax is treated differently depending on how the asset is acquired. (See the aforementioned details for depreciable property, nondepreciable property, and property held for sale or resale.)

A compensating use tax is treated as a sales tax. This type of tax is imposed on the use, storage, or consumption of an item brought in from another taxing jurisdiction. Typically, it is imposed at the same percentage as a sale tax.

To learn about obtaining a resale number needed for the collection of sales taxes and your sales tax obligations, contact your state tax department (you can find it through your telephone directory or at <www.sba.gov>).

Employment Taxes

If you have employees and pay the employer portion of FICA for them, you can deduct this amount as a tax. Tax under the Federal Insurance Contribution Act (FICA) is comprised of a Social Security tax and a Medicare tax. The employer portion of the Social Security tax is 6.2 percent. This tax is applied to a current wage base of up to $87,900 in 2004, which is adjusted annually for inflation. The employer portion of the Medicare tax is 1.45 percent. This is applied to all wages paid to an employee; there is no wage base limit. If you, as an employer, pay both the employer and employee portion of the tax, you may claim a deduction for your full payments.

You may also be liable for federal unemployment tax (FUTA) for your employees. The gross federal unemployment tax rate is 6.2 percent. This is applied to employee wages up to $7,000, for a maximum FUTA tax of $434 per employee. However, you may claim a credit of up to 5.4 percent for state unemployment tax that you pay. If your state unemployment tax rate is 5.4 percent or more, then the net FUTA rate is 0.8 percent. Even if your state unemployment rate is less than 5.4 percent, you are permitted to claim a full reduction of 5.4 percent. However, if you are exempt from state unemployment tax, you must pay the full FUTA rate of 6.2 percent. These tax payments are deductible by you as an employer.

State Benefit Funds

An employer who pays into a state disability or unemployment insurance fund may deduct the payments as taxes. An employee who must contribute to the following state benefit funds can deduct the payments as state income taxes on Schedule A:

- *California*—Nonoccupational Disability Benefit Fund
- *New Jersey*—Nonoccupational Disability Benefit Fund
- *New York*—Nonoccupational Disability Benefit Fund
- *Rhode Island*—Nonoccupational Disability Benefit Fund
- *West Virginia*—Unemployment Compensation Trust Fund

Franchise Taxes

Corporate franchise taxes (which is another term that may be used for state corporate income taxes and has nothing to do with whether the corporation is a franchise) are a deductible business expense. Your state may or may not impose franchise taxes on S corporations, so check with your state corporate tax department.

Excise Taxes

Excise taxes paid or incurred in a trade or business are deductible as operating expenses. A credit for federal excise tax on certain fuels may be claimed as explained in the following section.

Fuel Taxes

Taxes on gas, diesel fuel, and other motor fuels used in your business are deductible. As a practical matter, they are included in the cost of the fuel and are not separately stated. Thus, they are deducted as a fuel cost rather than as a tax.

However, in certain instances, you may be eligible for a credit for the federal excise tax on certain fuels. The credit applies to fuel used in machinery and off-highway vehicles (such as tractors), and kerosene used for heating, lighting, and cooking on a farm.

You have a choice: claim a tax credit for the federal excise tax or claim a refund of this tax. You can claim a quarterly refund for the first three quarters of the year if the refund is $750 or more. If you do not exceed $750 in a quarter, then you can carry over this refund amount to the following quarter and add it to the refund due at that time. But if, after carrying the refund forward to the fourth quarter you do not exceed $750, then you must recoup the excise tax through a tax credit.

Alternatively, if you have pesticides or fertilizers applied aerially, you may waive your right to the credit or refund, allowing the applicator to claim it (something that would reduce your application charges). If you want to waive the credit or refund, you must sign an irrevocable waiver and give a copy of it to the applicator. For further information on this credit, see IRS Publication 378, *Fuel Tax Credits and Refunds.*

Foreign Taxes

Income taxes paid to a foreign country or U.S. possession may be claimed as a deduction or a tax credit. To claim foreign income taxes as a tax credit, you must file Form 1116, Foreign Tax Credit (unless as an individual you have foreign tax of $300 or less, or $600 or less on a joint return). Corporations claim the foreign tax credit on Form 1118, Foreign Tax Credit—Corporations. The same rules apply for foreign real property taxes paid with respect to real property owned in a foreign country or U.S. possession.

Other Rules

If a corporation pays a tax imposed on a shareholder and the shareholder does not reimburse the corporation, then the corporation, and not the shareholder, is entitled to claim the deduction for the payment of the tax.

NONDEDUCTIBLE TAXES

You may not deduct federal income taxes, even the amount paid with respect to your business income. Other nondeductible taxes include assessments on real property for local benefits that tend to add to the value of the property, employee contributions to private or voluntary disability plans, fines imposed by a governmental authority, penalties imposed by the federal government on taxes or for failing to file returns, and occupational taxes.

DEDUCTIBLE INTEREST
General Rules

Interest paid or incurred on debts related to your business generally is fully deductible as business interest. Business interest is deductible without limitation, except when such interest is required to be capitalized. (Remember, for example, that construction period interest and taxes must be capitalized, as explained earlier in this chapter.) There is one main exception to the general deductibility rule for business interest: interest on life insurance policies.

Interest is characterized by how and what the proceeds of the loan that generated the interest are used. *Personal interest* is nondeductible (except to the extent of qualified home mortgage interest and a limited amount of student loan interest). *Investment interest* is deductible only to the extent of net investment income. Interest characterized as incurred in a passive activity is subject to the passive loss rules. The characterization is not dependent on what type of property—business or personal—was used as collateral for the loan. For example, if you borrow against your personal life insurance policy and use the proceeds to buy equipment for your business, you can deduct the interest as business interest. On the other hand, if you take a bank loan using your corporate stock as collateral, and use the proceeds to invest in the stock market, the interest is characterized as investment interest. Interest on a tax deficiency relating to Schedules C, E, or F is nondeductible personal interest.

If the proceeds are used for more than one purpose, you must make an allocation based on the use of the loan's proceeds. When you repay a part of the loan, the repayments are treated as repaying the loan in this order:

- Amounts allocated to personal use
- Amounts allocated to investments and passive activities
- Amounts allocated to passive activities in connection with rental real estate in which you actively participate
- Amounts allocated to business use

The interest obligation must be yours in order for you to claim an interest deduction. If you pay off someone else's loan, you cannot deduct the interest you pay. If you are contractually obligated to make the payment, you may be able to deduct your payment as some other expense item, but not as interest.

Debt Incurred to Buy an Interest in a Business

If you use loan proceeds to buy an interest in a partnership, LLC, or S corporation or to make a contribution to capital, this is treated as a *debt-financed acquisition*. In this case, you must allocate the interest on the loan based on the assets of the pass-through business. The allocation can be based on book value, market value, or the adjusted bases of the assets.

> **example**
>
> You borrow $25,000 to buy an interest in an S corporation. The S corporation owns $90,000 of equipment and $10,000 of stocks (based on fair market value (FMV)). In this case, nine-tenths of the interest on the loan is treated as business interest ($90,000 ÷ $100,000); one-tenth of the interest is treated as investment interest ($10,000 ÷ $100,000).

If you, as an S corporation shareholder, LLC member, or partner, receive proceeds from a debt, you must also allocate the debt proceeds. These are called *debt-financed distributions*. Under a general allocation rule, debt proceeds distributed to an owner of a pass-through entity are allocated to the owner's use of the proceeds. Thus, if the owner uses the proceeds for personal purposes, the pass-through entity must treat the interest as nondeductible personal interest. Under an optional allocation rule, the pass-through entity may allocate the proceeds (and related interest) to one or more of the entity's expenditures other than distributions. The expenditures to which the debt is allocated are those made in the same year as the allocation is made (see IRS Notice 89-35 for allocations in pass-through entities).

If you borrow money to buy stock in a closely held C corporation, the Tax Court considers the interest to be investment interest. The reason: C corporation stock, like any publicly traded stock, is held for investment. This is so even if the corporation never pays out investment income (*dividends*) or the purchase of the stock is made to protect one's employment with the corporation.

Loans between Shareholders and Their Corporations

Special care must be taken when shareholders lend money to their corporation, and vice versa, or when shareholders guarantee third-party loans made to their corporation.

Corporation's Indebtedness to Shareholders

If a corporation borrows from its shareholders, the corporation can deduct the interest it pays on the loan. The issue sometimes raised by the IRS in these types of loans is whether there is any real indebtedness. Sometimes loans are used in place of dividends to transform nondeductible dividend payments into deductible interest. In order for a loan to withstand IRS scrutiny, be prepared to show a written instrument bearing a fixed maturity date for the repayment of the loan. The instrument should also state a fixed rate of interest. There should be a valid business reason for this borrowing arrangement (such as evidence that the corporation could not borrow from a commercial source at a reasonable rate of interest). If the loan is subordinated to the claims of corporate creditors, this tends to show that it is not a true debt, but other factors may prove otherwise. Also, when a corporation is heavily indebted to shareholders, the debt-to-equity ratio may indicate that the loans are not true loans but are merely disguised equity.

Shareholder Guarantees of Corporate Debt

Banks or other lenders usually require personal guarantees by the corporation's principal shareholders as a condition for making loans to the corporation. This arrangement raises one of the basic rules for deducting interest discussed earlier: The obligation must be yours in order for you to deduct the interest.

---

example

A sole shareholder paid interest on a loan made by a third party to his corporation. He agreed that he would pay any outstanding debt if the corporation failed to do so. He was not entitled to claim an interest deduction because it was the corporation, not he, who was primarily liable on the obligation. The shareholder was only a guarantor.

Below-Market and Above-Market Loans

When shareholders and their corporations arrange loans between themselves, they may set interest rates at less than or more than the going market rate of interest. This may be done for a number of reasons, including to ease the financial burden on a party to the loan or to create tax advantage. Whatever the reason, it is important to understand the consequences of the arrangement.

Below-Market Loans

If you receive an interest-free or below-market-interest loan, you may still be able to claim an interest deduction. You can claim an interest deduction equal to the sum of the interest you actually pay, plus the amount of interest that the lender is required to report as income under the below-market loan rules. The amount that the lender is required to report as income is fixed according to interest rates set monthly by the IRS. Different rates apply according to the term of the loan.

Rates required to be charged in order to avoid imputed interest are called the *applicable federal rates* (AFRs). You can find an index of AFRs by entering "applicable federal rules" in the search box at <www.irs.gov>. If a loan is payable on demand, the short-term rate applies. However, if the loan is outstanding for an entire year, you can use a blended annual rate (1.98 percent for 2004) provided by the IRS to simplify the computation of the taxable imputed interest. The blended rate for 2004 is 1.98 percent.

Whether you are required to report this amount as income (which would, in effect, offset the interest deduction) depends on the amount of the loan and the context in which it was made. If it was treated as compensation or a dividend, you have to include it in income; if it was considered a gift loan, you do not have additional income. Gift loans are loans up to $10,000 (as long as the loan is not made for tax avoidance purposes). The corporation (lender) must report the interest as income. If the loan is to an employee, an offsetting deduction can be taken for compensation. But if the loan is to a nonemployee, such as a shareholder who does not work for the corporation, no offsetting deduction can be taken.

Above-Market Loans

Instead of borrowing from a bank, your corporation may be able to borrow from a relative of yours, such as your child or parent, to whom you want to make gifts. You can turn the arrangement into a profitable one for both your corporation and your relative (the lender). Set the interest rate at more than what would be charged by the bank. Provided that the interest is still considered "reasonable" and the loan is an arm's-length transaction, your corporation deducts the interest and the lender receives it. If an unreasonably high rate of interest is charged and the arrangement is not at arm's length, however, the IRS will attack the arrangement and may disallow the interest as being a disguised dividend payment to you.

Home Mortgage Interest and Home Offices

If you are self-employed, use a portion of your home for business, and claim a home office deduction, you must allocate the home mortgage interest. The portion of the interest on the mortgage allocated to the business use is deducted on Form 8829, Home Office Expenses. The balance is treated as personal mortgage interest deductible as an itemized expense on Schedule A.

NONDEDUCTIBLE INTEREST AND OTHER LIMITATIONS ON DEDUCTIBILITY

If you borrow additional funds from the same lender to pay off a first loan for business, you cannot claim an interest deduction. Once you begin paying off the new loan, you can deduct interest on both the old and new loans. Payments are treated as being applied to the old loan first and then to the new loan. All interest payments are then deductible.

As in the case of taxes, if interest is paid to acquire a capital asset for resale, you must capitalize the interest expense. The interest is recovered when the asset is sold.

Commitment Fees

Fees paid to have business funds available for drawing on a standby basis are not treated as deductible interest payments. They may, however, be deductible as business expenses. Fees paid to obtain a loan may be treated as deductible interest. However, the fees are not immediately deductible; rather, they are deductible only over the term of the loan. If the loan falls through, the fees can be deducted as a loss.

Similarly, points paid to acquire a loan on business property are treated as prepaid interest. They are not currently deductible as such. Instead, they are deductible over the term of the loan. If you pay off the loan before the end of the term (before you have fully deducted the prepaid interest), you can deduct the remaining balance of prepaid interest in the final year of payment.

Interest Paid on Income Tax Deficiencies

If you pay interest on a tax deficiency arising from business income from your sole proprietorship, S corporation, partnership, or LLC, you cannot deduct the interest on your individual return. This interest is treated as nondeductible personal interest even though business income generated the deficiency.

While a C corporation can deduct interest it pays on any tax deficiency, it cannot deduct tax penalties.

Interest Related to Tax-Exempt Income

No deduction is allowed for interest paid or incurred to buy or carry tax-exempt securities.

chapter 12

first-year expensing and depreciation, amortization, and depletion

First-year expensing, which is also called the Section 179 deduction after the section in the Tax Code that creates it, is a write-off allowed for the purchase of equipment used in your business. This deduction takes the place of depreciation—the amount expensed is not depreciated. For example, if you buy a computer for your business for $2,500, you can opt to deduct its cost in full in the year you place the computer into service. If you don't make this election, you must write off the cost over a number of years fixed by law.

Depreciation is an allowance for a portion of the cost of equipment or other property owned by you and used in your business. Depreciation is claimed over the life of the property, although it may be accelerated, with a greater amount claimed in the early years of ownership. For example, *bonus depreciation* is claimed in the first year. The thinking behind depreciation is that equipment wears out. In theory, if you were to put into a separate fund the amount you claim each year as a depreciation allowance, when your equipment reaches the end of its usefulness you will have sufficient funds to buy a replacement (of course, the replacement may not cost the same as the old equipment). To claim a depreciation deduction, you do not necessarily have to spend any money. If you have already bought equipment, future depreciation deductions do not require any additional out-of-pocket expenditures.

Amortization is conceptually similar to depreciation. It is an allowance for the cost of certain capital expenditures, such as goodwill and trademarks, acquired in the purchase of a business. Amortization can be claimed only if it is specifically allowed by the tax law. It is always deducted ratably over the life of the property. As you will see, amortization is also allowed as an election for some types of expenditures that would otherwise not be deductible.

Depletion is a deduction allowed for certain natural resources. The tax law carefully controls the limits of this deduction.

For a further discussion of depreciation, amortization, and depletion, see IRS Publication 463, *Travel, Entertainment, Gifts, and Car Expenses*; IRS Publication 534, *Depreciating Property Placed in Service Before 1987*; and IRS Publication 946, *How to Depreciate Property*.

FIRST-YEAR EXPENSING

Instead of depreciating the cost of tangible personal property over a number of years, you may be able to write off the entire cost in the first year. This is *first-year expensing* or a *Section 179 deduction* (named after the section in the Internal Revenue Code that governs the deduction). A first-year expense deduction may be claimed whether you pay for the item with cash or credit. If you buy the item on credit, the first-year expense deduction can be used to enhance your cash flow position (you claim an immediate tax deduction but pay for the item over time).

You can elect to deduct up to a set dollar amount of the cost of tangible personal property used in your business. In 2004, you can deduct $102,000 (and more in certain economically distressed communities).

The property must be acquired by purchase. If you inherit property, for example, and use it in your business, you cannot claim a first-year expense deduction. If you acquire property in whole or in part by means of a trade, you cannot claim a first-year expense deduction for the portion of the property acquired by trade.

---

example

You buy a new car that is used 100 percent for business. You pay cash and trade in your old car. You cannot compute the first-year expense deduction for the portion of the new car's basis that includes the adjusted basis of the car you traded in.

First-year expensing may be claimed for property that has been pre-owned (i.e., used property), as long as the property is new to you (and you acquire it by purchase).

If you buy property on credit, you can still use the first-year expense deduction even though you are not yet out-of-pocket for the purchase price. A purchase on credit that entitles you to a first-year expense deduction is a strategy for aiding your cash flow (i.e., you gain a tax deduction even though you have not expended the cash).

The property must have been acquired for business. If you buy property for personal purposes and later convert it to business use, you cannot claim a first-year expense deduction. If you are an employee, be prepared to show the property you expense was acquired for business (not personal) purposes.

Off-the-shelf software is eligible for expensing. (In the past its cost had to be amortized over a period of up to 36 months.)

Generally, the first-year expense deduction does not apply to property you buy and then lease to others. (There is no restriction on leased property by corporations.) However, a first-year expense deduction is allowed for leased property you manufactured and leased if the term of the lease is less than half of the property's class life and, for the first 12 months the property is transferred to the lessee, the total business deductions for the property are more than 15 percent of the rental income for the property.

Limits on First-Year Expensing

Three limits apply for first-year expensing: a *dollar limit*, an *investment limit*, and a *taxable income limit*.

Dollar Limit

You cannot deduct more than the applicable dollar amount in any one year. This dollar limit ($102,000 in 2004) applies on a per-taxpayer basis. For businesses within empowerment zones, renewal communities, the District of Columbia, or the New York City Liberty Zone, the dollar limit is increased by the smaller of $35,000 or the cost of qualified Section 179 property within these areas. If you qualify for a higher dollar limit, simply cross out the preprinted $102,000 limit on Form 4562 and write in your applicable dollar limit in the margin.

note

A special dollar limit for cars used in business supersedes the first-year expense deduction limit. (See Chapter 7 for more details on deducting the costs of business cars.) No first-year expense deduction can be claimed for listed property unless it is used more than 50 percent for business.

If an individual owns more than one business, he or she must aggregate first-year expense deductions from all businesses and deduct no more than a total of $102,000 in 2004. Married persons are treated as one taxpayer. They are allowed only one $102,000 deduction regardless of which spouse placed the property in service. If they file separate returns, each can claim only one-half or $51,000.

for the future

The dollar limit on expensing in 2005 is $105,000.

Investment Limit

The first-year expense deduction is really designed for small businesses. This is because every dollar of investments in equipment over $410,000 reduces the dollar limit.

example

In 2004 you buy equipment costing $420,000. Your first-year expense deduction is limited to $92,000 ($102,000 − $10,000).

If a business buys equipment costing $512,000, the deduction limit is fully phased out, so no first-year expense deduction is allowed.

Taxable Income Limit

The total first-year expense deduction cannot exceed taxable income from the active conduct of a business. You are treated as actively conducting a business if you participate in a meaningful way in the management or operations of a business.

Taxable income for purposes of this limit has a special meaning. Start with your net income (or loss) from all businesses that you actively conduct. If you are married and file jointly, add your spouse's net income (or loss). This includes certain gains and losses, called Section 1231 gains and losses (see Chapter 6), and interest from working capital in your business. It also includes salary, wages, and other compensation earned as an employee, so even though a moonlighting business that bought the equipment has little or no income, you may still be eligible for a full first-year expense deduction if your salary from your day job is sufficient. Reduce your net income (or loss) by any first-year expense deduction, the deduction for one-half of self-employment tax, and net operating loss carrybacks or carryforwards. This, then, is your taxable income for purposes of the taxable income limitation. If your taxable income limits your deduction, any unused deduction can be carried forward and used in a future year.

---

example

Your taxable income (without regard to a first-year expense deduction) is $12,000. You place in service in 2004 a machine costing $14,000. Your first-year expense deduction is limited to $12,000. You can carry forward the additional $2,000 to next year.

Carryforwards of unused first-year expense deductions can be used if there is sufficient taxable income in the next year. You can choose the properties for which the costs will be carried forward. You can allocate the portion of the costs to these properties as long as the allocation is reflected on your books and records.

Special Rules for Pass-Through Entities

The dollar limit, investment limit, and taxable income limit apply at both the entity and owner levels. This means that partnerships, as well as their partners, and S corporations, as well as their shareholders, must apply all the limits. The same is true for LLCs and members.

---

example

You are a 50-percent shareholder in an S corporation that claims a first-year expense deduction in 2004 of $102,000. Your allocable share as reported on your Schedule K-1 is $50,000. You also own a business that you run as a sole proprietor. You place in service a machine costing $75,000. (Assume sufficient taxable income by the S corporation and for your sole proprietorship.) Your first-year expense deduction for this machine is limited to $51,000. The balance of the cost of the machine, $24,000, cannot be expensed in the current year because of the dollar limit.

Should the First-Year Expensing Election Be Made?

You don't automatically claim this deduction; you must elect it on Form 4562. While first-year expensing provides a great opportunity for matching your tax write-off with your cash outlay, it is not always advisable to take advantage of this opportunity. Consider forgoing the election in the following situations:

- You receive the write-off through a pass-through entity but could claim it for purchases made through a sole proprietorship (see the preceding example).

- You are in a low tax bracket this year but expect to be more profitable in the coming years so that depreciation deductions in those years will be more valuable.

Dispositions of First-Year Expense Property

If you sell or otherwise dispose of property for which a first-year expense deduction was claimed, or cease using the property for business, there may be recapture of your deduction. This means that you must include in your income a portion of the deduction you previously claimed. The amount you must recapture depends on when you dispose of the property. The longer you hold it, the less recapture you have. If you sell property at a gain, recapture is not additional income; it is merely a reclassification of income. If you realize gain on the sale of first-year expense property, instead of treating the gain as capital gain, the recapture amount is characterized as ordinary income.

Recapture is calculated by comparing your first-year expense deduction with the deduction you would have claimed had you instead taken ordinary depreciation.

---

example

In 2001, you placed in service office furniture (seven-year property) costing $10,000, which you fully expensed. In 2004 you used the property only 40 percent for business (and 60 percent for personal purposes). You calculate your recapture as shown in Table 12.1.

If you transfer first-year expense property in a transaction that does not require recognition of gain or loss (e.g., if you make a tax-free exchange or contribute the property to a corporation in a tax-free incorporation), an adjustment is made in the basis of the property. The adjusted basis of the property is increased before the disposition by the amount of the first-year expense deduction that is disallowed. The new owner cannot claim a first-year expense deduction with respect to this disallowed portion.

TABLE 12.1 Calculating Recapture

First-Year Expense Deduction:		$10,000
Allowable Depreciation		
$10,000 × 14.29%*	$1,429	
10,000 × 24.49	2,449	
10,000 × 17.49	1,749	
10,000 × 12.49 × 40%	500	$6,127
Recapture amount		$3,873

*MACRS percentages from Table 12.2.

GENERAL RULES FOR DEPRECIATION

Depreciable Property

Depreciation is a deduction allowed for certain property used in your business. It is designed to offset the cost of acquiring it, so you cannot depreciate leased property. To be depreciable, the property must be the kind that wears out, decays, gets used up, becomes obsolete, or loses value from natural causes. The property must have a determinable useful life that is longer than one year. Antiques, for example, generally cannot be depreciated because they do not have a determinable useful life; they can be expected to last indefinitely. The same is true for goodwill you build up in your business (though if you buy a business and pay for its goodwill, you may be able to amortize the cost, as explained later in this chapter).

Land is not depreciable because it, too, can be expected to last indefinitely. However, some land preparation costs can be depreciated if they are closely associated with a building on the land rather than the land itself. For example, shrubs around the entry to a building may be depreciated; trees planted on the perimeter of the property are nondepreciable land costs. Also, the cost of the minerals on the land may not be depreciated but may be subject to depletion.

When you own a building, you must allocate the **basis** of the property between the building and the land, since only the building portion is depreciable.

Basis   Generally, basis is the amount you pay for property. It does not matter whether you finance your purchase or pay cash. You add to basis sales taxes and other related expenses (such as nondeductible closing costs if you get a mortgage, or attorney's fees). But you cannot include the value of trade-ins in your basis.

There is no special rule for making an allocation of basis. Obviously you would prefer to allocate as much as possible to the building and as little as possible to the land. However, the allocation must have some logical basis. It should be based on the relative value of each portion. What is the land worth? What is the building worth? You may want to use the services of an appraiser to help you derive a fair yet favorable allocation that will withstand IRS scrutiny.

---

example

In 2004, you begin to use a personal computer for a business you have just started up. You paid $2,500 for it in 2002 and it is now worth $1,200. Your basis for depreciation is $1,200. At the same time, you begin to use one room in your home as a home office. You bought your home in 1996 for $200,000 and it is now worth $300,000 (exclusive of land). Assuming that the home office allocation is 12.5 percent of the home, your basis for depreciation is $25,000 (12.5 percent of $200,000, which is lower than 12.5 percent of $300,000, or $37,500).

If you convert personal property to business use, the basis for purposes of depreciation is the lower of its adjusted basis (generally cost) or fair market value at the time of the conversion to business use. If you acquire replacement property in a like-kind exchange or an involuntary conversion, special rules govern basis for purposes of depreciation (see IRS Publication 946, *How to Depreciate Property*).

Property that can be expected to last for one year or less is simply deducted in full as some other type of deduction. For example, if you buy stationery that will be used up within the year, you simply deduct the cost of the stationery as supplies. In order to claim depreciation, you must be the owner of the property. If you lease property, like an office, you cannot depreciate it; only the owner can, since it is the owner who suffers the wear and tear on his or her investment.

Depreciable property may be tangible or intangible. *Tangible property* is property you can touch—office furniture, a machine, or a telephone. Tangible property may be personal property (a machine) or real property (a factory). *Intangible property* is property you cannot touch, such as copyrights, patents, and franchises. *Personal property* does not mean you use the property for personal purposes; it is a legal term for tangible property that is not real property.

If you use property for both business and personal purposes, you must make an allocation. You can claim depreciation only on the business portion of the property. For example, if you use your car 75 percent for business and 25 percent for personal purposes (including commuting), you can claim depreciation on only 75 percent of the property.

Certain property can never be depreciated. In addition to land, you cannot depreciate your inventory. *Inventory* is property held primarily for sale to customers in the ordinary course of your business.

When to Claim Depreciation

You claim depreciation beginning with the year in which the property is **placed in service.** You continue to claim depreciation throughout the life of the asset. The life of the asset is also called its *recovery period*. Different types of assets have different recovery periods. The length of the recovery period has nothing to do with how durable a particular item may be. You simply check the classifications of property to find the recovery period for a particular item.

Placed in service   When an item is ready and available for a specific use, whether or not the item is actually used.

You stop claiming depreciation on the item when the property's cost has been fully depreciated or when the property is retired from service. Property is retired from service when it is permanently withdrawn from use, by selling or exchanging it, abandoning it, or destroying it.

---

example

A machine with a five-year recovery period is no longer needed after three years for the task for which it was purchased. The machine is sold to another company that still has a use for it. Once the machine is sold, it has been permanently removed from your service. You cannot claim depreciation after this occurs.

Even if you do not actually claim depreciation, you are treated as having done so for purposes of figuring the basis of property when you dispose of it.

---

example

You place a piece of machinery in service in 2002 and claim a depreciation deduction on your 2002 return. In 2003, your revenues are low and you forget to report your depreciation deduction on your 2003 return. In 2004, you sell the machine. In calculating gain or loss on the sale, you must adjust basis for the depreciation you actually claimed in 2002 and the depreciation you should have claimed in 2003.

If you failed to claim depreciation in the past, file an amended return to fix the error if the tax year is still open (the statute of limitation on amending the return has not expired). Alternatively, you can correct the underdepreciation (even for a closed tax year) by filing for a change in accounting method on Form 3115. Under a special IRS procedure, you simply adjust your income in the current year. Be sure to write on Form 3115 "Automatic Method Change under Rev. Proc. 98-60."

If you abandon property before it has been fully depreciated, you can deduct the balance of your depreciation deductions in the year of abandonment. For instance, if you have a machine with a seven-year recovery period that you abandon in the fifth year because it is obsolete, you can claim the depreciation that you would have claimed in the sixth, seventh, and eighth years in the fifth year along with depreciation allowable for that year.

MODIFIED ACCELERATED COST RECOVERY SYSTEM

Modified Accelerated Cost Recovery System (MACRS) is a depreciation system that went into effect for tangible property placed in service after 1986. It is composed of two systems: a basic system, called the *General Depreciation System* (GDS), and an alternate system, called the *Alternative Depreciation System* (ADS). The difference between the two systems is the recovery period over which you claim depreciation and the method for calculating depreciation. You use the basic system unless the alternate system is required or you make a special election to use the alternate system. You cannot use either system for certain property: intangible property (patents, copyrights, etc.), motion picture films or videotapes, sound recordings, and property you elect to exclude from MACRS so that you can use a depreciation method based on some other measuring rod than a term of years (these other methods are not discussed in this book).

Basic System

You can use the basic system (GDS) to depreciate any tangible property unless you are required to use the alternate system, elect to use the alternate system, or are required to use some other depreciation method. To calculate your depreciation deduction, you need to know:

- *The property's basis.* If you purchase property, basis is your cost. If you acquire property in some other way (get it by gift, inheritance, or in a tax-free exchange), basis is figured in another way. For example, if your corporation acquires property from you upon its formation in a tax-free incorporation, then the corporation steps into your shoes for purposes of basis.

---

example

You form a corporation (C or S) and contribute cash and a computer. In exchange you receive all of the stock of the corporation. Your basis for the computer was $4,000. The corporation assumes your basis—$4,000.

A similar rule applies to property you contribute to a partnership or LLC upon its formation. If you are a sole proprietor or an employee and convert property from personal use to business use, your basis for depreciation is the lesser of the fair market value (FMV) on the date of conversion to business use or the adjusted basis of the property on that date.

The cost of property includes sales taxes. If you hire an architect to design a building, the fees are added to the basis of the property and recovered through depreciation. The following are more items to consider when calculating your depreciation deduction.

- *The property's recovery period.* Recovery periods are fixed according to the claim in which a property falls. In the past, recovery period was referred to as the useful life of the property and you may periodically see this old phase still in use.

- *The date the property is placed in service.* Remember, this is the date the property is ready and available for its specific use.

- *The applicable convention.* These are special rules that govern the timing of deductions (explained later in this chapter).

- *The depreciation method.* MACRS has five different depreciation methods.

Recovery Periods

The class assigned to a property is designed to match the period over which the basis of property is recovered (e.g., cost is deducted). Five-year property allows the cost of certain equipment to be deducted over five years (subject to adjustment for conventions discussed later).

Three-Year Property

This property includes taxis, tractor units for use over the road, racehorses over two years old when placed in service, any other horse over 12 years old when placed in service, breeding hogs, certain handling devices for manufacturing food and beverages, and special tools for manufacturing rubber products.

Five-Year Property

This property includes cars, buses, trucks, airplanes, trailers and trailer containers, computers and peripheral equipment, some office machinery (calculators, copiers, typewriters), assets used in construction, logging equipment, assets used to manufacture organic and inorganic chemicals, and property used in research and experimentation. It also includes breeding and dairy cattle and breeding and dairy goats.

Seven-Year Property

This property includes office fixtures and furniture (chairs, desks, files); communications equipment (fax machines); breeding and workhorses; assets used in printing; recreational assets (miniature golf courses, billiard establishments, concert halls); assets used to produce jewelry; musical instruments; toys; sporting goods; motion picture and television films and tapes; and any property not assigned to another class.

10-Year Property

This property includes barges, tugs, vessels, and similar water transportation equipment; single-purpose agricultural or horticultural structures placed in service after 1988; and trees or vines bearing fruits or nuts.

15-Year Property

This property includes certain depreciable improvements made to land (bridges, fences, roads, shrubbery).

20-Year Property

This property includes farm buildings (other than single-purpose agricultural or horticultural structures) and any municipal sewers.

Residential Rental Realty

Rental buildings qualify if 80 percent or more of the gross rental is from dwelling units. The recovery period is 27.5 years.

Nonresidential Realty

This class applies to factories, office buildings, and any other realty other than residential rental realty. The recovery period is 39 years (31.5 years for property placed in service before May 13, 1993).

Components of Realty

Structural components of a building are part and parcel of the realty and generally must be depreciated as such (e.g., over 39 years). However, certain components, such as electrical systems and wiring, carpeting, floor covering, plumbing connections, exhaust systems, handrails, room partitions, tile ceilings, and steam boilers, can be treated as tangible personal property instead of realty. As such, they can be depreciated over shorter recovery periods rather than being treated as part of realty subject to longer recovery periods. Obtain a cost segregation analysis when buying, building, or improving realty.

---

example

You install a fake floor to cover wiring needed for your computers. The IRS originally said that the floor can be depreciated as personal property over five years rather than as part of the realty depreciated over 39 years. However, it later said it would take another look at this conclusion, so beware.

Improvements or Additions

In general, improvements or additions to property are treated as separate property and are depreciated separately from the property itself. The recovery period for improvements begins on the later of the date the improvements are placed in service or the date the property to which the improvements are made is placed in service. Use the same recovery period for the improvements that you would for the underlying property (unless an improvement is a component of realty that can be depreciated according to its own recovery period).

Property Acquired in a Like-Kind Exchange

The property acquired in a like-kind exchange is depreciated over the remaining recovery period of the old property. Thus, the new property, which has the basis of the old property, also has the old property's remaining recovery period. This enables you to write off the newly acquired asset more rapidly than if the recovery period of the new asset were used.

Conventions

There are three conventions that affect the timing of depreciation deductions. Two apply to property other than residential or nonresidential real property (essentially personal property such as equipment); the other applies to residential or nonresidential real property (rental units, offices, and factories).

Half-Year Convention

The *half-year convention* applies to all property (other than residential or nonresidential real property) unless superseded by the mid-quarter convention (explained next). Under the half-year convention, property is treated as if you placed it in service in the middle of the year. You are allowed to deduct only one-half of the depreciation allowance for the first year. This is so even if you place the property in service on the first day of the year. Under this convention, property is treated as disposed of in the middle of the year, regardless of the actual date of disposition.

The half-year convention means that property held for its entire recovery period will have an additional year for claiming depreciation deductions. Only one-half of the first year's depreciation deduction is claimed in the first year; the balance of depreciation is claimed in the year following the last year of the recovery period.

---

example

A desk (seven-year property) is placed in service on January 1, 2004. Without regard to expensing or bonus depreciation, one-half of the depreciation deduction that would otherwise be claimed in the first year is allowed. Normal depreciation is claimed in years two through seven. The remaining depreciation is claimed in the eighth year.

Mid-Quarter Convention

Under the *mid-quarter convention*, all property placed in service during the year (or disposed of during the year) is treated as placed in service (or disposed of) in the middle of the applicable quarter. The mid-quarter convention applies (and the half-year convention does not) if the total bases of all property placed in service during the last three months of the year (the final quarter) exceeds 40 percent of the total bases of property placed in service during the entire year. In making this determination, do not take into consideration residential or nonresidential real property or property placed in service and then disposed of in the same year.

---

example

You are on a calendar year. In January 2004, you place in service machine A, costing $3,000. In November 2004 you place in service another machine, machine B, costing $10,000. You must use the mid-quarter convention to calculate depreciation for both machines. This is because more than 40 percent of all property placed in service during the year ($13,000) was placed in service in the final quarter of the year ($10,000). (Actually, 77 percent of all property placed in service in the year was placed in service in the final quarter of the year.)

---

example

Continuing with the same machine situation, except that machine B is placed in service in January and machine A is placed in service in November. In this instance, the mid-quarter convention does not apply because only 23 percent of all property placed in service in 2004 was placed in service in the final quarter of the year.

Mid-Month Convention

This convention applies only to real property. You must treat all real property as if it were placed in service or disposed of in the middle of the month. The mid-month convention is taken into account in the depreciation tables from which you can take your deduction. Simply look at the table for the type of realty (residential or nonresidential) you own, and then look in the table for the month in which the property is placed in service.

Depreciation Methods

There are five ways to depreciate property: the 200-percent declining balance rate, the 150-percent declining balance rate, the straight-line election, the 150-percent election, and the ADS method. Both 200-percent and 150-percent declining balance rates are referred to as accelerated rates.

You may use the 200-percent rate for three-year, five-year, seven-year, and 10-year property over the GDS recovery period. The half-year or mid-quarter convention must be applied. The 200-percent declining balance method is calculated by dividing 100 by the recovery period and then doubling it. However, as a practical matter you do not have to compute the rates. They are provided for you in Tables 12.2 and 12.3, which take into account the half-year or mid-quarter conventions.

If the 200-percent declining balance rate is used, you can switch to

TABLE 12.2 MACRS Rates—Half-Year Convention

Year	Three-Year Property	Five-Year Property	Seven-Year Property
1	33.33%	20.00%	14.29%
2	44.45	32.00	24.49
3	14.81	19.20	17.49
4	7.81	11.52	12.49
5		11.52	8.93
6		5.76	8.92
7			8.93
8			4.46

TABLE 12.3 MACRS Rates—Mid-Quarter Convention (200% Rate)

Year	First Quarter	Second Quarter	Third Quarter	Fourth Quarter
Three-Year Property			
1	58.33%	41.67%	25.00%	8.33%
2	27.78	38.89	50.00	61.11
3	12.35	14.14	16.677	20.37
4	1.54	5.30	8.33	10.19
Five-Year Property			
1	35.00	25.00	15.00	5.00
2	26.00	30.00	34.00	38.00
3	15.60	18.00	20.40	22.80
4	11.01	11.37	12.24	13.68
5	11.01	11.37	11.30	10.94
6	1.38	4.26	7.06	9.58
Seven-Year Property			
1	25.00	17.85	10.71	3.57
2	21.43	23.47	25.51	27.55
3	15.31	16.76	18.22	19.68
4	10.93	11.97	13.02	14.06
5	8.75	8.87	9.30	10.04
6	8.74	8.87	8.85	8.73
7	8.75	8.87	8.86	8.73
8	1.09	3.33	5.53	7.64

the straight line in the year when it provides a deduction of value equal to or greater than the accelerated rate. Of course, total depreciation can never be more than 100 percent of the property's basis. The switch to straight line merely accelerates the timing of depreciation (the total depreciation is, of course, limited to the basis of the property). Table 12.4 shows you when it becomes advantageous to switch to the straight-line rate.

You use the 150-percent rate for 15- and 20-year property over the GDS recovery period. Again, you must also apply the half-year or mid-quarter convention. You change over to the straight-line method when it provides a greater deduction. Tables for this rate may be found in IRS Publication 946, *How to Depreciate Property.*

TABLE 12.4 When to Change to Straight-Line Method

Class	Changeover Year
Three-year property	3rd
Five-year property	4th
Seven-year property	5th
10-year property	7th
15-year property	7th
20-year property	9th

Residential and nonresidential realty must use the straight-line rate (see Tables 12.5 and 12.6). *Straight line* is simply the cost of the property divided by the life of the property. However, you begin depreciation with the month in which the property is placed in service. This makes the rate vary slightly over the years. The tables can be used to calculate depreciation for residential and nonresidential real property using basic depreciation (GDS). For all tables, find your annual depreciation rate by looking in the column for the month in which the property was placed in service (for example, for calendar-year businesses, March is 3; August is 8). Then look at the year of ownership you are in (e.g., the year in which you place property in service, look at year number one).

TABLE 12.5 Rates for Residential Realty Years (27 years), Straight-Line, Mid-Month Convention

	Month in the First Recovery Year the Property Is Placed in Service					
Year	1	2	3	4	5	6
1	3.485%	3.182%	2.879%	2.576%	2.273%	1.970%
2–9	3.636	3.636	3.636	3.636	3.636	3.636
Year	7	8	9	10	11	12
1	1.677%	1.364%	1.061%	0.758%	0.455%	0.152%
2–9	3.636	3.636	3.636	3.636	3.636	3.636

TABLE 12.6 Rates for Nonresidential Realty Years (39 Years), Straight-Line, Mid-Month Convention

	Month in the First Recovery Year the Property Is Placed in Service					
Year	1	2	3	4	5	6
1	2.461%	2.247%	2.033%	1.819%	1.605%	1.391%
2–39	2.564	2.564	2.564	2.564	2.564	2.564
Year	7	8	9	10	11	12
1	1.177%	0.963%	0.749%	0.535%	0.321%	0.107%
2–39	2.564	2.564	2.564	2.564	2.564	2.564

---

example

You are on a calendar year and placed in service a factory in April 2001. In 2004, your depreciation rate is 2.564 percent. You found this rate by looking at the table for 39-year nonresidential property under month 4, year 4.

Tables for depreciation of residential and nonresidential real property using ADS as well as years after year 9 for residential and pre-May 13, 1993, nonresidential realty may be found in Appendix A of IRS Publication 946, *How to Depreciate Property.*

Alternative Depreciation System

You must use the alternative system (ADS) (and not the basic system, GDS) for listed property not used more than 50 percent for business, property used predominantly in farming and placed in service during any year in which you elect not to apply the uniform capitalization rules to certain farming costs, and certain other property. Listed property includes cars and other transportation vehicles, computers and peripherals (unless used only at a regular business establishment), and cellular telephones.

The ADS requires depreciation to be calculated using the straight-line method (see Table 12.7). This is done by dividing the cost of the property by the alternate recovery period. In some cases, the recovery period is the same as for the basic system; in others, it is longer.

TABLE 12.7 Recovery Periods under
Alternative Depreciation System

Property	Years
Cars, computers, light-duty trucks	5
Furniture and fixtures	10
Personal property with no class life	12
Nonresidential/residential real estate	40

You can elect to use ADS for other property in order to claim more gradual depreciation. The election applies to all property within the same class placed in service during the year (other than real estate). For residential rental and nonresidential real property, you can make the election to use ADS on a property-by-property basis.

An election to use ADS may be helpful, for example, if you are first starting out and do not have sufficient income to offset large depreciation deductions. Use of ADS can help to avoid alternative minimum tax and the special depreciation computations required for alternative minimum tax.

For property placed in service after December 31, 1999, you can calculate depreciation for regular tax purposes using the same recovery periods as required for alternative minimum tax purposes. This eliminates the need to make any adjustments for alternative minimum tax and to keep separate records of depreciation taken for regular and alternative minimum tax purposes.

Recapture of Depreciation

If you sell or otherwise dispose of depreciable or amortizable property at a gain, you may have to report all or some of your gain as ordinary income. The treatment of what would otherwise have been capital gain as ordinary income is called *recapture*. In effect, some of the tax benefit you enjoy from depreciation deductions may be offset later on by recapture.

Also, if you sell or otherwise dispose of real property (e.g., residence containing a home office) on which straight-line depreciation was claimed after May 6, 1997, all such depreciation is taxed as capital gain up to 25 percent. This taxable portion is referred to as *unrecaptured depreciation*. The treatment of income from depreciation recapture is explained in Chapter 6.

Recordkeeping for Depreciation

Since depreciation deductions go on for a number of years, it is important to keep good records of prior deductions. It is also necessary to maintain records since depreciation deductions may differ for regular income tax purposes and the alternative minimum tax. Recordkeeping is explained in Chapter 3.

BONUS DEPRECIATION

There is a special first-year depreciation allowance that can be claimed for property purchased after September 10, 2001, and before January 1, 2005. The special *bonus depreciation* allowance for 2004 is 50 percent of the adjusted basis of the property (generally the cost of the property minus any first-year expensing). Alternatively, you can opt *not* to use the 50 percent rate, but instead claim bonus depreciation at a 30 percent rate or waive it entirely.

If you claim bonus depreciation, you reduce the adjusted basis of the property by this amount for purposes of figuring regular depreciation.

---

example

On October 1, 2004, you buy and place in service a machine costing $130,000. You elect to expense $100,000 of its cost. You can claim bonus depreciation of $15,000 (50 percent of [$130,000 – $100,000]). You can apply regular depreciation to the remaining adjusted basis of $15,000. So, for example, if the machine is five-year property, the regular depreciation deduction for 2004 is $3,000 (20 percent of $15,000). Of the $130,000 cost of the machine, you can deduct $118,000 in the year of acquisition ($100,000 + $15,000 + $3,000).

If you claim bonus depreciation, there is no adjustment made for alternative minimum tax purposes (see Chapter 17).

Eligible Property

To qualify for bonus depreciation, you must meet three conditions:

1. The original use of the property must commence with you (i.e., bonus depreciation cannot be claimed for used property). There is a limited exception for sale-leaseback arrangements.

2. The acquisition must be after September 10, 2001. If you manufacture, construct, or produce property for your own use, the manufacturing, construction, or production must have begun after September 10, 2001.

3. The property must be placed in service before January 1, 2005. However, property considered to have a "longer production period," such as property with a recovery period of at least 10 years, must be placed in service before January 1, 2006.

Computer software acquired separately from hardware qualifies for bonus depreciation (but software that is Section 197 property does not qualify for bonus depreciation).

A leasehold improvement qualifies for bonus depreciation as long as it is an improvement to an interior portion of nonresidential realty made pursuant to the lease by the lessee, it is placed in service more than three years after the building is first placed in service, and the interior of the building is occupied exclusively by the lessee or sublessee.

Election Out of Bonus Depreciation

Bonus depreciation applies automatically; you do not have to elect it as you do first-year expensing. However, you can elect *not* to claim it. This may be advisable if you do not have substantial income and would benefit more from claiming depreciation in future years to offset anticipated income. If you do not make this election, then you are deemed to have claimed bonus depreciation, even if you failed to take the deduction (i.e., you must reduce the basis of the property by the amount you could have claimed).

You can elect out of bonus depreciation for a class of assets (for example, all five-year property); however, you cannot use it for some assets within the class but not for others within the same class.

To make the election out of bonus depreciation, attach your own statement to the return saying you are electing not to claim the additional allowance and specifying for which class of property you are making the election. Or, if you wish, you can opt to claim 30 percent bonus depreciation in lieu of the 50 percent rate.

LIMITATIONS ON LISTED PROPERTY

Certain property is called *listed property* and is subject to special depreciation limits. Listed property includes:

- Cars
- Other transportation vehicles (including boats)
- Computers and peripherals, unless used only at a regular business establishment owned or leased by the person operating the establishment. (A home office is treated as a business establishment.)
- Cellular telephones (or similar telecommunication equipment)

These are the only items considered listed property because they have been specified as such in the tax law. For example, fax machines and noncellular telephones are not treated as listed property.

It is advisable to keep a log or other record for the use of listed property. This will help you show that business use is more than 50 percent. However, if you use listed property, such as a computer, in a home office whose expenses are deductible, the Tax Court says you do not need records. The reason: Recordkeeping for business use does not apply to computers used at a place of business (which includes a home office that is the principal place of business and that is used regularly and exclusively for that business).

If business use of listed property is not more than 50 percent during the year, the basic depreciation system cannot be used. In this case, you must use the ADS. Under this system, depreciation can be calculated only with the straight-line method. Divide the cost of the property by the alternative recovery period. For cars, computers, and other listed property, the alternative recovery period happens to be the same as the basic recovery period—five years.

Use of the ADS means that instead of accelerating depreciation deductions to the earlier years of ownership, depreciation deductions will be spread evenly over the recovery period of the property.

PUTTING PERSONAL PROPERTY TO BUSINESS USE

You may already own some items that can be useful to your business, such as a home computer, office furniture, and a cell phone. You don't have to go out and buy new items for the business; you can convert what you already own from personal to business use.

For depreciation purposes, the basis of each item is the lower of its adjusted basis (usually its cost) or its value at the time of conversion. For most items that decline in value over time, this means that depreciation is usually based on value. But for other property, such as realty that increases in value, depreciation is usually based on adjusted basis.

---

example

In 2002, you purchased a computer for home use at a cost of $3,000. In 2004, you start a business and begin to use the computer for business activities. Its value in 2004 is $1,000. For depreciation purposes, you are limited to $1,000; in this case the computer's value is lower than its adjusted basis.

---

example

In 2002, you bought your home for $200,000. In 2004, you start a business from home and use 10 percent of the space exclusively for this purpose. The house is now worth $240,000. For depreciation purposes, you are limited to $20,000 (10 percent of $200,000); in this case the adjusted basis is lower than the home's current value.

You cannot use first-year expensing for property you convert from personal to business use in a year that is after the year you acquired the property. The law limits expensing to the year in which property is initially placed in service (and that is usually prior to the year it is first used in business).

AMORTIZATION

Certain capital expenditures can be deducted over a term of years. This is called *amortization*. This deduction is taken evenly over a prescribed period of time. Amortization applies only to the following expenditures:

- Intangibles acquired on the purchase of a business
- Business start-up costs and organizational expenses
- Construction period interest and taxes
- Research and experimentation costs
- Bond premiums
- Reforestation costs
- Pollution control facilities
- Costs of acquiring a lease

Intangibles Acquired on the Purchase of a Business

If you buy a business, a portion of your cost may be allocated to certain intangible items; such as goodwill; going concern value; workforce in place; patents, copyrights, formulas, processes, designs, patterns, and know-how; customer-based intangibles; supplier-based intangibles; licenses, permits, and other rights granted by a governmental unit or agency; covenants not to compete; trademarks, or trade names. These items are called *Section 197 intangibles*, named after a section in the Internal Revenue Code. You may deduct the portion of the cost allocated to these items ratably over a period of 15 years.

---

example

You buy out the accounting practice of someone else. As part of the sale, the other accountant signs a covenant not to compete with you for two years within your same location. You may amortize the portion of the cost of the practice relating to the covenant over 15 years.

Section 197 intangibles do not include interests in a corporation, partnership, trust or estate, or sports franchise, interests in land, certain computer software, and certain other excluded items. Also, you cannot amortize the cost of self-created items. Thus, if you generate your own customer list, you cannot claim an amortization deduction.

Dispositions

If a Section 197 intangible is sold at a loss but other such intangibles are still owned, no loss can be taken on the sale. Instead the bases of the remaining Section 197 intangibles are reduced by the unclaimed loss. The same rule applies if a Section 197 intangible becomes worthless or is abandoned. No loss is recognized on the worthlessness or abandonment. Instead, the bases of remaining Section 197 are increased by the unrecognized loss.

Business Start-Up Costs and Organizational Expenses

When you start up a business, you may incur a variety of expenses. Ordinarily these are capital expenditures that are not currently deductible. They are expenses incurred to acquire a capital asset, namely, your business. However, the tax law allows amortization for certain business start-up costs. More specifically, for costs incurred before October 23, 2004, for businesses that commence before this date, you can elect to deduct these costs ratably over a period of 60 months or more. After October 22, 2004, you can deduct the first $5,000 of costs and amortize the balance over 15 years. If you later sell your business before the end of the amortization period or the business folds before that time, you can deduct the unamortized amount in your final year.

Business Start-up Costs

Generally, you think of start-up costs as expenses you pay during the first few years of your business. But for tax purposes, the term "start-up costs" has a very specific meaning. These include amounts paid to investigate *whether* to start or purchase a business and *which* business to start or purchase (this is called the *whether and which* test for determining amortization of start-up costs). Expenses related to these activities, such as a survey of potential markets and travel costs to meet potential suppliers, are treated as start-up expenses.

Other similar expenses are amortizable if they would have been deductible if paid or incurred to operate a going business and were actually paid or incurred prior to the commencement of business operations. Otherwise such expenses must be treated as part of the cost of acquiring a capital asset—the business. For example, legal fees to prepare contracts for the purchase of a business are no longer start-up fees but, rather, are expenses that must be added to the cost of the business.

Once you have passed the start-up phase and identified a target business you want to acquire, you can no longer amortize related expenses under this rule.

---

example

You are looking for a business to buy and have your accountant review the financial data from several prospects. You then zero in on one business and examine its financial data in detail. The accountant's fee related to the general search is amortizable, but the fee related to the detailed examination of the target business is not.

Organizational Costs for a Corporation

If you set up a corporation (C or S), certain expenses unique to this form of business can be written off under the same rules for start-up costs. These expenses include the cost of temporary directors, organizational meetings, state incorporation fees, accounting services for setting up the corporate books, and legal services to draft the charter, bylaws, terms of the original stock certificates, and minutes of organizational meetings.

You can deduct any other organizational costs if they are incident to the creation of a corporation, they are chargeable to the capital account, and the cost could have been amortized over the life of the corporation if the corporation had a fixed life.

You cannot amortize expenses related to selling stock, such as commissions, professional fees, and printing costs.

Organizational Costs of a Partnership

If you set up a partnership, certain expenses unique to this form of business can be written off under the same rules for start-up costs. As in the case of corporate organizational costs, partnership organizational costs include those that are incident to the creation of a partnership, are chargeable to the capital account, and would have been amortizable over the life of the partnership if the partnership had a fixed life.

Syndication costs to sell partnership interests are not treated as amortizable organizational costs. These nonamortizable costs include commissions, professional fees, and printing costs related to the issuing and marketing of partnership interests.

Computer Software

There are several different rules for treating the cost of software:

- If it is purchased separately from the purchase of a computer (i.e., it is not bundled with the hardware), the cost can be expensed. Alternatively, if expensing is not elected, the cost can be amortized over 36 months. However, if the useful life of the software is less than 36 months, amortize it over its useful life. If it has a useful life of less than one year (e.g., an annual tax preparation program), deduct it in full in the year of purchase (in effect, the same write-off as expensing but there is no taxable income limitation in this instance as there is for expensing).

- If it is bundled with hardware, depreciate as part of the hardware (generally over five years as explained earlier in this chapter).

- If it is purchased as part of the acquisition of a business, it is amortized as a Section 197 asset over 15 years.

- If it is developed by you for use in your business, treat it as a research and development cost (explained later).

- If it is leased, deduct the lease payments over the term of the lease as you would any other rental expense.

Research and Experimentation Costs

If you have research and experimentation costs, you have a choice of ways to deduct them. You can claim a current deduction for amounts paid or incurred in the year.

Alternatively, you can elect to amortize them over a period of not less than 60 months. Where you do not have current income to offset the deduction, it may be advisable to elect amortization.

You may be able to claim a tax credit for increasing your research and experimentation program. For further information on this credit, see Chapter 18.

Costs of Acquiring a Lease

If you pay a fee to obtain a lease, you can amortize the cost over the term of the lease. The lease term includes all renewal options if less than 75 percent of the cost is attributable to the term of the lease remaining on the acquisition date. The remaining term of the lease on the acquisition date does not include any period for which the lease may be subsequently renewed, extended, or continued under an option exercisable by the lessee.

DEPLETION

Depletion is a deduction allowed for certain mineral properties or timber to compensate the owner for the use of these resources. *Mineral properties* include oil and gas wells, mines, other natural deposits, and standing timber. In order to claim depletion, you must be an owner or operator with an economic interest in the mineral deposits or standing timber. This means that you are adversely affected economically when mineral properties or standing timber is mined or cut. Depletion is claimed separately for each mineral property, which is each mineral deposit in each separate tract or parcel of land. Timber property is each tract or block representing a separate timber account.

> **note**
>
> Claiming depletion may result in alternative minimum tax (AMT) both for individuals and C corporations (not otherwise exempt from AMT).

Methods of Depletion

There are two ways to calculate depletion: *cost depletion* and *percentage depletion.*

Cost Depletion

Cost depletion is determined by dividing the adjusted basis of the mineral property by the total number of recoverable units in the property's natural deposit (as determined by engineering reports). This figure is multiplied by the number of units sold if you use the accrual method of accounting, or the number of units sold and paid for if you use the cash method. Cost depletion is the only method allowed for timber. The depletion deduction is calculated when the quantity of cut timber is first accurately measured in the process of exploitation. Special rules are used to determine depletion for timber, and the deduction is taken when standing timber is cut.

Percentage Depletion

Percentage depletion is determined by applying a percentage, fixed by tax law according to each type of mineral, to your gross income from the property during the tax year (see Table 12.8).

The deduction for percentage depletion is limited to no more than 50 percent (100 percent for oil and gas properties allowed to use percentage depletion) of taxable income from the property calculated without the depletion deduction and certain other adjustments. Only small producers are allowed to use percentage depletion for oil and gas properties. If you use percentage depletion for mineral properties but it is less than cost depletion for the year, you must use cost depletion.

Partnership Oil and Gas Properties

The depletion allowance, whether cost depletion or percentage depletion, must be calculated separately for each partner and not by the partnership. Each partner can decide on the depletion method. The partnership simply allocates to the partner his or her proportionate share of the adjusted basis of each oil and gas property. Each partner

TABLE 12.8 Percentage for Mineral Properties

Type of Property	Percentage
Oil and gas—small producers	15.0%
Sulfur, uranium, and U.S. asbestos, lead, zinc, nickel, mica, and certain other ores and minerals	22.0
Gold, silver, copper and iron ore, and certain U.S. oil shale	15.0
Coal, lignite, sodium chloride	10.0
Clay and shale used for sewer pipe	7.5
Clay used for flowerpots and so on, gravel, sand, stone	5.0
Most other minerals and metallic ores	14.0

must keep this information separately. In separate records the partner must reduce the share of the adjusted basis of each property by the depletion taken on the property each year by that partner. The partner will use this reduced adjusted basis to figure gain or loss if the partnership later disposes of the property. (This partnership rule also applies to members in LLCs.)

S Corporation Oil and Gas Properties

The depletion allowance, whether by cost or by percentage, must be computed separately by each shareholder and not by the S corporation. The same rules apply to S corporations that apply to partnerships, with some modifications. To enable a shareholder to calculate cost depletion, the S corporation must allocate to each shareholder his or her adjusted basis of each oil and gas property held by the S corporation. This allocation is made on the date the corporation acquires the property. The shareholder's share of the adjusted basis of each oil and gas property is adjusted by the S corporation for any capital expenditures made for each property. Again, each shareholder must separately keep records of his or her pro rata share of the adjusted basis of each property and must reduce that share by depletion taken on the property. The reduced adjusted basis is used by the shareholder to determine gain or loss on the disposition of the property by the S corporation.

chapter 13

retirement plans

The Social Security benefits you may expect to receive will make up only a portion of your retirement income. In order to help you save for your own retirement and to encourage employers to provide retirement benefits to employees, the tax laws contain special incentives for retirement savings. Broadly speaking, if a retirement plan conforms to special requirements, then contributions are deductible while earnings are not currently taxable. What is more, employees covered by such plans are not immediately charged with income. If you have employees, setting up retirement plans to benefit them not only gives you a current deduction for contributions you make to the plan but also provides your staff with benefits. This helps to foster employee goodwill and may aid in recruiting new employees. Dramatic law changes in recent years permit greater retirement savings opportunities than ever before.

The type of plan you set up governs both the amount you can deduct and the time when you claim the deduction. Certain plans offer special tax incentives designed to encourage employers to help with employee retirement benefits. Even though you may be an employer, if you are self-employed (a sole proprietor, partner, or LLC member), you are treated as an employee for purposes of participating in these plans.

For further information about retirement plans, see IRS Publication 560, *Retirement Plans for Small Business,* and IRS Publication 590, *Individual Retirement Arrangements.*

QUALIFIED RETIREMENT PLANS

Qualified retirement plans provide retirement benefits and meet stringent requirements under federal law. Some of these laws fall under the jurisdiction of the Treasury Department and the IRS; others fall under the Department of Labor. Qualified plans allow employees to defer reporting income from benefits until retirement while at the same time allowing employers to claim a current deduction for contributions to the plans.

Income earned by the plan is not currently taxed. Eventually it is taxed to employees when distributed to them as part of their benefits.

Types of Retirement Plans

There are two main categories of plans: *defined benefit plans* and *defined contribution plans.*

Defined Benefit Plans

Defined benefit plans predict what an employee will receive in benefits upon retirement. This prediction is based on the employee's compensation, age, and anticipated age of retirement. It is also based on an estimation of what the plan can earn over the years. Then an actuary determines the amount that an employer must contribute each year in order to be sure that funds will be there when the employee retires. The employer takes a deduction for the actuarially determined contribution.

There are, however, variations of defined benefit plans. For example, in a cash balance defined benefit plan, benefits payable upon retirement depend in part on plan performance.

Defined Contribution Plans

Defined contribution plans are more like savings accounts. The employer contributes to an account for each employee. The contribution is based on a defined formula, such as a percentage of the employee's compensation. The account may not really be a separate account. In corporate plans it is a bookkeeping notation of the benefits that belong to each employee. The benefits that are ultimately paid to an employee are based on what the contributions actually earn over the years.

There are a variety of plans under the umbrella of defined contribution plans. The most common is the *profit-sharing plan*. Under this plan, the employer agrees to contribute a percentage of employee compensation to the plan. The allocation is usually based purely on an employee's relative compensation (other factors, such as age, can be taken into account).

Another common plan is a *money purchase plan*. Under this plan, the employer also agrees to contribute a fixed percentage of compensation each year. Perhaps the most popular type of defined contribution plan today is the 401(k) plan (also called a cash and deferred compensation arrangement). The reason for its popularity: Contributions are made by employees through salary reduction arrangements that let them fund their retirement plan with pretax dollars. These employee contributions are called *elective deferrals*. Employers often match to some extent employee elective deferrals as a way of encouraging participation, something desirable so that owners, executives, and other highly-paid employees can benefit.

Regardless of the plan selected, all plans have the same requirements designed to ensure that they do not benefit only owners and top executives but also ordinary workers. Many of these requirements are highly technical. They are explained here so that you will recognize how complicated the use of qualified plans can become. It may be helpful to discuss your retirement plans or anticipated plans with a retirement plan expert.

Businesses that do not want to become involved with the complexities of qualified plans can use simplified employee pensions (SEPs) or savings incentive match plans for employees (SIMPLEs), discussed later in this chapter in connection with plans for self-employed persons.

Covering Employees

Plans must be maintained on a nondiscriminatory basis. They cannot favor owners and top employees over rank-and-file employees.

Compensation Limit

Benefits and contributions are based on a participant's taxable compensation reported on an employee's W-2 form. It does not include tax-free fringe benefits or other excludable wages.

The law limits the amount of compensation that can be taken into account. For 2004 there is a $205,000 limit. If an employee earns $225,000, only the first $205,000 is used to compute benefits and contributions. For 2005, the limit is $210,000.

Contribution Limit

The contribution limit depends on the type of plan involved. For defined contribution plans, the 2004 limit is the lesser of 25 percent of compensation or $41,000 ($42,000 for 2005). This percentage is the top limit. Plans can adopt lesser percentages for contributions.

For defined benefit plans, there is no specific limit on contributions. Rather, the limit is placed on the benefits that can be provided under the plan. Contributions are then actuarially determined to provide these benefits. For 2004, the plan cannot provide benefits exceeding $165,000 per year, adjusted annually for inflation. For 2005, the limit is $170,000.

Making Contributions

Contributions to defined benefit plans must be made on a quarterly basis. In order to avoid a special interest charge, contributions made in quarterly installments must be at least 90 percent of contributions for the current year or 100 percent of contributions for the prior year. If contributions are based on the current year, the balance of the contributions may be made as late as the due date for the employer's return, including extensions.

Contributions for defined contribution plans can be made at any time up to the due date of the employer's return, including extensions. In fact, contributions can be made even after the employer's tax return is filed as long as they do not exceed the return's due date. In effect, contributions can be funded through a tax refund.

---

example

An employer (C corporation), whose 2004 return is ordinarily due on March 15, 2005, obtains a filing extension to September 15, 2005. The return is filed on June 1, 2005, and a refund is received on August 15, 2005. The employer has until September 15, 2005, to complete contributions to its profit-sharing plan, a deduction for which was reported on the return. The employer can use the refund for this purpose.

The only way to extend the deadline for making contributions is to obtain a valid filing extension. For example, an owner of a professional corporation on a calendar year who wants to extend the time for making contributions must obtain an extension of time to file Form 1120, the return for that corporation. To do this, Form 7004,

> **note**
>
> Contributions to defined benefit plans subject to minimum funding requirements must be made no later than September 15 (even if there is an extension of time to file the return until October 15).

Application for Automatic Extension of Time to File Corporation Income Tax Return, must be filed no later than March 15, the due date for Form 1120 for calendar-year corporations.

Filing Form 7004 gives the corporation six months (to September 15) to file its return and complete its contributions.

Contributions generally must be made in cash. When cash flow is insufficient to meet contribution requirements (and there are no refunds available for this purpose, as explained earlier), employers may be forced to borrow to make contributions on time. In some instances, contributions can be made by using employer stock.

Borrowing from the Plan

Owners may be able to borrow from the plan without adverse tax consequences. The plan must permit loans, limiting them to the lesser of:

a. $50,000, or

b. The greater of one-half your accrued benefit or $10,000.

The loan must be amortized over a period of no more than five years (except for loans that are used to buy personal residences) and charge a reasonable rate of interest. As an owner, you cannot deduct interest on the loan.

The plan must also allow rank-and-file employees the opportunity to borrow from the plan on the same basis as owners and top executives.

ADDED COSTS FOR RETIREMENT PLANS

In addition to the contributions you make to the plan, there may be other costs to consider. The type of plan you have affects the nature and amount of these added costs.

Whether you have a defined contribution or a defined benefit plan, you may be required to maintain a bond for yourself or someone else who acts as a fiduciary in your plan. You also must update your plan documents so that they reflect the latest law changes.

If you are approaching retirement age and want to obtain the maximum retirement benefits for your contributions (the biggest bang for your buck), you may want to adopt a defined benefit plan. Before doing so, it is important to recognize that these types of plans entail two additional costs not associated with defined contribution plans.

Bonding Requirement

To ensure that you will not run off with the funds in your company retirement plan, leaving participants high and dry, you are required to be bonded if you have any control over the plan or its assets. This includes, for example, authority to transfer funds or make disbursements from the plan. The bond must be at least 10 percent of the amount over which you have control. The bond cannot be less than $1,000, but it need not exceed $500,000.

No bond is required if the plan covers only you as the owner (a self-employed person or a single shareholder-employee) or only partners and their spouses.

Plan Amendments

You are required to keep your plan up to date and operate it in accordance with law changes that are enacted from time to time. The deadline for document compliance for law changes made in 2001 in most cases is the last day of the plan year beginning in 2005.

If you discover errors in your plan (either in how it is written or how it is being operated), you can correct the errors and avoid or minimize penalties. If you do not take the initiative and the IRS discovers the problems, you can be subject to greater penalties, interest, and even plan disqualification. To correct problems, you can use the IRS's Employee Plans Compliance Resolution System (see IRS Rev. Proc. 2003-44, as modified by Rev. Proc. 2003-72, for details).

Actuarial Costs for Defined Benefit Plans

If you have a defined benefit plan, you must use the services of an enrolled actuary to determine your annual contributions. You must expect to pay for this service year after year.

Pension Benefit Guaranty Corporation Premiums for Defined Benefit Plans

The Pension Benefit Guaranty Corporation (PBGC) is a quasi-federal agency designed to protect employee pension plans in the event that the employer goes under. In order to provide this protection, the PBGC charges annual premiums for each participant in the plan. First, there is a flat-rate premium, which is currently $19 per participant (a different rate applies to multiemployer plans). Then, for underfunded plans of a single employer, there is an additional variable-rate premium of $9 for every $1,000 of underfunding. (*Underfunding* means that the employer has not contributed sufficient amounts to pay all anticipated pensions that have already vested.)

There is now an online system, call My Plan Administration Account (PPA), for paying premiums and filing returns. For information, go to <www.pbgc.gov>.

Plan Start-Up Costs

If you set up a plan, you may be eligible for a special tax credit designed to encourage small business owners to start retirement plans. A small employer eligible for the credit is one with no more than 100 employees who received at least $5,000 of compensation from the company in the preceding year. However, the plan must cover at least one employee who is not a highly compensated employee. Thus, a self-employed individual with no employees who sets up a profit-sharing plan cannot claim a tax credit for any of her start-up costs.

In addition to the employee requirement, to qualify for the credit you must not have had a qualified plan in any of the three preceding years.

The credit is 50 percent of eligible start-up costs, for a maximum credit of $500. The credit can be claimed for three years starting with the year in which the plan is effective. However, you can opt to first claim the credit in the year immediately preceding the start-up year.

---

example

Your corporation sets up a 401(k) plan in 2004 and the business qualifies as a small employer. The corporation can opt to take a credit for expenses incurred in 2004 on its 2003 return.

The credit applies only to qualified start-up costs. These include ordinary and necessary expenses to set up the plan, run it, and educate employees about the plan and participation in it. Qualified expenses in excess of the $1,000 taken into account in figuring the $500 maximum credit can be deducted as ordinary and necessary business expenses.

RETIREMENT PLANS FOR SELF-EMPLOYED INDIVIDUALS

Self-employed individuals have three main options in retirement plans. First, they can set up qualified retirement plans, which used to be called Keogh plans. These plans may also known by other names. They have been called H.R.10 plans, reflecting the number of the bill in Congress under which qualified plans for self-employed individuals were created. They may also be called Basic Plans or some other name created by a bank, brokerage firm, insurance company, or other financial institution offering plan investments. A second option in retirement plans for self-employed individuals is a simplified employee pension plan (SEP). A third option in retirement plans is savings incentive match plan for employees (SIMPLE).

Self-Employed Qualified Plans in General

Qualified plans for self-employed individuals are subject to the same requirements as qualified plans for corporations. (Banks, brokerage firms, mutual funds, and insurance companies offering plans for self-employed individuals generally may denominate them as Keoghs, basic plans, or simply by the type of plan established, such as a profit-sharing plan.) Like corporate qualified plans, self-employed qualified plans must cover employees of a self-employed person on a nondiscriminatory basis. Also like corporate plans, they are limited in the amount that can be contributed and deducted.

There is an important distinction between self-employed qualified plans and corporate qualified plans: the way in which contributions are calculated on behalf of owner-employees.

Contributions to Self-Employed Qualified Plans

Contributions to all retirement plans are based on compensation. For self-employed individuals under self-employed qualified plans, the basis for contributions is net earnings from self-employment. But this is not merely the net profit from your business on which self-employment tax is paid. Net earnings from self-employment must be further reduced by the deduction for one-half of the self-employment tax.

To calculate compensation of the owner-employee, start with the profit from Schedule C or Schedule C-EZ (or Schedule F in the case of farming) or the net earnings from self-employment on Schedule K-1 of Form 1065. For partners, this is essentially your distributive share of partnership income plus any guaranteed payments. Net earnings from self-employment from various activities are totaled on Schedule SE, Self-Employment Tax. After you have your compensation amount, subtract from this amount one-half of the self-employment tax computed on Schedule SE. This net amount is the figure upon which contributions to qualified retirement plans are based.

In order to make contributions on your own behalf, you must have net earnings from self-employment derived from your personal services. If you merely invest capital in a partnership while your personal services are not a material income-producing factor, you cannot make a plan contribution. If you are a limited partner, you cannot base a plan contribution on your distributive share of partnership income. Similar rules apply to members in LLCs. Income received from property, such as rents, interest, or dividends, is not treated as net earnings from self-employment.

Calculating Your Contribution Rate

For self-employed individuals, the contribution rate must be adjusted for the employer deduction on behalf of yourself. This is a roundabout way of saying that the base percentage rate you use to determine contributions on behalf of employees, if any, must be adjusted for determining contributions on your own behalf. To arrive at this reduced percentage rate, divide the contribution rate, expressed as a decimal number, by one plus the contribution rate. In effect, if the contribution rate for your profit-sharing plan is 25 percent, you divide 0.25 by 1.25 to arrive at the contribution rate on your behalf: 20 percent.

Remember, the maximum deduction for 2004 contributions cannot exceed the lesser of $41,000 or, $205,000 times your contribution rate.

---

example

You maintain a 25-percent profit-sharing plan for your sole proprietorship, of which you are the only worker. In 2004 your net profit reported on Schedule C is $210,000. Your net earnings from self-employment for purposes of calculating plan contributions are $201,561 ($210,000 – $8,439 [one-half of the self-employment tax]). Your contribution is limited to $41,000 (20 percent of $205,000). You cannot base your contribution on your full net earnings from self-employment because of the $205,000 compensation limit and $41,000 deduction limit.

Simplified Employee Pensions in General

Simplified employee pensions, or SEPs, are another type of retirement plan that self-employed individuals can use to save for retirement on a tax-advantaged basis. (Corporations can use SEPs as well.) As the name implies, they do not entail all the administrative costs and complications associated with other qualified retirement plans. There are no annual reporting requirements, as is the case for qualified plans and qualified corporate retirement plans.

Simplified employee pensions are individual retirement accounts set up by employees to which an employer makes contributions, then deducts them. The contributions are a fixed percentage of each employee's compensation. To set up a SEP, an employer need only sign a form establishing the percentage rate for making contributions and for setting eligibility requirements. This is a one-page form, Form 5305-SEP, Simplified Employee Pension-IRA Contribution Agreement.

The form is not filed with the IRS. Instead, it serves merely as an agreement under which the employer makes contributions. The employer then instructs employees where to set up SEP-IRAs to receive employer contributions. Banks, brokerage firms, and insurance companies generally have prototype plans designed for this purpose.

The maximum deduction for a contribution under a SEP is essentially the same as for a deferred contribution plan: 25 percent of compensation or $41,000, whichever is less. For contributions made on behalf of self-employed individuals, this percentage works out to 20 percent. As with other qualified plans, no more than $205,000 of compensation in 2004 can be taken into account in computing contributions.

Covering Employees

You must cover all employees who meet an age and service test. The SEP must cover employees who are 21 or older, earn over $450 in 2004, and have worked for you at any time in at least three out of five years. You can provide for more favorable coverage (for example, you can cover employees at age 18).

Employees over the age of $70\frac{1}{2}$ can continue to participate in a SEP and receive employer contributions. However, required minimum distributions must also be made to these employees.

Salary Reduction Arrangements

Before 1997, a SEP of a small business (with no more than 25 employees who were eligible to participate in the SEP at any time during the prior year) could be designed so that employees funded all or part of their own retirement plans. If you had a SARSEP plan in 1996, you can continue to fund it with salary reduction amounts in 2004.

Savings Incentive Match Plans for Employees

Self-employed individuals have another retirement plan alternative: Savings Incentive Match Plans for Employees (SIMPLE). These plans are open to **small employers** who want to avoid complicated nondiscrimination rules and reporting requirements. These SIMPLE plans can be used by corporations as well as by self-employed business owners.

Small employers   Those employers with 100 or fewer employees who received at least $5,000 in compensation in the preceding year.

Simple Incentive Match Plans for Employees plans may be set up as either IRAs or 401(k) plans. The rules for both types of SIMPLE plans are similar but not identical. Employees can contribute to the plans on a salary reduction basis up to $9,000 in 2004 ($10,000 in 2005). Those age 50 or older by the end of the year can contribute an additional $1,500 in 2004 ($2,000 in 2005). Self-employed individuals can make similar contributions based on earned income.

Employers satisfy nondiscrimination rules simply by making required contributions. Employers have a choice of contribution formulas:

- Matching contributions (dollar-for-dollar) up to three percent of employee's compensation for the year (or a lower percentage in some cases). For example, in 2004, if an employee under age 50 earning $35,000 makes the maximum salary reduction contribution of $9,000, the employer must contribute $1,050 (three percent of $35,000). The maximum matching contribution per employee in 2004 to a SIMPLE 401(k) is $6,120 (100 percent of the matching employee contribution, which is up to three percent of $205,000). However, there is no limit on compensation taken into account for employer matching contributions to a SIMPLE-IRA.

- Nonelective contributions of two percent of compensation (regardless of whether the employee makes any contributions) for any employee earning at least $5,000. For example, in 2004, if an employee's compensation is $25,000, the employer's contribution is $500 (two percent of $25,000). The maximum contribution per employee in 2004 is $41,000 (two percent of $205,000, the maximum compensation that can be used to determine contributions).

Self-employed persons can make employer contributions to SIMPLE IRAs on their own behalf as well as make their own contributions. In effect, they are treated as both employer and employee.

Employee and employer contributions vest immediately. This means that employees can withdraw contributions at any time (although withdrawals prior to age 59½ are subject to a 25-percent penalty if taken within the first two years of beginning participation, and 10 percent if taken after that period).

Employers who want to let employees choose their own financial institutions can adopt SIMPLE plans merely by completing Form 5304-SIMPLE. Employers who want to choose the financial institutions for their employees use Form 5305-SIMPLE. Whichever option is chosen, the form is not filed with the IRS but is kept with the employer's records. This form has the necessary notification to eligible employees and a model salary reduction agreement that can be used by employees to specify their salary reduction contributions. Employers who use SIMPLE plans cannot maintain any other type of qualified retirement plan.

SALARY REDUCTION ARRANGEMENTS

Salary reduction arrangements are not limited to SIMPLE plans. Perhaps the most common form of salary reduction arrangement is elective deferrals to regular 401(k) plans. In fact, these plans have become the most popular form of retirement plans in recent years.

These 401(k) plans allow employers to offer retirement benefits to employees that are largely funded by the employees themselves. To encourage employees to participate in the plans (employers cannot force employees to make contributions), employers may offer matching contributions. For example, an employer may match each dollar of employee deferral with a dollar of employer contributions or some other ratio. Employers who offer 401(k) plans must be careful that stringent nondiscrimination rules are satisfied.

Essentially, these rules require that a sufficient number of rank-and-file employees participate in the plan and make contributions. If the nondiscrimination rules are not satisfied, the plan will not be treated as a qualified plan and tax benefits are not available. Explaining the advantages of participating to rank-and-file employees and offering matching contributions are two ways to attract the necessary participation.

Employees who take advantage of elective deferral options cannot deduct their contributions to the 401(k) plan. They have already received a tax benefit by virtue of the fact that deferrals are excluded from taxable income for income tax purposes. They are still treated as part of compensation for purposes of FICA and FUTA.

From an employer perspective, using 401(k) plans can shift the investment responsibility to employees. Instead of making all of the investment decisions, the employer simply has to offer a menu of investment options to employees. Then the employees decide how they want their funds invested. Employees can be as conservative or as aggressive as they choose. Treasury and Department of Labor regulations detail the number and types of investment options that must be offered and what must be communicated to employees about these investment options.

There is a dollar limit on the elective deferral. In 2004 the elective deferral cannot exceed $13,000. The catch-up elective deferral limit for those who attain age 50 by December 31, 2004, is $3,000. For 2005, the deferral limits increase to $14,000 and $4,000 respectively.

Those who work for certain tax-exempt organizations—schools, hospitals, and religious organizations—may be able to make elective deferrals used to buy tax-deferred annuities, called 403(b) annuities. The same elective deferral limit applies here.

One-Person 401(k) Plans

If you work alone, with no employees, can you have a 401(k) plan? The answer is yes, even if you are self-employed. This type of plan may enable you to maximize contributions because you can make both employee salary reduction contributions (elective deferrals) and employer contributions.

example

You are self-employed, age 45, and have net earnings from self-employment of $140,000. If you have a profit-sharing plan, your contribution is limited to $28,000 (20% of $140,000). But with a one-person 401(k) plan, the maximum contribution of $41,000 can be attained with these earnings (salary reduction contribution of $13,000, plus employer contribution of $28,000). For those with an incorporated business, the maximum contribution is attained with salary of $112,000.

Loans from 401(k) Plans

The rules governing loans from 401(k) plans are the same as those discussed earlier in connection with loans from corporate plans. However, it should be noted that all participants, not just owners, are prohibited from deducting interest on plan loans. But the interest is really being paid to the participant's own account, so the loss of a deduction is not so important.

NONQUALIFIED RETIREMENT PLANS

If you have a business and want to provide retirement benefits without the limitations and requirements imposed on qualified plans, you can use nonqualified plans. These plans have been growing in popularity in recent years because of restrictions and costs associated with qualified plans. Nonqualified plans are simply plans you design yourself to provide you and/or your employees with whatever benefits you desire. Benefits under the plan are not taxed to the employees until they receive them and include them in their income.

There are no nondiscrimination rules to comply with. You can cover only those employees you want to give additional retirement benefits, and this can be limited to owners or key executives. There are no minimum or maximum contributions to make to the plan. However, because nonqualified plans give you all the flexibility you need to tailor benefits as you see fit, the law prevents you, as the employer, from enjoying certain tax benefits. You cannot deduct amounts now that you will pay in the future to employees under the plan. Your deduction usually cannot be claimed until benefits are actually paid to employees. However, there is one circumstance under which you can deduct these amounts: If you segregate the amounts from the general assets of your business so that they are not available to meet the claims of your general creditors, the amounts become immediately taxable to the employees and thus deductible by you.

How a Nonqualified Plan Works

Suppose you want to allow your key employees the opportunity to defer bonuses or a portion of their compensation until retirement. To do this, you set up a nonqualified plan. These employees can defer specified amounts until termination, retirement, or some other time or event. The employees in the plan must agree to defer the compensation before it is earned. They generally have no guarantee that the funds they agree to defer will, in fact, be there for them upon retirement. If your business goes under, they must stand in line along with all your other creditors. Employees should be made to understand the risk of a deferred compensation arrangement.

Once you set up the terms of the plan, you simply set up a bookkeeping entry to record the amount of deferred compensation. You may also want to credit each employee's deferred compensation account with an amount representing interest. In the past, there had been some controversy on the tax treatment of this interest. One court allowed a current deduction for the interest. The IRS, on the other hand, had maintained that no deduction for the interest could be claimed until it, along with the compensation, was paid out to employees and included in their income. However, that court changed its view and now agrees with the IRS. As long as receipt of the interest is deferred, so, too, is your deduction for the interest.

chapter 14

casualty and
theft losses

Earthquakes in Montana, floods in North Dakota, droughts in New Jersey, hurricanes in Texas, ice storms in New York—these are just some examples of the types of weather-related events that can do severe damage to your business property. Terrorist attacks are another means of causing damage to business property. If you suffer casualty or theft losses to your business property, you can deduct the losses. You may also suffer a loss through condemnation or a sale under threat of condemnation. Again, the loss is deductible. Certain losses—those from events declared to be federal disasters—may even allow you to recover taxes you have already paid in an earlier year. And special breaks apply to those who suffered losses in the September 11, 2001, terrorist attacks. But if you receive insurance proceeds or other property in return, you may have a gain rather than a loss. The law allows you to postpone reporting of the gain if certain steps are taken.

For further information about deducting casualty and theft losses, see IRS Publication 547, *Casualties, Disasters, and Thefts (Business and Nonbusiness);* IRS Publication 2194B, *Disaster Losses Kit for Businesses;* and IRS Publication 3921, *Help from the IRS for Those Affected by the Terrorist Attacks on America.*

CASUALTY AND THEFT

If you suffer a casualty or theft loss to business property, you can deduct the loss. There are no dollar limitations on these losses, as there are on personal losses. Nor are there adjusted gross income (AGI) limitations on these losses, as there are on casualty and theft losses to personal property.

Definition of Casualty

If your business property is damaged, destroyed, or lost because of a storm, earthquake, flood, or some other "sudden, unexpected or unusual event," you have experienced a *casualty*. For losses to nonbusiness property (such as your personal residence), the loss must fall squarely within the definition of a casualty loss. Losses to business property need not necessarily satisfy the same definition.

The tax law details what is considered a "sudden, unexpected or unusual event." To be sudden, the event must be one that is swift, not one that is progressive or gradual. To be unexpected, the event must be unanticipated or unintentional on the part of the one who has suffered the loss. To be unusual, the event must be other than a day-to-day occurrence. It cannot be typical of the activity in which you are engaged.

note

Business losses are deductible without having to establish that the cause of the loss was a casualty. Thus, if your equipment rusts or corrodes over time, you can deduct your loss even though it does not fit into the definition of a casualty loss (assuming you can fix the time of the loss). The reason for understanding the definition of the term "casualty" is that it determines where the loss is reported. It also comes into play in connection with deferring tax on gains from casualties, as discussed later in this chapter.

Examples of Casualties

Certain events in nature automatically are considered a casualty: earthquake, hurricane, tornado, cyclone, flood, storm, and volcanic eruption. Other events have also come to be known as casualties: sonic booms, mine cave-ins, shipwrecks, and acts of vandalism. The IRS has also recognized as a casualty the destruction of crops due to a farmer's accidental poisoning of his fields. Fires are considered casualties if you are not the one who started them (or did not pay someone to start them). Car or truck accidents are casualties provided they were not caused by willful negligence or a willful act.

Progressive or gradual deterioration, such as rust or corrosion of property, is not considered a casualty.

Proof of Casualties

You must show that a specific casualty occurred and the time it occurred. You must also show that the casualty was the direct cause of the damage or destruction to your property. Finally, you must show that you were the owner of the property. If you leased property, you must show that you were contractually liable for damage so that you suffered a loss as a result of the casualty.

Definition of Theft

The taking of property must constitute a theft under the law in your state. Generally, *theft* involves taking or removing property with the intent to deprive the owner of its use. Typically, this includes robbery, larceny, and embezzlement.

If you are forced to pay extortion money or blackmail in the course of your business, the loss may be treated as a theft loss if your state law makes this type of taking illegal.

Proof of Theft

You must show when you discovered the property was missing. You must also show that a theft (as defined by your state's criminal law) took place. Finally, you must show that you were the owner of the property.

Determining a Casualty or Theft Loss

To calculate your loss, you must know your **adjusted basis** in the property.

Adjusted basis   This is generally your cost of the property, plus any improvements made to it, less any depreciation claimed. Basis is also reduced by any prior casualty losses claimed with respect to the property.

You also need to know the fair market value (FMV) of the property. If the property was not completely destroyed, you must know the extent of the damage. This is the difference between the FMV of the property before and after the casualty.

---

example

Your business car is in an accident and you do not have collision insurance. The car's FMV before the accident was $9,000. After the accident, the car is worth only $6,000. The decrease in the FMV is $3,000 ($9,000 value before the loss, less $6,000 value after the loss).

How do you determine the decrease in FMV? This is not based simply on your subjective opinion. In most cases, the decrease in value is based on an appraisal by a competent appraiser. If your property is located near an area affected by a casualty that causes your property value to decline, you cannot take this general decline in value into account. Only a direct loss of value may be considered. Presumably, a competent appraiser will be able to distinguish between a general market decline and a direct decline as a result of a casualty. The IRS looks at a number of factors to determine whether an appraiser is competent and his or her appraisal can be relied upon to establish FMV. These factors include:

- Familiarity with your property both before and after the casualty
- Knowledge of sales of comparable property in your area
- Knowledge of conditions in the area of the casualty
- Method of appraisal

Remember that if the IRS questions the reliability of your appraiser, it may use its own appraiser to determine value. This may lead to legal wrangling and ultimately to litigation on the question of value. In order to avoid this problem and the costs entailed, it is advisable to use a reputable appraiser, even if this may seem costly to you.

Appraisals used to secure a loan or loan guarantee from the government under the Federal Emergency Management Agency (FEMA) are treated as proof of the amount of a disaster loss. Disaster losses are explained later in this chapter.

You may be able to establish value without the help of an appraiser in certain situations.

If your car is damaged, you can use "blue book" value (the car's retail value, which is printed in a book used by car dealers). You can ask your local car dealer for your car's retail value reported in the blue book (or look it up at <www.kbb.com>). You can modify this value to reflect such things as mileage, options, and the car's condition before the casualty. Book values are not official, but the IRS has come to recognize that they are useful in fixing value.

Repairs may be useful in showing the decrease in value. To use repairs as a measure of loss, you must show that the repairs are needed to restore the property to its precasualty condition and apply only to the damage that resulted from the casualty. You must also show that the cost of repairs is not excessive and that the repairs will not restore your property to a value greater than it had prior to the casualty. Making repairs to property damaged in a casualty can result in double deductions: one for the cost of repairs and the other for the casualty loss.

---

example

Severe flooding destroys a business owner's property. He is not compensated by insurance. The IRS, in a memorandum to a district counsel, allows him to claim a casualty loss for the damage as well as deducting the cost of repairs to the property where such repairs merely restore it to its precasualty condition.

The last piece of information necessary for determining a casualty or theft loss is the amount of insurance proceeds or other reimbursements, if any, you received or expect to receive as a result of the casualty or theft. While insurance proceeds are the most common reimbursement in the event of a casualty or theft, there are other types of reimbursements that are taken into account in the same way as insurance proceeds. Examples: court awards for damages as a result of suits based on casualty or theft, payment from a bonding company for a theft loss, and forgiveness of a federal disaster loan under the Disaster Relief and Emergency Assistance Act.

What happens if you have not received an insurance settlement by the time you must file your return? If there is a reasonable expectation that you will receive a settlement, you treat the anticipated settlement as if you had already received it. In other words, you take the expected insurance proceeds into account in calculating your loss. Should it later turn out that you received more or less than you anticipated, adjustments are required in the year you actually receive the insurance proceeds, as explained later in this chapter.

If the amount of insurance proceeds or other reimbursements is greater than the adjusted basis of your property, you do not have a loss. Instead, you have a gain as a result of your casualty or theft loss. How can this be, you might ask? Why should a loss of property turn out to be a gain for tax purposes? Remember that your adjusted basis for business property in many instances reflects deductions for depreciation. This brings your basis down. But your insurance may be based on the value of the property, not its basis to you. Therefore, if your basis has been adjusted downward for depreciation but the value of the property has remained constant or increased, your insurance proceeds may produce a gain for you. Gain and how to postpone it are discussed later in this chapter.

Calculating Loss When Property Is Completely Destroyed or Stolen

Reduce your adjusted basis by any insurance proceeds received or expected to be received and any salvage value to the property. The result is your casualty loss deduction. The FMV of the property does not enter into the computation.

---

example

Your machine is completely destroyed by a flood. You have no flood insurance, and the destroyed machine has no salvage value. The adjusted basis of the machine is $6,000. Your casualty loss is $6,000 (adjusted basis of the property [$6,000], less insurance proceeds [zero]).

If the casualty or theft involves more than one piece of property, you must determine the loss (or gain) for each item separately. If your reimbursement is paid in a lump sum and there is no allocation among the items, you must make an allocation. The allocation is based on the items' FMV before the casualty.

Calculating Loss When Property is Partially Destroyed

Calculate the difference between the FMV of the property before and after the casualty. Reduce this by any insurance proceeds. Compare this figure with your adjusted basis in the property, less any insurance proceeds. Your casualty loss is the smaller of these two figures.

---

example

Your machine is damaged as a result of a flood. You do not have flood insurance. The machine is valued at $8,000 before the flood and $3,000 after it. Your adjusted basis in the machine is $6,000. Your loss is $5,000, the difference between the FMV of the machine before and after the flood, which is smaller than your adjusted basis.

If you lease property from someone else (e.g., if you lease a car used for business), your loss is limited to the difference between the insurance proceeds you receive, or expect to receive, and the amount you must pay to repair the property.

Inventory and Crops

You cannot deduct a loss with respect to inventory or crops damaged or destroyed by a casualty. Your inventory account is simply adjusted for the loss. In the case of crops, the cost of raising them has already been deducted, so no additional deduction is allowed if they are damaged or destroyed by a casualty.

Recovered Property

What happens if you deduct a loss for stolen property and the property is later recovered? Do you have to go back and amend the earlier return on which the theft loss was taken? The answer is no. Instead, you report the recovered property as income in the year of recovery.

But what if the property is not recovered in good shape or is only partially recovered? In this instance, you must recalculate your loss.

You use the smaller of the property's adjusted basis or the decrease in the FMV from the time it was stolen until you recovered it. This smaller amount is your recalculated loss. If your recalculated loss is less than the loss you deducted, you report the difference as income in the year of recovery. The amount of income that you must report is limited to the amount of loss that reduced your tax in the earlier year.

Insurance Received (or Not Received) in a Later Year

If you had anticipated the receipt of insurance proceeds or other property and took that anticipated amount into account when calculating your loss but later receive more (or less) than you anticipated, you must account for this discrepancy. As with recovered stolen property, you do not go back to the year of loss and make an adjustment. Instead, you take the insurance proceeds into account in the year of actual receipt.

If you receive more than you had expected (by way of insurance or otherwise), you report the extra amount as income in the year of receipt. You do not have to recalculate your original loss deduction. The additional amount is reported as ordinary income to the extent that the deduction in the earlier year produced a tax reduction. If the additional insurance or other reimbursement, when combined with what has already been received, exceeds the adjusted basis of your property, you now have a gain as a result of the casualty or theft. The gain is reported in the year you receive the additional reimbursement. However, you may be able to postpone reporting the gain, as discussed later in this chapter.

If you receive less than you had anticipated, you have an additional loss. The additional loss is claimed in the year in which you receive the additional amount.

---

example

In 2004, your business car was completely destroyed in an accident. Your adjusted basis in the car was $8,000. The car had a value of $10,000 before the accident and no value after the accident. You expected the driver responsible for the accident to pay for the damage. In fact, a jury awarded you the full extent of your loss. However, in 2005, you learn that the other driver will not pay the judgment and does not have any property against which you can enforce your judgment. In this instance, you have received less than you anticipated. You do not recalculate your 2004 taxes. Instead, you deduct your loss (limited to your adjusted basis of $8,000) in 2005.

Basis

If your property is partially destroyed in a casualty, you must adjust the basis of the property:

- Decrease basis by insurance proceeds or other reimbursements and loss deductions claimed.
- Increase basis by improvements or repairs made to the property to rebuild or restore it.

Year of the Loss

In general, the loss can be claimed only in the year in which the casualty or other event occurs. However, in the case of the theft, the loss is treated as having occurred in the year in which it is discovered.

CONDEMNATIONS AND THREATS OF CONDEMNATION

The government can take your property for public use if it compensates you for your loss. The process by which the government exercises its right of eminent domain to take your property for public use is called *condemnation*. In a sense, you are being forced to sell your property at a price essentially fixed by the government. You can usually negotiate a price; sometimes you are forced to seek a court action and have the court fix the price paid to you. Typically, an owner is paid cash or receives other property upon condemnation of property.

When property is condemned because it is unsafe, this is not a taking of property for public use. It is simply a limitation on the use of the property by you.

For tax purposes, a condemnation or threat of condemnation of your business property is treated as a sale or exchange. You may have a gain or you may have a loss, depending on the condemnation award or the proceeds you receive upon a forced sale. But there is something special in the tax law where condemnations are concerned. If you have a gain, you have an opportunity to avoid immediate tax on the gain. This postponement of reporting the gain is discussed in Chapter 6.

Condemnation Award

The amount of money you receive or the value of property you receive for your condemned property is your *condemnation award.* Similarly, the amount you accept in exchange for your property in a sale motivated by the threat of condemnation is also treated as your condemnation award. The amount of the condemnation award determines your gain or loss for the event.

If you are in a dispute with the city, state, or federal government over the amount that you should be paid and you go to court, the government may deposit an amount with the court. You are not considered to have received the award until you have an unrestricted right to it. This is usually after the court action is resolved and you are permitted to withdraw the funds for your own use.

Your award includes moneys withheld to pay your debts. For example, if the court withholds an amount to pay a lien holder or mortgagee, your condemnation award is the gross amount awarded to you, not the net amount paid to you.

The condemnation award does not include **severance damages** and **special assessments.**

Severance damages   Compensation paid to you if part of your property is condemned and the part not condemned suffers a reduction in value as a result of the condemnation. Severance damages may cover the loss in value of your remaining property or compensate you for certain improvements you must make to your remaining property (such as replacing fences, digging new wells or ditches, or planting trees or shrubs to restore the remaining property to its condition prior to the condemnation of your other property).

Special assessments   Charges against you for improvements that benefit the remaining property as a result of the condemnation of your other property (such as widening of the streets or installing sewers).

Severance damages are not reported as income. Instead, they are used to reduce the basis of your remaining property.

Special assessments serve to reduce the condemnation award. They must actually be withheld from the award itself; they cannot be levied after the award is made, even if it is in the same year.

DISASTER LOSSES

In the past several years, our country has experienced a large number of major disasters, including hurricanes, floods, fires, blizzards, earthquakes, and terrorist attacks. When large areas suffer sizable losses, the president may declare the areas eligible for special federal disaster relief. This disaster assistance comes in the form of disaster relief loans, special grants (money that does not have to be repaid), special unemployment benefits, and other types of assistance. Still, despite all these efforts by the federal government, as well as state, local, and private agencies, you may experience serious disruption to your business and loss to your business property. The tax law provides a special rule for certain disaster losses that will give you up-front cash to help you get back on your feet.

Typically, you deduct your loss in the year in which the disaster occurred. However, you may elect to deduct your loss on a prior year's return, which can result in a tax refund that may provide you with needed cash flow.

---

example

In January 2005, you suffer an uninsured disaster loss of $25,000. You may, of course, deduct the loss on your 2005 return, which is filed in 2006 (assuming you are on a calendar-year basis). Alternatively, you may elect to deduct your loss on your 2004 return.

If your loss occurs later in the year, after you have already filed your tax return for the prior year, you can still get a tax refund by filing an amended return for the prior year. For example, if in the Example your loss occurred in December 2005 (after you filed your 2004 return), you can file an amended return for 2004 to claim the disaster loss.

If you suffer a loss in your inventory due to a disaster, you need not account for your loss simply by a reduction in the cost of goods sold. Instead, you can claim a deduction for your loss. The loss can be claimed on the return for the year of the disaster or on a return (or amended return) for the preceding year. If you choose to deduct your inventory loss, then you must also reduce your opening inventory for the year of the loss so that the loss is not also reflected in the inventory; you cannot get a double benefit for the loss.

DEDUCTING PROPERTY INSURANCE AND OTHER CASUALTY/THEFT-RELATED ITEMS

It is well and good that you can write off your casualty and theft losses. But as a practical matter, you should carry enough insurance to cover these situations so that you will not suffer any financial loss should these events befall your business. If you carry insurance to cover fire, theft, flood, or any other casualty related to your business, you can deduct your premiums.

The same rule that applies to business property insurance also applies to insurance for your car or other vehicles used in your business. This insurance covers liability, damages, and other losses in accidents involving your business car. However, if you use your car only partly for business, you must allocate your insurance premiums. Only the portion related to business use of your car is deductible. The portion related to personal use of your car is not deductible.

If you use the standard mileage allowance to deduct expenses for business use of a car, you cannot deduct any car insurance premiums. The standard mileage rate already takes into account an allowance for car insurance.

If your property is damaged by a casualty and you pay a qualified appraiser to establish the FMV of the property in order to prove your damage and the extent of your loss, you claim a separate deduction for appraisal fees. You do not take the appraisal fees into account when calculating your casualty loss deduction.

chapter 15

home office deductions

Today over 40 million Americans work at home at least some of the time, and the number is growing. Computers, faxes, modems, and the information highway make it easier and, in some cases, more profitable to operate a home office. As a general rule, the cost of owning or renting your home is a personal one and, except for certain specific expenses (such as mortgage interest, real estate taxes, and casualty losses), you cannot deduct personal expenses. However, if you use a portion of your home for business, you may be able to deduct a number of expenses, including rent or depreciation, mortgage and real estate taxes, maintenance, and utilities. These are collectively referred to as home office deductions. They are claimed as a single deduction item. The deduction is allowed for both self-employed individuals and employees who meet special requirements.

This chapter covers home *office* expenses; however, you need not use your home as an office to claim this deduction. Home office is simply a name assigned to a category of deductible business expenses. For example, you may use your garage to do mechanical repairs, or a greenhouse to grow plants for sale. The expenses related to these uses may be treated as home office expenses.

It has long been thought that claiming a home office deduction is an automatic red flag for an audit. However, there are no statistics to show that this is true. If you meet the tests for claiming a home office deduction as explained in this chapter and you have proof of your expenses, you should have nothing to fear, even if your return is questioned.

For more information about home office deductions see IRS Publication 587, *Business Use of Your Home.*

HOME OFFICE DEDUCTIONS IN GENERAL

Whether you own your home or rent it, you may be able to deduct a portion of the costs of your home if you use it for business. This is so for both employees and self-employed individuals. However, the law is very strict on what constitutes business use of a home. First, you must use the portion of your home exclusively and regularly for business. Then you must meet one of three tests. The home office must be:

- Your principal place of business,
- A place to meet or deal with patients, clients, or customers in the normal course of your business, or
- A separate structure (not attached to your house or residence) that is used in connection with your business.

Exclusively and Regularly

Exclusive use of a home office means that it is used solely for your business activities and not for personal purposes, including investment activities. If you have a spare bedroom or a den that you have equipped with a computer, telephone, and perhaps a fax/modem, you cannot meet the exclusive use test for a home office if you also use that room as a guest room or family den.

The exclusive use test does not require you to set aside an entire room for business purposes. You can meet this test if you clearly delineate a portion of a room for business. It must be a separately identifiable space. However, you need not mark off this separate area by a permanent partition to satisfy the separately identifiable space requirement.

There are two important exceptions to the exclusive use requirement: day-care facilities and storage space. Each of these exceptions is discussed later in this chapter.

The home office must also be used on a regular basis for your business activity. This determination is based on all the facts and circumstances. Occasional or incidental use of a home office will not satisfy this requirement, even if such space is used exclusively for business purposes.

Principal Place of Business

Your home office is treated as your principal place of business if it is the place where you conduct your business. It may be your prime activity or a sideline business. As long as it is the main location for the particular activity, it is your principal place of business. Generally this means the location where you earn your money. However, one court has recognized that a musician who spends considerably more time using one room in a home for practice so that she can perform with symphonies and make recordings can treat that room as the principal place of business. It remains to be seen whether this reasoning will be extended to other types of professionals—for example, an attorney who prepares and rehearses his opening and closing arguments in a home office.

Your home office is considered to be your principal place of business if it is used for substantial managerial or administrative activities (e.g., keeping books and records and scheduling appointments) and there is no other fixed location for such activities.

---

example

You run an interior design business, seeing clients in their homes and offices. You use your home office to schedule appointments, keep your books and records, and order supplies. You can treat your home office as your principal place of business because you use it for substantial managerial or administrative activities and you do not have a store front or other office for such work.

More Than One Business

If you are an employee and also conduct a sideline business from a home office, you may deduct your home office expenses for the sideline business. The business activity from the home office need not be your main activity; the home office simply must be the principal place of business for the sideline activity.

However, if you conduct more than one activity from a home office, be sure that each activity meets all home office requirements. Otherwise you may lose out on deductions. For example, if you are an employee and also have a business that you run from your home, if you use the home office for your employment-related activities (and not for the convenience of your employer), then you fail the exclusive use test for the home-based business. You will not be able to deduct any home office expenses even though the home office is the principal place of business for the home-based activity.

Place to Meet or Deal with Patients, Clients, or Customers

If you meet with patients, clients, or customers in a home office, you can deduct home office expenses. The home office need not be your principal place of business. You can conduct business at another location, and your home office can be a satellite office. However, if you use your home office only to make or receive phone calls with patients, clients, and customers, you do not meet this test. While making or receiving phone calls can arguably be viewed as dealing with patients, clients, or customers, the IRS will not view it as such.

Separate Structure

If you have a separate freestanding structure on your property, you can treat it as a home office if you use it exclusively and regularly for your home office activity. A separate structure may be a garage, a studio, a greenhouse, or even a barn. It need not be an office in order for expenses to be deducted as home office expenses. Nor does the separate structure need be the principal place of your business activity. Further, it need not be a place to meet or deal with patients, clients, or customers in the normal course of your business. It simply must be used in connection with your business.

> **example**
>
> You own a flower shop in town. You have a greenhouse on your property in which you grow orchids. You can deduct the home office expenses of the greenhouse.

What constitutes a separate structure? The answer is not always clear. In one case, the Tax Court treated a separate structure in a taxpayer's backyard as part of the house itself because of the close relationship to it. If your local real estate law treats a separate structure as *appurtenant* to the house, then it is not a separate structure for purposes of the home office deduction rules.

Examples of separate structures that may qualify as home offices include an artist's studio, a florist's greenhouse, and a carpenter's workshop.

SPECIAL REQUIREMENTS FOR EMPLOYEES

Telecommuters take heart. If you use your home for business, you can deduct home office expenses provided your use is for the convenience of your employer. However, this is not an easy standard to satisfy. There is no hard-and-fast rule for proving that your use of a home office is for the convenience of your employer. Neither the tax law nor regulations provide any guidelines.

Your home office use is not treated as being for the convenience of your employer simply because it is appropriate or helpful to your job; there must be a real need on the part of your employer for you to use an office at home (e.g., no space at your employer's location).

If you employ your spouse, you may be able to deduct home office expenses by requiring your spouse to use the home office for your convenience. There have been no cases or rulings testing this arrangement, but if there is a real need on your part for it, the arrangement just might work.

You cannot claim a home office deduction if you rent a portion of your home to your employer and then perform services in it as an employee. If you do rent space to your employer, the rent is still taxable to you.

ALLOCATING THE BUSINESS PART OF HOME EXPENSES

Some expenses of the home office are directly related to business use. For example, if you paint your home office, the entire cost of the paint job is a business expense. Other expenses are indirectly related to business use of your home office; rather, they relate to your entire home. Indirect expenses include deductible mortgage interest, real estate taxes, depreciation, rent, utilities, insurance, general repairs to the home (such as servicing the heating system), security systems, snow removal, and cleaning.

Only the portion of indirect expenses related to the business use of your home is deductible. How do you make an allocation of expenses? If you have five rooms and use one for business, can you allocate one-fifth of expenses, or 20 percent, for business? The answer is yes if the rooms are more or less the same size. This is often not the case. If rooms are of unequal size, you allocate expenses based on the square footage of business use. Determine the size of your home; then determine the size of your home office. Divide the size of your home office by the size of your home to arrive at a percentage of business use.

---

example

Your home is 1,800 square feet. Your home office is 12 feet × 15 feet, or 180 square feet. Therefore, your home office use is 10 percent (180 divided by 1,800).

Once you have determined your business percentage, you apply this percentage against each indirect expense.

---

example

Your business percentage is 20 percent, and instead of owning your home you rent it. If your annual rent is $12,000, you may treat $2,400 ($12,000 × 20) as part of your home office deduction. The balance of your rent is not deductible, since it is a personal expense.

You apply the business percentage against deductible mortgage interest. You can include a second mortgage and deductible points in this figure. Again, the portion of your mortgage interest not treated as part of your home office deduction continues to be deductible as an itemized deduction on Schedule A.

Casualty losses may be either an indirect or direct expense, depending upon the property affected by the casualty. If, for example, your home office is damaged in a storm and you are not fully compensated by insurance, you claim your loss as a direct expense. If, however, the damage is to your entire home (such as a roof leak), you treat the loss as an indirect expense. See Chapter 14 for more information on deducting casualty losses.

If you rent your home, you can deduct the business portion of rent as an indirect expense. If you own your home, you cannot deduct the fair rental value of your home office. However, you can claim depreciation on your home office. See Chapter 12 for more information on depreciation.

Generally, utility expenses are treated as indirect expenses. The business portion is part of your home office deduction; the nonbusiness portion is not deductible. However, in some instances you may be able to deduct a greater portion of a utility expense. For example, if you can show that electrical use for your home office is greater than the allocable percentage of the whole bill, you can claim that additional amount as a direct expense.

The business portion of a homeowner's insurance policy is part of your home office deduction. It is an indirect expense. If you also pay additional coverage directly related to your home office, treat the additional coverage as a direct expense. You may, for example, carry special coverage for your home office equipment (computer, library, etc.).

Repairs may be direct or indirect expenses, depending on their nature. A repair to a furnace is an indirect expense; a repair to a window in the home office itself is a direct expense.

A home security system for your entire home can give rise to two types of write-offs. First, the business portion of your monthly monitoring fees is an indirect expense. Second, the business portion of the cost of the system itself may be depreciated. This depreciation also becomes part of your indirect expenses.

The cost of landscaping and lawn care is not a deductible expense.

Telephone Expenses

Telephone expenses are not part of your home office deduction. They are separately deductible. However, if you maintain a home office, you may not deduct the basic monthly service charge for the first telephone line to your home as a business expense. You can deduct business-related charges, such as long-distance calls for business or call answering, call waiting, and call forwarding. You can also deduct the entire phone bill of a second phone line used exclusively for business.

Deduction Limits

Home office deductions cannot exceed your gross income from the home office activity. For those who conduct their primary business from home, this gross income limit poses no problem. Income from the home office activity will more than exceed home office expenses. Thus, for example, if a dentist conducts his or her practice from a home office, there should be no problem in deducting all home office expenses. For those who use a home office for a sideline activity, however, the gross income limit may pose a problem.

What Is Gross Income?

For purposes of limiting home office deductions, *gross income* is income from the business activity conducted in the home office.

---

example

A teacher who teaches full-time at school conducts a retail business from a home office. For purposes of limiting home office deductions, gross income includes only the income from the retail business.

To calculate gross income, look to your profit reported on Schedule C if you are self-employed, or the portion of your salary earned in the home office if you are an employee. You can adjust your Schedule C profit for certain items. If you sold your home, the portion of the gain related to the home office increases your gross income for purposes of limiting home office deductions. If you suffer a loss on the home office portion, you reduce your gross income.

If your gross income from your home office business activity is less than your total business expenses, your home office deduction is limited. Your deduction for otherwise nondeductible expenses (such as utilities or depreciation) cannot exceed gross income from the business activity, reduced by the business portion of otherwise deductible expenses (such as home mortgage interest or real estate taxes) and business expenses not attributable to business use of the home (such as salaries or supplies). This sounds rather complicated, but Form 8829, Expenses for Business Use of Your Home, incorporates this limitation.

You can carry forward the unused portion of a home office deduction to a future year and deduct it when there is gross income from the same home office activity to offset it. There is no time limit on the carryforward. You can claim it even though you no longer live in the home in which the deduction arose, as long as there is gross income from the same activity to offset the deduction. Be sure to keep adequate records to support your carryforward deduction.

SPECIAL BUSINESS USES OF A HOME

There are two exceptions to the exclusive use requirement: day-care facilities and storage space. If either of these exceptions apply, you can deduct your home office expenses even though the space is also used for personal purposes.

Day-Care Facilities

If you use all or part of your home on a regular basis as a facility to provide day-care services, you figure your deductible home office expenses in a different way as explained in IRS Publication 587, *Business Use of Your Home*.

Storage

If space is used on a regular basis for the storage of your inventory or sample products, you can deduct home office expenses even though you also use the space for personal purposes and thus fail the exclusive use test. The storage space that is deductible is only the actual space used. For example, if a portion of a basement is used for storage, only the expenses related to that portion are deductible even if the rest of the basement is not used for other purposes.

Expenses of storage space are deductible even though the exclusive use test is not satisfied if:

- The home is the fixed location of the business activity (you run the business from home).
- The business activity is selling goods wholesale or retail.
- The space is used as a separately identifiable space suitable for storage.

---

example

An individual runs from home a gift basket business and uses her family room to store samples. She may deduct the portion of the family room used to store her samples even though the family room is also used for personal purposes.

ANCILLARY BENEFITS OF CLAIMING HOME OFFICE DEDUCTIONS

Claiming home office deductions means more, tax-wise, than simply deducting the expenses related to that office. It means additional tax benefits may be available.

Having a home office means that travel to and from the office for business is fully deductible (there is no such thing as commuting from a home office). So travel from your home to a customer's location and back again is a fully deductible business expense.

Having a home office also means it is not necessary to keep a log of computer use. A computer used in a regular business establishment is not treated as listed property for which an owner must prove business use exceeds 50 percent in order to claim first-year expensing or accelerated depreciation. A home office for which a deduction is allowed is treated as a regular business establishment.

IMPACT OF HOME OFFICE DEDUCTIONS ON HOME SALES

Claiming a home office deduction does *not* impact your ability to claim the home sale exclusion (up to $250,000 of gain; $500,000 on a joint return) if you otherwise qualify for it. However, any depreciation taken on a home office after May 6, 1997, must be *recaptured* at the rate of 25 percent (for taxpayers in tax brackets over this amount). This means you must report your total depreciation deductions related to home office use after this date and must pay tax on the total amount at the rate of 25 percent. You cannot use the exclusion to offset this tax.

You cannot avoid this recapture by choosing not to report depreciation to which you are entitled. Recapture applies to depreciation both allowed (the amount you actually claimed) *and* allowable (what you were entitled to claim). If you want to avoid depreciation recapture, you must sidestep the home office deduction entirely by disqualifying your home office. You can do this easily by *not* using the space exclusively for business. By disqualifying your home office, you lose out on depreciation but can still claim many related costs, such as office maintenance and utility costs, as ordinary and necessary business expenses.

chapter 16

medical coverage and other deductions

Medical coverage is an expensive personal expense for most people. So, for many, a job that provides medical coverage offers an important benefit. For the small business owner there is often a need to obtain personal coverage. It may also be imperative to offer medical coverage as a benefit to attract and keep good employees. A deduction of all or a portion of the cost of medical coverage is a significant cost-saving feature of providing such coverage. In addition to medical coverage, you can write off a wide array of expenses.

For more information about deducting medical coverage and other costs, see IRS Publication 535, *Business Expenses*, and IRS Publication 969, *Medical Savings Accounts*.

DEDUCTING MEDICAL INSURANCE

With rare exceptions, you are not required to provide medical insurance for employees. However, according to the Kaiser Family Foundation, 60 percent of all small businesses (with 3 to 24 employees) offer this benefit to their employees. If you choose to provide medical insurance, you can deduct the cost of their group hospitalization and medical insurance. Deductible medical coverage also includes premiums for **long-term care insurance**.

Long-term care insurance An insurance contract that provides coverage for long-term care services necessary for diagnostic, preventive, therapeutic, curing, treating, mitigating, and rehabilitative services, as well as maintenance or personal care services required by a chronically ill person and provided pursuant to a plan of care prescribed by a licensed health care practitioner.

Medical coverage provided to employees is treated as a tax-free fringe benefit. According to the IRS, medical coverage provided to a domestic partner is taxable to the employee because a domestic partner is not a spouse under state law. However, an employer providing such medical coverage can still deduct it (since the employee is taxed on the cost of coverage for a domestic partner as additional compensation).

The value of long-term care insurance provided through a cafeteria plan or other flexible spending arrangement is not excludable from the employees' income.

You cannot deduct amounts you set aside or put into reserve funds for self-insuring medical costs (see medical reimbursement plans). However, your actual losses (when you pay for uninsured medical costs) are deductible.

Coverage for Retirees

You are not required to continue providing medical coverage for employees who retire (beyond COBRA requirements discussed later in this chapter). If you choose to pay for such coverage, you may deduct it. You may terminate your obligation for this coverage as long as you retained the right to do so in any plan or agreement you made to provide the coverage (for example, in an employee's early retirement package).

Special Rules for Partnerships and S Corporations

The business may provide coverage not only for rank-and-file employees but for owners as well. Partnerships and S corporations follow special rules for health insurance coverage provided to owners because owners cannot receive this benefit on a tax-free basis.

First, partnerships deduct accident and health insurance for their partners as guaranteed payments made to partners. Alternatively, partnerships can choose to treat the payment of premiums on behalf of their partners as a reduction in distributions. In this alternative, the partnership cannot claim a deduction.

S corporations deduct accident and health insurance for its shareholder-employees in the same way that it does for other employees.

Payment of accident and health insurance for a shareholder means the premiums are not treated as wages for purposes of FICA (includes Social Security and Medicare taxes) if the insurance is provided under a plan or system for employees and their dependents. Of course, even where the payment is not treated as wages for FICA, it is still taxable to the shareholder for income tax purposes.

A partnership or S corporation must report the medical insurance that it provides to owners on the owners' Schedule K-1. This is picked up by the partners and S corporation shareholders as income (unless, in the case of the partnership, the partnership does not claim a deduction). Owners may be entitled to deduct a percentage of health insurance, as explained in the next section.

DEDUCTING HEALTH COVERAGE BY SELF-EMPLOYED PERSONS AND MORE-THAN-2-PERCENT S CORPORATION SHAREHOLDERS

Self-employed persons (sole proprietors, partners, and LLC members), as well as more-than-2-percent S corporation shareholders, may deduct the cost of health insurance (including long-term care coverage) they buy directly or receive through their business, but not as a business expense.

The deduction is taken from gross income on page one of Form 1040. This means the deduction is allowed even if the self-employed person does not itemize deductions.

The deduction cannot exceed the net earnings from the business in which the medical insurance plan is established. For S corporation shareholders, the deduction cannot be more than wages from the corporation (if this was the business in which the insurance plan was established).

You cannot take the deduction for any month if you were eligible to participate in any employer (including your spouse's) subsidized health plan at any time during the month. For example, suppose you are a single, self-employed individual and pay for your own health coverage. On July 1, 2004, you begin a job in which your employer provides you with health insurance. You can deduct your health insurance from January 1 through June 30, 2004 (the time you did not receive any subsidized health coverage).

USING MEDICAL REIMBURSEMENT PLANS

Businesses can set up special plans, called *medical reimbursement plans*, to pay for medical expenses not otherwise covered by insurance. For example, medical reimbursement plans can pay for the cost of eye care or cover co-payments and other out-of-pocket costs. Medical reimbursement plans are self-insured plans; they are not funded by insurance.

Medical reimbursement plans can cover only employees. These include owners of C corporations (but not S corporations). The plans cannot discriminate in favor of highly compensated employees, such as owners and officers.

The IRS has endorsed a way around the ban on deducting medical costs of self-employed owners. If the business has a medical reimbursement plan for employees and your spouse is an employee (nonowner), the medical reimbursement plan can cover the medical expenses of your spouse-employee and your employee's spouse (you) and dependents. In this way, your medical costs are deductible by the business and are not taxable to you.

While self-insured medical reimbursement plans provide advantages to employers, there is a significant risk of substantial economic exposure (that claims will run higher than anticipated and planned for). This problem can be addressed by setting a dollar limit (such as $2,500) on medical reimbursements for the year.

Another disadvantage to this type of plan is the administration involved (reviewing and processing reimbursement claims). For a very small employer, however, this may not be significant.

SHIFTING THE COST OF COVERAGE TO EMPLOYEES

Health insurance is increasingly costly to employers. There are several ways in which business owners can reduce their costs without putting employees out in the cold.

Sharing the Cost of Premiums

Instead of employers paying the entire cost of insurance, employers can shift a portion of the cost to employees. For example, employers may provide free coverage for employees but shift the cost of spousal and dependent care coverage to employees.

Flexible Spending Arrangements

Businesses can set up flexible spending arrangements (FSAs) to allow employees to decide how much they want to pay for medical expenses. Employees pay for medical expenses on a pretax basis. At the beginning of the year, they agree to a salary reduction amount that funds their FSA. Contributions to an FSA are not treated as taxable compensation (and are not subject to FICA). Employees then use the amount in their FSA to pay for most types of medical-related costs, such as medical premiums, orthodontia, or other expenses during the year that are not covered by medical insurance (including over-the-counter medications, such as pain relievers and cold remedies, not prescribed by a doctor). This plan cannot be used to pay for cosmetic surgery unless it is required for medical purposes (such as to correct a birth defect).

---

example

Your employee agrees to a monthly salary reduction amount of $100. This means that the employee has $1,200 during the year to spend on medical costs.

The downside for employers is that employees can use all of their promised contributions for the year whenever they submit proof of medical expenses. This means that if employees leave employment after taking funds out of their FSA but before they have fully funded them, the employer winds up paying the difference. So, for example, if an employee who promises to contribute $100 per month submits a bill for dental expenses of $1,200 on January 15 and leaves employment shortly thereafter, the employee has contributed only $100; the employer must bear the cost of the additional $1,100 submission.

Of course, the flip side benefits the employer. If employees fail to use up their FSA contributions before the end of the year (referred to as the "use it or lose it" rule), the employer keeps the difference. Nothing is refunded to the employees.

Cafeteria Plans

Employers can set up cafeteria plans to let employees choose from a menu of benefits. This makes sense for some employers, since cafeteria plans allow working couples to get the benefits they need without needless overlap. For example, if one spouse has health insurance coverage from his employer, the other spouse can select dependent care assistance or other benefits offered through a cafeteria plan. Cafeteria plans do not require employees to reduce salary or make contributions to pay for benefits. Benefits are paid by the employer. Health Savings Accounts (HSAs) cannot be part of cafeteria plans.

Premium-Only Plans

In these plans, employees choose between health coverage or salary. If they select the coverage, it is paid by means of salary reduction. In effect, employees are paying for their own coverage, but with pretax dollars. The employer deducts the compensation (whether the employee chooses the coverage or takes the salary). The only cost to the employer under this type of plan is the cost of administering it. (Many payroll service companies will administer the plan for a modest charge.) Bonus: Both the employer and employee save on FICA if the medical coverage is chosen.

SETTING UP HEALTH SAVINGS ACCOUNTS (HSAs)

The high cost of health insurance is considered by many small-business owners to be their number-one concern. Now there's a way to cut costs by 40 percent or more by combining a high-deductible (lower-cost) health policy with a special savings account called a Health Savings Account (HSA).

Eligibility

HSAs are open to anyone who, on the first day of the month, is covered by a high-deductible health plan (HDHP), is not covered by another type of health insurance plan (other than worker's compensation, long-term care, disability, and vision and eye care), and is not eligible for Medicare. This means that self-employed individuals, small-business owners, and those who work for small businesses and are under age 65 can use HSAs to obtain necessary health coverage.

For a list of insurers offering HDHP coverage and trustees for HSA accounts, go to <www.hsainsider.com>.

Archer medical savings accounts, which are similar to HSAs, can be used by small employers and self-employed individuals instead of HSAs.

High-Deductible Plan

This is defined as a plan with an annual deductible of at least $1,000 for self-only coverage or $2,000 for family coverage and the sum of the annual deductible and other annual out-of-pocket expenses is no more than $5,000 for self-only or $10,000 for family coverage (these dollar limits will be adjusted annually for inflation).

Benefits of HSAs

HSAs give you an affordable way to offer health coverage for yourself and your employees. This example from the National Small Business Association shows you how.

---

example

A company with 15 employees is currently paying $72,000 for a low-deductible health insurance. It changes to a high-deductible health plan with a $2,500 deductible for participants. The annual cost of the new plan is $40,000. The company also contributes $1,000 to each participant's HSA, so its total cost is $55,000 ($40,000 insurance premiums + $15,000 HSA contributions). This is $17,000 less than the company was paying for high-deductible health coverage.

Contributions to HSAs are *not* subject to payroll taxes, which makes HSAs a better option than paying additional compensation to employees as a way to cover unreimbursed medical expenses.

Contributions

For 2004, contributions are limited to $2,600 for those with self-only coverage or $5,150 for family coverage (any plan other than self-only); these limits will be adjusted annually for inflation.

For those age 55 or older by year-end, the contribution limit is increased by $500 in 2004 (increasing in $100 increments to $1,000 by 2009). Contributions are fully deductible.

You are not required by law to make contributions for your employees, but if you choose to do so, it must be on a nondiscriminatory basis (you can't simply contribute for owners and not for rank-and-file employees).

Like IRAs, contributions to HSAs can be made up to the due date of the return (e.g., April 15, 2005, for 2004).

Taxation of HSAs

There is no current tax on earnings in HSAs. Funds withdrawn from HSAs to pay medical costs are not subject to tax. Money can be taken out for any purpose, but nonmedical withdrawals are taxable and there is a 10 percent penalty (the penalty is waived for disability or attainment of age 65).

When taking withdrawals for medical purposes, you are not required to prove this to the financial institution acting as the account's trustee or custodian. If you maintain the accounts for your employees, they are not required to prove the purpose of their withdrawal to you (it is their responsibility). But you should save receipts and other proof to show that the withdrawals should not be subject to a 10 percent penalty if you are under age 65.

Note: Employees own their HSAs and can take them when they leave the company.

HEALTH REIMBURSEMENT ARRANGEMENTS

If you want to limit your outlays for employee medical costs, consider a relatively new option called a health reimbursement arrangement (HRA). You contribute a fixed amount to an account for each employee that can be tapped to cover unreimbursed medical expenses. You complement the HRA by switching medical insurance to a less extensive, less costly plan. Overall you save on your medical costs. And the HRA does not entail any costly and complex design requirements associated with other types of plans such as flexible spending arrangements within cafeteria plans (for details on HRAs see Rev. Rul. 2002-41).

The benefit to your employee is that neither contributions to nor qualified reimbursements from the plan are taxable. Funds in the account can be accessed by credit or debit cards that you set up for this purpose. Also, unused amounts in an employee's account can be carried forward and used in future years (there is no use-it-or-lose-it feature).

COBRA COVERAGE

Employers who normally employ 20 or more employees and who provide coverage for employees must extend continuation coverage (referred to as COBRA—the initials for the law that created continuation coverage). COBRA entitles employees who are terminated (whether voluntarily or otherwise) to pay for continued coverage of what they received while employed. It also covers families of deceased employees and former spouses of divorced employees. COBRA coverage generally applies for 18 months (36 months in some cases).

Employers can charge for COBRA coverage but only up to the cost of the coverage to the employer plus an administrative fee. This limit on the total cost to the individual for COBRA coverage is 102 percent of the cost of the insurance. Employers who fail to provide COBRA and/or to provide proper notice of COBRA can be subject to a substantial penalty.

A number of states have their own COBRA rules, referred to as *mini-COBRA*. Be sure to check any state law requirements on providing continuation health coverage to terminated employees.

Federal COBRA does not include the cost of long-term care insurance.

OTHER DEDUCTIONS

The types of deductions discussed throughout this book are not exclusive. You may be entitled to many other business deductions. In general, most types of **ordinary** and **necessary** business expenses are deductible, although there may be some limitations that affect the timing or amount you can claim. The following discussion is designed to give you a flavor of the range of expenses you can write-off in your business.

Ordinary   Common and accepted in your business.

Necessary   Helpful or appropriate to your business. To be necessary, an expense need not be indispensable. For example, if you send flowers to your employee in the hospital, you may deduct the cost of the flowers.

Advertising

Ordinary advertising costs that are reasonable in amount can be deducted. Examples of such costs include business cards, print or media ads, ads in telephone directories, prizes for contests and other promotional activities and signs with a useful life of not more than one year (signs with a longer life can be depreciated as explained in Chapter 12).

Charitable Contributions

Business donations to charitable organizations are deductible. Special enhanced deductions are allowed to C corporations that donate certain types of property, such as computer equipment to schools and libraries.

For C corporations, the deduction for charitable contributions is limited to 10 percent of taxable income. For owners of other types of businesses, limitations apply on your personal return based on your adjusted gross income.

Dues and Subscriptions

Dues to business, professional and civic organizations, such as annual dues to a bar or medical association or a chamber of commerce, are deductible. But no deduction can be claimed for dues to clubs to country clubs, airline clubs and other clubs organized for pleasure or social purposes (even though you do business at the clubs).

Employees' Pay

You can deduct employee compensation that is reasonable in amount. You can also deduct employment taxes on this pay, including the employer share of Social Security and Medicare (FICA) taxes and federal (FUTA) and state unemployment taxes.

You may also deduct a wide array of employee benefits, including assistance for adoption, dependent care and education, group-term life insurance and meals and lodging. But many of these benefits, which are tax free to your employees and deductible by the business, may not be tax free to you as the business owner.

Your employment tax obligations, including income tax withholding on employee wages, are discussed IRS Publication 15, *Circular E, Employer's Tax Guide.*

Insurance

The cost of most types of business-related insurance is deductible. In addition to medical coverage discussed earlier in this chapter, premiums for the following types of coverage can be deducted: casualty insurance, errors and omissions coverage, employer practices liability, overhead insurance professional liability coverage, performance and fidelity bonds and premiums to the Pension Benefit Guaranty Corporation (PBGC) if you have a defined benefit retirement plan.

Legal and Professional Fees

Fees paid to lawyers, accountants and other professional advisors generally are currently deductible. However, legal fees incurred to acquire a capital asset (e.g., purchase a building) are not separately deductible but, rather, are added to the cost of the asset. Legal and accounting fees to form a business are discussed in Chapter 12.

Payments to Independent Contractors

Payments to workers who are not your employees are deductible and are not subject to employment taxes. If annual amounts are $600 or more, you may have to file Form 1099-MISC with the IRS to report the payments.

Penalties, Fines, and Damages

If you contract to perform work and are subject to a penalty for noncompletion or lateness, you can deduct the penalty. Similarly, compensatory damages paid to the government or to other parties as a result of a lawsuit are deductible.

However, you cannot write off nonconformance penalties imposed by the Environmental Protection Agency for failing to meet certain standards, governmental fines and penalties for violating the law, or punitive damages from lawsuits.

Supplies, Materials, and Uniforms

The cost of incidental supplies and materials used in your business are deductible. Examples of deductible items include postage, books, software and equipment with a useful life of less than one year, uniforms and clothing that are not suitable for ordinary street use (e.g., protective gear for construction sites).

Travel and Entertainment Expenses

Travel and entertainment costs for business are deductible. However, only 50 percent of the cost of business meals and entertainment generally is deductible. A deduction for business gifts is limited to $25 per person per year.

To claim a deduction for these costs, strict substantiation requirements must be satisfied. See IRS Publication 463, *Travel, Entertainment, Gifts, and Car Expenses*.

chapter 17

deductions for alternative minimum tax

Reducing regular tax is only half the battle that a small business owner wages to increase after-tax returns. Minimizing or avoiding alternative minimum tax (AMT) where applicable is a second important front that must be addressed. Some business owners may find themselves subject to AMT if they have certain substantial deductions and/or credits.

ALTERNATIVE MINIMUM TAX BASICS

Alternative minimum tax is designed to ensure that all taxpayers pay at least some tax. Years ago, with tax shelters and other loopholes, wealthy individuals and corporations often paid little or no tax. In an effort to make all taxpayers share the tax burden, an AMT was imposed.

The AMT is a separate tax system, with its own deductions and tax rates. A taxpayer computes the regular income tax as well as a tentative AMT. The extent to which the tentative AMT exceeds regular tax liability is reported as AMT. Alternative minimum tax liability for individuals can be reduced by certain personal tax credits, including a limited foreign tax credit (corporations can reduce their AMT liability only by a limited foreign tax credit). There are two different AMT structures: one for C corporations and another for individuals.

---

for the future

As the individual income tax rates decline over the next several years, an increasing number of business owners may find themselves subject to the AMT on their share of business preferences and adjustments as well as on personal items.

C corporations pay AMT at the rate of 20 percent. This rate is applied to *alternative minimum taxable income* (AMTI) reduced by an exemption amount of $40,000 (reduced by 25 percent of the amount by which AMTI exceeds $150,000). Alternative minimum taxable income includes an *adjusted current earnings* (ACE) adjustment. This adjustment is designed to measure income tax on as broad a basis as it is for financial reporting purposes.

Individuals have a two-tier AMT rate structure of 26 percent on the first $175,000 of income subject to AMT, plus 28 percent on any excess amount. The amount subject to these tax rates is reduced by an exemption amount of $58,000 on a joint return, $40,250 for singles, and $27,000 for married filing separately. This exemption amount is phased out for high-income taxpayers (e.g., no exemption may be claimed on a joint return when AMT income exceeds $330,000).

Who is subject to AMT? Potentially all businesses are subject to AMT. However, small C corporations may be exempt, as explained later in this chapter. Owners of pass-through entities (partnerships, LLCs, and S corporations) figure AMT on their individual returns. They include business items passed through to them and identified as AMT items on their Schedule K-1.

Exemption for Small Corporations

Small corporations are entirely exempt from AMT. However, despite this exemption thousands continue to pay this tax needlessly. If you meet the definition of a small corporation, review prior tax returns to make sure you did not pay this tax in vain.

Small corporation   A C corporation with average gross receipts of $7.5 million or less for the prior three tax years ($5 million for the first three years, or portion of time, in business).

---

example

X, Inc., a C corporation, had average gross receipts of $275,000 for the three-year period that included 2001, 2002, and 2003. For 2004, X is a small corporation and therefore is exempt from AMT.

New C corporations (those with the first tax year being 2004), other than those aggregated with other corporations, are exempt from AMT in 2004 without regard to gross receipts. The tax law simply assumes that start-ups are small corporations.

note

While a C corporation generally can claim a tax credit with respect to AMT liability incurred in a prior year, a small corporation can claim only a limited AMT credit.

Once your business is established as a small corporation, it retains that status (and is exempt from AMT) as long as its average gross receipts for the prior three-year period do not exceed $7.5 million. The first year of small corporation status is ignored for purposes of this three-year period.

Loss of Small Corporation Status

If your business succeeds to the extent that it loses its small corporation status, special AMT rules continue to apply to *formerly small corporations*. These rules simplify AMT for such corporations. In general, these corporations start fresh for certain AMT items and never have to make certain AMT adjustments.

DEDUCTION LIMITS FOR ALTERNATIVE MINIMUM TAX

Certain deductions that were allowed for regular tax purposes may be disallowed or modified for AMT.

The following deductions that were claimed on individual returns must be modified for AMT purposes:

- Investment interest.
- Depreciation.
- Net operating losses (NOLs).
- Mining exploration and development costs (the regular tax deduction must be amortized over 10 years).
- Research and experimentation expenditures (costs must be amortized over 10 years if you are not a material participant in the business).
- Passive activity losses from nonfarming activities (losses are adjusted for items not deductible for AMT purposes).

Adjustments for Depreciation

The depreciation method that you use for regular tax purposes may require that an adjustment be made for AMT purposes. For AMT purposes you are allowed only a limited depreciation deduction. If you claimed more for regular tax purposes, you must adjust your AMT income accordingly.

For property (other than real property) acquired after 1986, your AMT depreciation is limited to the 150-percent declining balance method, switching to straight line when a larger depreciation deduction results. For real property acquired after 1986, your AMT depreciation is limited to straight line over 40 years.

For real property placed in service after December 31, 1998, an AMT adjustment is no longer required. For personal property placed in service after this date, a depreciation election can be made to use the same depreciation method for regular and AMT purposes so that an AMT adjustment is avoided. By making this election, depreciation is figured using the 150-percent declining balance method over the regular tax recovery period (instead of the 200-percent declining balance method).

> **note**
>
> Different adjustments apply to property placed in service before 1987. Follow the instructions to Form 6251.

Preference Items

Certain items that may have escaped the regular tax is subject to AMT. These include tax-exempt interest on private activity bonds issued after August 7, 1986; exclusion of 50 percent of the gain on the sale of small business stock; oil and gas preferences; and accelerated depreciation on real property acquired before 1987.

Net Operating Losses

The NOL deduction for regular tax purposes must be adjusted for AMT. This is because only a limited NOL deduction is allowed for AMT purposes. The NOL for AMT purposes is the regular tax NOL except that the nonbusiness deduction adjustment includes only AMT itemized deductions (i.e., state and local taxes and certain other deductions cannot be used to figure the NOL deduction).

You may be able to eliminate your AMT liability because of your NOL deduction. However, the NOL deduction cannot be more than 90 percent of AMT income (without regard to the NOL deduction). If you cannot use all of your NOL because of the 90-percent limit, you may carry it back and forward under the applicable carryback/carryforward periods (explained in Chapter 4). However, the carryback and carryforward NOLs are also subject to the 90-percent limit.

Other Adjustments and Preferences

In figuring AMT income on which AMT tax is imposed, certain income items are also given special treatment. These include incentive stock options, long-term contracts, tax-exempt interest on private activity bonds, and basis adjustments for AMT gain or loss.

For C corporations other than small C corporations, the key adjustment that can trigger AMT is the ACE adjustment. However, since small corporations are exempt from AMT, this adjustment is not explained further.

MINIMUM TAX CREDIT

If you paid AMT last year, you may be eligible for a tax credit this year. Different minimum tax credits apply for individuals and corporations.

Individuals

You qualify for a minimum tax credit if you meet any of the following three conditions:

1. You paid any AMT in 2003.
2. You had an unused minimum tax credit that you carried forward from 2003 to 2004.
3. You had certain unallowed business-related credits in 2003.

The credit is the amount of AMT paid in 2003 reduced by the part of the tax related to exclusion items (standard deduction, medical expenses, taxes, miscellaneous itemized deductions, gains on small business stock, tax-exempt interest from private activity bonds, and depletion). The credit may be increased by minimum tax credit carryforwards and unallowed credits for nonconventional-source fuel, orphan drugs, and electric vehicles.

Compute the credit on Form 8801, Credit for Prior Year Minimum Tax—Individuals, Estates, and Trusts. If the credit exceeds your AMT liability for 2004, the excess amount may be carried forward and used to offset AMT liability in a future year. There is no limit on the carryforward period.

Corporations

Unlike an individual's minimum tax credit which is limited to exclusion items, corporations that paid AMT in a prior year may claim a tax credit in 2004 if they have no AMT liability this year. Compute the credit on Form 8827, Credit for Prior Year Minimum Tax—Corporations.

chapter 18

roundup of
tax credits

Just as deductions offset business income, tax credits offset tax liability. In effect, tax credits are considerably more valuable than deductions since they offset taxes on a dollar-for-dollar basis.

Businesses may be entitled to a variety of credits that Congress created to encourage certain activities—hiring special workers, using alternative energy sources, pouring money into research, and so on. Not every business credit applies to small business owners (but are all listed within this chapter to alert you to their existence).

Many of these credits have been discussed throughout this book in the chapter to which they relate.

EMPLOYMENT-RELATED CREDITS

The tax law encourages you to hire certain workers by permitting you to claim tax credits for certain wages you have paid. These credits include the work opportunity credit, welfare-to-work credit, credit for tips on FICA, empowerment zone employment credit, Indian employment credit, and community renewal employment credit.

Work-Related Personal Credits

If you work as an employee or as a self-employed person, you may be eligible for certain personal tax credits. Workers whose income is below threshold amounts may be eligible to claim an earned income credit, and whether you are an employee or a business owner, if you hire someone to look after your children under age 13 or a disabled spouse or child of any age so that you can go to work, you may claim a dependent care credit.

CAPITAL CONSTRUCTION-RELATED CREDITS

The tax law encourages certain types of construction.

Disabled Access Credit

If you make capital improvements to make your premises more accessible to the handicapped, you may qualify for a credit of 50 percent of expenditures over $250, but not over $10,250. Thus, the top credit is $5,000. If you claim this credit you cannot claim depreciation on these costs.

Low-Income Housing Credit

If you invest in the construction or rehabilitation of housing for low-income individuals, you may be eligible for a tax credit of 70 percent of new construction or 30 percent of federally subsidized buildings. The credit is claimed over a 10-year period.

Rehabilitation Credit

If you rehabilitate or reconstruct certain buildings, you may claim a credit of 10 percent of your costs if the building was originally placed in service before 1936. If the building is a certified historic structure listed on the National Register of Historic Places, the credit is 20 percent of your expenditures. To qualify, your expenditures must be more than the greater of $5,000 or your adjusted basis in the building and its structural components.

New Markets Credit

To encourage investments in certain economically-disadvantaged areas, you may claim a credit for purchasing stock in a community development entity (CDE). A CDE is a domestic corporation or partnership that provides investment capital for low-income communities or persons, maintains accountability to the residents of the area, and has been certified as a CDE by the Community Development Financial Institutions (CDFI) Fund of the Department of the Treasury. The credit is claimed over a period of seven years. The amount of the credit is the equity investment multiplied by 5 percent in years one through three and 6 percent in years four through seven. The credit is subject to recapture if the CDE ceases to be qualified, the proceeds cease to be used to make qualified investments, or the investment is redeemed by the entity (there is no recapture if you merely sell your investment).

OTHER TAX CREDITS

Other tax credits in the law are intended to encourage specific things— research, alternative energy consumption, and so on.

Credit for Employer-Provided Child Care Facilities and Services

You can claim a credit for providing child care facilities and child care referral services. The credit is 25 percent of qualified facility expenses, plus 10 percent of referral service costs, for a maximum credit of $150,000. If a company builds a child care facility, the basis of the facility for purposes of depreciation must be reduced by the expenses taken into account in figuring the credit. If the facility ceases to be used for child care within 10 years, the credit is subject to recapture.

Research Credit

If you engage in research and experimentation, you may claim a credit of 20 percent of increased research activities (increased costs this year compared with a base period that is usually the three preceding years). Alternatively you may claim a flat percentage of gross receipts on average for a four-year period. The credit percentage (2.65%, 3.2%, or 3.75%) scales up with the percentage of gross receipts. There is no dollar limit on the credit, but the credit cannot exceed taxable income from the business that produced the credit.

Alcohol Fuels Credit

The credit applies to alcohol (ethanol and methanol) you sold or used as fuel in your business.

Enhanced Oil Recovery Credit

The credit applies to certain oil recovery costs if you are in the oil and gas business.

Federal Excise Tax on Fuels

The federal excise tax you pay on certain fuels used in your business (particularly farming activities) may be claimed either as a credit or a tax refund. The credit is the amount of this tax paid on fuel used in machinery and off-highway vehicles (such as tractors) and on kerosene used for heating, lighting, and cooking on a farm.

Foreign Tax Credit

If you pay tax to a foreign country—on business income or investments made abroad—you may be eligible for a tax credit. The purpose of the tax credit is to prevent you from paying tax twice on the same income (once to a foreign country and again on your federal income tax).

Renewable Energy Production Credit

The credit is the cost of selling electricity produced from alternative energy sources within 10 years of placing the production facility in service.

Credit for Small Employer Pension Plan Start-Up Costs

Small employers (those with no more than 100 employees who received at least $5,000 of compensation in the preceding year) may claim a tax credit for starting up a qualified retirement plan. The credit is 50 percent of administrative and employee-education expenses up to $1,000, for a top credit of $500. The credit may be claimed for three years, starting with the year in which the plan becomes effective or the prior year.

Credit for Qualified Electric Vehicles.

If you buy an electric car for your business, you may claim a credit in 2004 of 10 percent of costs up to $40,000. (This credit is explained in Chapter 7.)

Puerto Rico Economic Activity Credit

A credit, based on certain wages and depreciation, can be claimed against any federal tax attributable to income from active business activities in Puerto Rico. However, wages taken into account for this credit may not be used for purposes of the research credit—no double-dipping is permitted.

Orphan Drug Credit

If your business engages in research on diseases and afflictions that are not widespread, you may claim a special credit for your related expenses.

Minimum Tax Credit

If you paid AMT in a prior year, you may be eligible for a tax credit this year. Different rules apply to individuals and C corporations. (This credit is explained in Chapter 17.)

GENERAL BUSINESS CREDIT

Most tax credits discussed in this chapter are part of the general business credit. This means that after figuring each separate credit, there is an overall limit to credits under the general business credit. Total credits in excess of these limits can be carried back and/or forward within limits.

The general business credit is comprised of the following:

> **note**
>
> The empowerment zone employment credit is not part of the general business credit and is not subject to the general business credit limitations. Excess empowerment zone credits may be carried over in a manner similar to the general business credit.

- Investment credit (rehabilitation credit, renewal energy credit, reforestation credit, and the credit from cooperatives)
- Work opportunity credit
- Welfare-to-work credit
- Credit for alcohol used as fuel
- Research credit
- Low-income housing credit

- Enhanced oil recovery credit
- Disabled access credit
- Renewable electricity production credit
- Indian employment credit
- Credit for FICA on tips
- Orphan drug credit
- Credit for contributions to selected community development corporations
- Renewal community employment credit
- Credit for employer-provided child care facilities and services
- Credit for small employer retirement plan start-up costs
- New markets credit

Credit Limitations

First you figure each separate credit of the general business credit and then total them. The total is then subject to special limits, determined by your regular and alternative minimum tax liability and certain other tax credits. Your limit is your net tax liability (regular tax reduced by certain personal credits, including the foreign tax credit), reduced by the greater of:

- Your tentative AMT liability (figured before comparing it with regular tax).
- Twenty-five percent of regular tax liability (before personal tax credits) over $25,000.

---

example

In 2004, your regular tax liability is $12,000. You are entitled to claim $1,000 in personal tax credits. You have no AMT liability. Your general business credit is limited to $11,000 (net tax liability of $11,000, reduced by zero since you do not have any AMT liability and 25 percent of your regular tax does not exceed $25,000).

Carrybacks and Carryforwards

If the credit limitation prevents you from claiming the full general business credit that you are otherwise entitled to, you do not lose the benefit of this excess amount—you simply cannot claim it in the current year. You may be able to use the excess credit to offset your tax liability in prior and/or future years.

You may carry back the excess amount to 2003. If there continues to be an excess (it exceeds the credit limitation for 2003), you may then carry forward the excess up to 20 years.

If you had credits arising in tax years beginning before 1998 that could not be currently claimed because of the credit limitation, this excess was subject to a three-year carryback period and a 15-year carryforward period. Be sure to segregate your pre-1998 and post-1997 excess credits. All excess pre-1998 amounts are added together and treated as one credit carryforward.

If you still have unused amounts and the carryforward period expires or the business ceases (or you die), the unused amounts may be deducted in the year after the carryforward expiration or in the year of business cessation (or death). However, to the extent the credit relates to the research credit, it must be cut in half before deducting it.

index

Abandonment of property, 88
Above-market loans, 148–149
Accelerated depreciation, 99
Accounting fees, 232
Accounting methods:
  accrual, 25–26, 129–130, 139–140
  cash, 22–24
  changing, 28
  installment, 27
  for long-term contracts, 26–27
  uniform capitalization rules and,
    27–28
Accounting periods, 19–22
Accrual method of accounting:
  bad debt and, 129–130
  description of, 25–26
  real estate taxes and, 139–140
Acquiring lease, cost of, 134–135
Acquisition, debt-financed, 146
Active participation, 61
Actual expense method for deducting
    car expenses:
  business use and, 99–100
  choosing, 96
  depreciation allowance, 98–99
  depreciation and, 97–98
  description of, 97
  dispositions of car, 103–105
  dollar limit on depreciation
    deduction, 100–102
  increasing dollar limit and, 102–103
  insurance premiums and, 210

Actuarial costs for defined benefit
    plans, 189
Adjusted basis, 64–65, 85–86, 201
Adjusted gross income, 12
Advance payments, 43–44
Advertising, 231
Agricultural payments, 47
Alcohol fuels credit, 239
All events test, 25
Alternative Depreciation System (ADS),
    170–171
Alternative minimum tax:
  deduction limits, 236–238
  minimum tax credit and, 238–239
  overview of, 234–235
  small corporations and, 235–236
Amendments to retirement plans,
    188–189
Americans with Disabilities Act,
    119–122
Amortization:
  business start-up costs, 177–178
  computer software costs, 179
  description of, 152
  dispositions, 177
  expenditures applicable to, 176
  intangibles acquired on purchase of
    business, 176–177
  lease acquisition costs, 180
  organizational costs, 178–179
  research and experimentation costs,
    179–180

Amount received, 64
Applicable federal rates, 148
Appraisal fees, 210
Appraiser, competence of, 202
Archer medical savings accounts, 228
Architectural barriers, removal of, 121
Asset classes, 91
Assets, capital:
    description of, 64
    transfer of, 65, 67
At-risk losses, 34
At-risk rules, 59–60
Audit chances:
    business organization and, 16
    home office deduction and, 212
Automobile, *see* Car; Car expenses

Bad debt:
    accrual method of accounting and,
        129–130
    business type, 126–127, 128
    collection of, 126
    debtor-creditor relationship and,
        123–124
    guarantees that result in, 128–129
    impact of loans with business or
        associates, 127
    loss due to, 125–126
    nonbusiness type, 127–128
    reporting on tax return, 130
    specific charge-off method and, 129
    types of, 126
    valuing, 127
    worthlessness and, 124–125
Bartering, 42
Basis, *see also* Adjusted basis
    adjusting as result of casualty, 207
    building and, 158
    business losses and, 56–58
    car and, 98–99
    recordkeeping for, 33
Below-market loans, 148
Blue book value of car, 203
Bonding requirement for retirement
    plans, 188

Bonus depreciation, 99, 151, 172–174
Bookkeeping method, 30
Boot, 68
Borrowing from retirement plan,
    187–188
Business organizations, *see also*
        C corporations; Corporations;
        Partnerships; S corporations
    changing form of, 17–18
    comparison of types of, 17
    factors in choosing type of, 13–17
    limited liability company, 6, 7–8,
        56–57, 75
    sole proprietorship, 3–6, 74,
        224–225
Business purpose, 21
Business use of car, 99–100

Cafeteria plans, 227
Calculating:
    contribution rate for self-employed
        individual, 192
    depletion, 180–181
    general business credit, 242
    gross income, 218–219
    net operating losses, 52–53
Calendar year, 19
Canceling lease, cost of, 135
Cancellation of debt, 49
Capital assets:
    description of, 64
    transfer of, 65, 67
Capital construction-related tax credits,
    238–239
Capital expenditures, 115, 116–117
Capital gains:
    for C corporations, 72
    deferring, 76, 77
    determining, 64–65
    excluding, 76–77
    holding period and, 66–67
    installment sales and, 68–70
    for pass-through entities, 70–71
    sale or exchange requirement,
        65–66

tax-free exchanges and, 67–68
tax on, and type of business
    organization, 15
tax rates on, 70–71
Capital losses:
    carryover period and, 34
    for C corporations, 72
    determining, 64–65
    holding period and, 66–67
    limitations on, 72–74
    for pass-through entities, 70–71
    sale or exchange requirement,
        65–66
Car:
    blue book value of, 203
    definition of, 95
    electric, tax credit for, 102, 110,
        204
    employee use of employer-provided,
        109
    ownership of by corporation, 109
Car expenses:
    actual expense method for deducting,
        96, 97–105
    deducting, 95–96
    leasing fees, 106–108, 136–137
    recordkeeping for, 111–114
    standard mileage allowance for, 96,
        105–106
Carryback:
    of general business credit, 243
    of net operating losses, 54–55
Carryforward of general business credit,
    243
Carryover:
    of net operating losses, 54
    recordkeeping for, 34–35
Cash method of accounting, 22–24
Casualty:
    basis, adjusting as result of, 207
    definition of, 200
    determining loss from, 201–205
    examples of, 200–201
    home office expense and, 217
    proof of, 201

C corporations:
    alternative minimum tax and,
        235–236
    capital gains and losses for, 72
    description of, 10–12
    income items for, 51
    loss limits on, 74
    sale of, 76
Charitable contributions, 32, 34,
    231
COBRA coverage, 230
Collection of bad debt, 126
Commitment fees, 149
Community development entity (CDE),
    241–242
Community renewal business, 77
Computer software:
    amortization of costs of, 179
    first-year expensing and, 153
Condemnation award, 208
Condemnations of property, 85–86,
    207
Conditional sales contract,
    132–133
Consignments, 43–44
Contributions:
    to corporate qualified plans,
        186–187
    to Health Savings Accounts,
        228–229
    to self-employed qualified plans,
        191–192, 194–195
Controlled entity, 73
Convenience of employer, home office
    deduction and, 215
Corporations, see also C corporations;
        S corporations
    car ownership and, 109
    minimum tax credit and, 239
    organizational costs for, 178
    renting property to, 132
    small, and alternative minimum tax,
        235–236
Cost depletion, 180–181
Cost of goods sold, 44–45

Credits, tax:
  alcohol fuels, 242
  capital construction-related, 241–242
  employer-provided child care
    facilities and services, 242
  employment-related, 240–241
  empowerment zone employment,
    240, 244
  enhanced oil recovery, 243
  federal excise tax on fuels, 243
  foreign tax, 243
  general business, 244–246
  minimum tax, 238–239, 244
  orphan drug, 244
  Puerto Rico economic activity, 244
  qualified electric vehicles, 102, 110,
    243
  recordkeeping and, 35
  renewable energy production, 243
  research, 242
  small employer pension plan start-up
    costs, 243

Daily business mileage and expense
    log, 111–112, 113
Damages:
  deduction for, 232
  to business property, 199
  to car used for business, 105
  reporting as income, 50
Day-care facilities, 219, 242
Debt, see also Bad debt
  cancellation of, 49
  guarantees by shareholders of
    corporate, 147
  incurred to buy interest in business,
    146
  nonrecourse type, 89
  recourse type, 88–89
Debt-financed acquisition, 146
Debt-financed distribution, 146
Deemed depreciation, 103
Deferring:
  compensation, risk of, 198
  gain, 76, 77

Defined benefit plans, 184, 189
Defined contribution plans, 184–185
Demolition expenses, 119
Depletion:
  calculating, 180–181
  description of, 152, 180
  partnership oil and gas properties,
    181–182
Depreciable property, 79, 158–160
Depreciation, see also Modified
    Accelerated Cost Recovery System
    (MACRS)
  accelerated, 99
  actual expense method for deducting
    car expenses and, 97–99
  alternative minimum tax and, 237
  bonus, 99, 151, 172–174
  claiming, 160–161
  deemed, 103
  description of, 151–152
  dollar limit on passenger cars,
    100–102
  electric cars and, 111
  excess, 100
  inventory and, 160
  methods of, 167–170
  property and, 79, 158–160
  recapture of, 83–84, 171–172
  recordkeeping for, 33, 172
  straight-line, 99, 167, 168–170
  timing of deductions, 165–167
  unrecaptured, 84
Disabled access credit, 119–120, 241
Disaster losses, 209–210
Dispositions, see also Sales
  of first-year expense property,
    156–157
  of Section 197 intangibles, 177
Distribution, debt-financed, 146
Distributive shares, 8
Dividends, 48
Dollar limit on first-year expensing,
    154
Double taxation, 11, 15, 17
Dues, 231

Economic performance test, 25

Election out of bonus depreciation, 173–174

Election to postpone gain by acquiring replacement property, 86–88

Elective deferrals, 185

Electric cars, tax credit for, 102, 110, 243

Electronic imaging systems, 31

Employees:
    business expenses of, 12–13
    independent contractors compared to, 4–5
    pay to, 231
    retirement plans for, 185
    shifting cost of medical coverage to, 225–227
    simplified employee pensions and, 193
    statutory, 5–6, 13

Employer identification number, 36

Employer-provided child care facilities and services credit, 242

Employer records, 36

Employment-related tax credits, 240–241

Employment tax, 142–143

Empowerment zone employment credit, 240, 244

Enhanced oil recovery credit, 243

Entertainment expenses, 32, 233

Environmental Protection Agency requirements, 117

Excess depreciation, 100

Excise tax, 143

Excluding gain, 76–77

Exclusive use of home office, 212

Expenditures:
    amortization and, 176
    capital, 115, 116–117
    qualifying, to meet requirements of Americans with Disabilities Act, 120

Expenses, *see also* Car expenses; Home office deductions
    demolition, 119
    prepaid, 35
    substantiation requirements for, 32
    telephone, 218
    utility, 217

Fair market value, 107, 201–202

Farming:
    cash method of accounting and, 24
    crops, casualty loss, and, 205
    income from, 46–47

Federal Emergency Management Agency (FEMA), 202

Federal excise tax on fuels credit, 243

Federal Insurance Contribution Act (FICA), 142

Federal unemployment taxes, 37, 142–143

Fifteen-year property, 163

Files, keeping, 31

Filing deadlines and extensions, 16–17

Fines, 232

First-in, first-out (FIFO) method, 45

First-year expensing:
    advantages of, 156
    car and, 99
    description of, 151, 152–153
    dispositions of property, 156–157
    limits on, 153–155
    pass-through entities and, 156

Fiscal year, 19–22

Five-year property, 163

Fixed and variable rate (FAVR) allowance, 114

Flexible spending arrangements, 226–227

Foreclosure on property, 88–89

Foreign taxes, 144, 240

Form 1099 income, 43

401(k) plans, 195–197

Franchise tax, 143
Fringe benefits and business
    organization, 14
Fuel taxes, 143–144

Gains, *see also* Capital gains
    deferring, 76, 77
    election to postpone by acquiring
        replacement property, 86–88
    excluding, 76–77
    on loss of property, 204
    net, 72
    ordinary, 66
    Section 1202, 76
    Section 1231 property and, 82–83
    short-term, 71
    unrecaptured, 71
General business credit, 244–246
General partnerships, 6–7
Gift-leaseback transactions, 133–134
Gross income, 218–219
Gross profits, 45
Gross receipts, 24
Guarantees:
    resulting in bad debt, 128–129
    by shareholders, of corporate debt,
        147

Half-year convention, 165–166,
    167
Health reimbursement arrangement,
    229–230
Health Savings Account (HSA),
    227–229
High-deductible health plan
    (HDHP), 228
Hobby losses, 58–59
Home mortgage interest, 149
Home office deductions:
    allocating business part of expenses,
        216–218
    benefits of claiming, 220
    carryover of, 34
    day-care facilities and, 219

exclusive and regular use
    requirements, 212–213
gross income and, 218–219
home mortgage interest, 149
impact of on home sale, 221
limits on, 218
meeting place and, 214
overview of, 211–212
principal place of business
    requirement, 213–214
rent and, 136
separate structure and, 214–215
for sideline business, 213–214
storage of inventory and, 219–220
telecommuting and, 215
Hybrid cars, 110

Inclusion amount, 107–108
Income:
    for corporations, 51
    from farming, 46–47
    gross, calculating, 218–219
    investment-type, 48–50
    miscellaneous, 50
    payment methods, 43–44
    from sale of goods, 44–46
    for service businesses, 43–44
    state taxes on, 51–52
Income tax withholding, 36–37
Independent contractors, 4, 232
Indirect expenses and home office,
    216–217
Individuals:
    alternative minimum tax and, 235
    capital loss limits on, 73–74
    minimum tax credit and, 238–239
Installment method, 27
Installment sales:
    capital gains and, 68–70
    recapture on, 83, 84–85
Insurance:
    long-term care, 222–223
    medical, deducting, 222–224
    premium, deduction for, 210, 217, 232

Insurance proceeds, 203–204, 206
Intangible property, 159
Intangibles, Section 197, 72, 176–177
Interest:
    above-market loan, 148–149
    below-market loan, 148
    deductible, 145–149
    on deferred payments, 69–70
    home mortgage, 149
    loans between shareholders and
        corporations, 147
    nondeductible, 149–150
    prepaid, 150
    on tax deficiency, 150
Interest income, 48
Inventory:
    casualty loss and, 205
    depreciation and, 160
    disaster loss and, 209–210
    physical, taking and reporting, 44–45
    small inventory-based business
        exception, 23–24
    storage of, and home office
        deduction, 219–220
Investment interest, 34, 145
Investment limit on first-year
    expensing, 154–155
Investment-type income, 48–50

Kickbacks, 42

Last-in, first-out (LIFO) method, 45, 51
Lease costs, 134–135, 180
Leased property, improvements made
    to, 136
Leasing car:
    inclusion amount, 107–108
    with option to buy, 107, 137
    overview of, 106–107, 136–137
Legal fees, 232
Lender and foreclosure or repossession
    of property, 89–90
Like-kind exchange, 165
Like-kind or like-class property, 67

Limited liability company (LLC):
    business losses and, 56–57
    description of, 7–8
    one-member, 6
    sale of, 75
Limited partnerships, 7
Listed property, limitations on,
    174–175
Livestock, sales of, 46
Loans:
    above-market, 148–149
    below-market, 148
    business income and, 43
    with business or associates, impact
        of, 127
    from 401(k) plans, 197
    from retirement plans, 187–188
    by shareholder-employees, 128, 147
Local taxes on business income, 140
Long-term care insurance, 222–223
Long-term contracts, accounting
        methods for, 26–27
Losses, see also Capital losses; Net
        operating losses (NOLs)
    at-risk, 34
    basis and, 56–58
    due to bad debt, 125–126
    due to casualty or theft, 201–205
    due to disaster, 209–210
    due to hobby, 58–59
    due to passive activity, 34–35,
        60–62
    nonrecaptured, 83
    ordinary, 66, 78–79
    rents and, 61–62
    Section 1231 property and, 82–83
    Section 1244, 77–79
    suspended, 62
Low-income housing credit, 241

MACRS, see Modified Accelerated Cost
        Recovery System (MACRS)
Material participation, 60–61
Materials, 232

Medical insurance:
  COBRA coverage, 230
  deducting, 222–224
  health reimbursement arrangement,
    229–230
  Health Savings Account (HSA),
    227–229
  shifting cost of to employees,
    225–227
Medical reimbursement plans, 225
Medicare tax, 15, 37, 142
Mid-month convention, 167, 169, 170
Mid-quarter convention, 166, 168
Mineral properties, 180, 181
Minimum tax credit, 238–239, 244
Modifications for disabled access,
  119–122
Modified Accelerated Cost Recovery
  System (MACRS):
  Alternative Depreciation System
    (ADS), 170–171
  basic system, 161–162
  cars and, 98
  conventions, 165–167
  depreciation methods, 167–170
  leased property and, 136
  recapture of depreciation, 171–172
  recovery periods, 162–165
Modifying lease, cost of, 135
Money purchase plan, 185
Mortgage interest, 217
Multistate operation and business
  organization, 16

National Tobacco Settlement payments,
  47
Net gains, 72
Net operating losses (NOLs):
  alternative minimum tax and, 238
  calculating, 52–53
  carrybacks and carryovers, 34,
    54–55
  description of, 52
  limitations on, 55–62

Netting process, 82
New markets credit, 238–239
Nonaccrual-experience method of
  accounting, 129–130
Nonqualified retirement plans,
  197–198
Nonrecaptured losses, 83
Nonrecourse debt, 89
Nonresidential realty, 164

Oil and gas properties, 181–182
150-percent declining balance rate,
  167
150-percent depreciation, 167
Ordinary gains or losses, 66
Ordinary loss treatment, 78–79
Orphan drug credit, 244

Parking fees, 105–106
Partnerships:
  business losses and, 56–57
  description of, 6–9
  medical insurance deduction and,
    223–225
  oil and gas properties, 181–182
  organizational costs for, 178–179
  sale of, 75
Passive activity losses, 34–35, 60–62
Pass-through entities:
  alternative minimum tax and, 235
  capital gains and losses for, 70–71
  description of, 8
  first-year expensing and, 156
  fiscal year and, 21–22
  profitability and, 14
  S corporations as, 9
Patronage dividends, 47
Payment methods, 43–44
Payments in kind, 42
Payments in services, 42
Penalties, 232
Pension Benefit Guaranty Corporation
  premiums for retirement plans,
  189

Percentage depletion, 181
Personal interest, 145
Personal liability and business
    organization, 13–14
Personal property:
  business use of, 175
  description of, 159
  tax on, 141
Personal service corporations:
  cash method of accounting and, 24
  description of, 11
Placed in service, 160
Preference items and alternative
    minimum tax, 238
Premium-only plans, 227
Prepaid expenses, 35
Prepayments, 43–44
Preventative maintenance, 115
Principal place of business requirement
    for home office deduction,
    213–214
Profitability and business organization,
    14
Profit motive, 59
Profit-sharing plan, 185
Property, *see also* Personal property;
    Section 1231 property
  abandonment of, 88
  bonus depreciation and, 173
  classes of, 162–164
  condemnations of, 85–86, 207
  damages to business, 199
  depreciable, 79, 158–160
  election to postpone gain by
    acquiring replacement, 86–88
  foreclosure or repossession of, 88–89
  gains on loss of, 204
  improvements or additions to, 136,
    164–165
  intangible, 159
  involuntary conversions of, 85–88
  like kind or like class, 67
  listed, limitations on, 174–175
  oil and gas, 181–182

renting to corporations, 132
  repairs to, 203
  theft and recovered, 205–206
Puerto Rico economic activity credit,
    244

Qualified electric vehicles, 111, 243
Qualified nonpersonal use vehicles,
    109–110
Qualified retirement plans, 184–188
Qualifying expenditures to meet
    requirements of Americans with
    Disabilities Act, 120

Real estate taxes, 139–140
Realty, components of, 164
Reasonable rate of interest, 69
Recapture:
  of depreciation, 83–85, 171–172
  dispositions of first-year expense
    property and, 156–157
  home office deduction, sale of home,
    and, 221
Recordkeeping:
  basis, 33
  car expenses and, 111–114
  carryovers, 34–35
  by computer, 30–31
  depreciation and, 33, 172
  electronic imaging systems and, 31
  employer records, 36
  income tax withholding, 36–37
  listed property and, 174–175
  modifications for disabled access,
    122
  overview of, 29
  substantiation requirements for
    expenses, 32
  taxes and, 30
  tax returns, 35–36
Recourse debt, 88–89
Recovery period, 160, 162–165
Rehabilitation credit, 241
Rehabilitation plans, 117–119

Related party:
    rent amount and, 131–132
    replacement property and, 87
    rule regarding, 26, 72–73
Renewable energy production credit,
    243
Rents:
    to corporation, 132
    deducting, 131–132
    farm income and, 46–47
    gift-leaseback transactions, 133–134
    home office deduction and, 136
    as income, 48–49
    losses and, 61–62
    with option to buy, 132–133
    payment of in advance, 133
Repairs:
    capital expenditures compared to,
        116–117
    to damaged property, 203
    deducting incidental, 115–116
    home office and, 217
Replacement property, 67, 86–88
Repossession of property, 88–89
Required year, 20
Research and experimentation costs,
    179–180
Research credit, 242
Resellers, 45
Residential rental realty, 164
Retirement plans:
    actuarial costs for, 189
    added costs for, 188
    amendments to, 188–189
    bonding requirement, 188
    borrowing from, 187–188
    compensation limit, 186
    contributions to, 186–187
    defined benefit plans, 184
    defined contribution plans, 184–185
    incentives for, 183–184
    nonqualified, 197–198
    Pension Benefit Guaranty
        Corporation premiums for, 189

qualified, 184
salary reduction arrangements,
    195–197
for self-employed individuals,
    190–195
start-up costs for, 189–190

Salary reduction arrangements,
    195–197
Sales, see also Dispositions
    of all assets of business, 90–91
    of cars used for business, 103–104
    fair market value and, 107, 201–202
    of home, and home office deduction,
        221
    installment, 68–70, 83, 84–85
    of qualified business stock, 76–77
Sales of business interests:
    corporations, 76
    partnerships and LLCs, 75
    sole proprietorship, 74
Sales tax, 141–142
Sampling and car expenses, 112, 114
Savings Incentive Match Plans for
        Employees (SIMPLE), 194–195
S corporations:
    business losses and, 57–58
    description of, 9–10
    income items for, 51
    loss limits on, 74
    medical insurance deduction and,
        223–225
    oil and gas properties, 182
    sale of, 76
Seasonal businesses, 20
Section 179 deduction, 98, 151,
    152–153
Section 197 intangibles, 72, 176–177
Section 444 election for fiscal year, 21
Section 1202 gain, 76
Section 1231 property:
    description of, 81–82
    determining gains or losses, 82–83
    recordkeeping and, 35

Section 1244 losses, 77–79
Securities:
    deferring gain from publicly traded, 77
    worthless, 79–80
Security system for home, 217
Self-employed individuals, retirement plans for:
    contributions to, 191–192
    overview of, 190–191
    Savings Incentive Match Plans for Employees, 194–195
    simplified employee pensions (SEPs), 192–193
Self-employment tax, 140–141
Separately stated items, 8–9
Separate structure and home office deduction, 214–215
SEPs (simplified employee pensions), 192–193
Seven-year property, 163
Severance damages, 208
Shareholders:
    in C corporations, 10, 11
    loans to corporation by, 128, 147
Short-term gain, 71
SIMPLE (Savings Incentive Match Plans for Employees), 194–195
Simplified employee pensions (SEPs), 192–193
Small business, definition of, 76
Small employer pension plan start-up costs credit, 240
Small employers, defined, 194
Social Security tax, 15, 37, 142
Software:
    amortization of costs of, 179
    first-year expensing and, 153
Sole proprietorship:
    description of, 3–6
    medical insurance deduction and, 224–225
    sale of, 74
Special assessments, 208

Specialized small business investment company, 77
Sport utility vehicles (SUVs), 101
Standard mileage allowance for car expenses:
    choosing, 96
    description of, 105–106
    insurance and, 210
    proving expenses with, 112, 114
    sale of car and, 103
Start-up costs:
    for business, 177–178
    for retirement plans, 189–190
    small employer pension plan credit, 243
State benefit funds, 143
State taxes on business income, 51–52, 140
Statute of limitations, 35
Statutory employees, 5–6, 13
Stock in small business, 77–79
Storage of inventory and home office deduction, 219–220
Straight-line depreciation, 99, 167, 168–170
Subscriptions, 231
Substantiation requirements for expenses, 32
Supplies, 232
Suspended losses, 62

Tangible property, 159
Taxable income limit on first-year expensing, 155
Tax attributes, 49
Tax credits, see Credits, tax
Taxes:
    deductions for, 138–139
    employment type, 142–143
    excise, 143
    foreign, 144
    franchise, 143
    fuel, 143–144

Taxes *(Continued)*
   Medicare and Social Security, 15, 37, 142
   nondeductible, 144–145
   personal property type, 141
   real estate type, 139–140
   recordkeeping and, 30
   sales and use type, 141–142
   self-employment, 140–141
   state and local income, 51–52, 140
Tax-free exchanges, 67–68
Tax penalties for C corporations, 11–12
Tax rates and business organization, 14–15
Tax returns, 35–36
Telecommuting and home office deduction, 215
Telephone expenses, 218
Ten-year property, 163
Termination of business, 17
Theft:
   of car used for business, 105
   definition of, 201
   determining loss from, 201–205
   proof of, 201
   recovered property and, 205–206
Threat of condemnation of property, 207
Three-year property, 163
Timing:
   of depreciation deductions, 165–167
   of placing replacement property in service, 87–88
   of tax-free exchanges, 68
Trade-in of cars used for business, 104–105

Transfer of first-year expense property, 157
Transportation barriers, removal of, 121
Travel expenses, 32, 233
Trucks, 109–110
Twenty-year property, 164
Two-and-a-half-month rule, 25–26
Two-hundred-percent declining balance rate, 167–168

Underfunding, 189
Uniform capitalization rules, 27–28
Uniforms, 232
Unrealized receivables, 75
Unrecaptured gain, 71
Use tax, 141–142
Utility expenses, 217

Valuing bad debt, 127
Vans, 109–110
Vehicle, *see* Car; Car expenses

Web sites:
   blue book value, 203
   insurers offering HDHP coverage and trustees for HSA accounts, 228
   Pension Benefit Guaranty Corporation, 189
Welfare-to-work credit, 244
Whether and which test for determining amortization of start-up costs, 177
Work opportunity credit, 244
Work-related personal credits, 237–238